PELICAN BOOKS
Poverty and Equality in Britain

J. C. Kincaid was brought up in a Scottish manse, and educated at Glasgow University and the London School of Economics. Between 1964 and 1971 he was Lecturer in Sociology at Aberdeen University and currently teaches in the Department of Social Policy at the University of Leeds.

He has written frequently on the social services, housing and taxation for the weekly paper *Socialist Worker* and the monthly review *International Socialism*. He is married with three children.

Poverty and Equality in Britain

A Study of Social Security and Taxation

REVISED EDITION

J. C. KINCAID

 *Penguin Books*

Penguin Books Ltd, Harmondsworth,
Middlesex, England
Penguin Books, 625 Madison Avenue,
New York, New York 10022, U.S.A.
Penguin Books Australia Ltd, Ringwood,
Victoria, Australia
Penguin Books Canada Ltd, 2801 John Street,
Markham, Ontario, Canada L3R 1B4
Penguin Books (N.Z.) Ltd,
182–190 Wairau Road,
Auckland 10, New Zealand

First published 1973
Reprinted 1974
Revised edition 1975
Reprinted 1977, 1979

Made and printed in Great Britain by
Hazell Watson & Viney Ltd,
Aylesbury, Bucks
Set in Monotype Times

Contents

Acknowledgements

For moral support, ideas, and the force of example, I am indebted to a number of friends, and in particular to Geoff Sharp, Graeme Reed, Nigel Harris, Peter Musgrave and Kim Hunter.

Most of all I wish to thank my wife, Audrey, who has patiently worked through all the arguments with me, and without whose help this book would have been neither started nor finished.

CHAPTER 1

Poverty and Equality

Each week, under the national-insurance scheme, more than eight million separate payments are made to individuals or families, to old-age pensioners, widows, the unemployed and to people unable to work because of sickness or industrial injury. At any one time as many as one in four of the households in Britain are dependent on national-insurance benefits as their major source of income. In addition, each week nearly three million supplementary pensions and allowances are paid out to people qualifying for them after a means test. And, finally, there are seven million children for whom a family allowance is paid.

Although social security benefits are anything but generous for the individual recipient, in terms of national finance the sums passing through the system are enormous. Government expenditure on social security currently equals about 8 per cent of gross national product, by far the largest single item in the Government's annual budget.

In 1973–4, over £5,200 million was paid out in social security benefits, more than 23 per cent of central Government expenditure. By comparison, the next biggest item was spending on education at just under £4,000 million. Defence cost £3,400 million, and the entire National Health Service less than £3,000 million.

Expressed in these broad terms, State provision for social security appears to be quite impressive. But behind the figures lies a familiar and depressing reality. For millions of people the social security system provides their sole, or at least their major, source of financial support. Yet, for many of the groups who depend on the system for an income, the level of benefits provided is quite inadequate to maintain a decent standard of living. Widespread

9

poverty is a direct consequence of the limited effectiveness of social security provision. Whatever may have been the case in the immediate post-war period, the social security schemes in Britain now fail to match the standard of those which operate in comparable industrial societies on the Continent. British entry into the Common Market does not, of itself, commit the British Government to effecting improvements in the social security system to bring it up to European standards. The Common Market treaty obligations are concerned only with the rights to welfare services of people moving from one country to another within the Community, and not with the level of welfare services available to people within their own country.

Radical improvements in social security provision in Britain are urgently needed and long overdue. This book is mostly concerned with one central question. How far does the present social security system operate to reduce inequality in British society? Huge sums of money are raised in taxation and by national-insurance contributions and are transferred in the form of social security benefits to millions of recipients. The sheer size of these income flows – equivalent to nearly one eighth of the total income provided by all wages and salaries – means that the social security system could have a major impact on the pattern of social class inequality in Britain. Certainly the common assumption is that social security, along with the other major components of the Welfare State, is substantially egalitarian in its effects. Such a view is carefully sustained within the political establishment and given wide currency by the mass media. It is usually accepted that the Welfare State operates as a gigantic funnel which transfers resources and purchasing power from the higher to the lower income groups in society. My argument is, on the contrary, that the social security system as established by the Labour Government in the late 1940s was much less egalitarian in its effects than was widely supposed at the time, and, more important, that over the past twenty years the modifications to the social security system which have been introduced by successive Governments have on the whole made it less and less egalitarian in its consequences.

If this view can be successfully established it undercuts most of the assumptions about welfare which are current within the major political parties. We are continually told that poverty can only be reduced, and social security provision improved, by modest steps and by a process of gradual reform. It is commonly accepted by the leadership of the Labour Party, as well as universally within the Conservative Party, that the present tax system and the Welfare State have made British society pretty well as egalitarian as it could reasonably become. For nearly fifteen years now, Labour's overriding objective has been to present itself to the electorate as the party of industrial efficiency and rapid economic growth. The Labour movement's traditional preoccupation with social justice has been completely subordinated to this end. In 1969, the late Richard Crossman, then Minister of Social Security, delivered an elaborate lecture to the Fabian Society on the problems of social security finance. He discussed at length the continuing necessity of effecting a shift in resources away from private spending and into the social services. But, in the very first paragraph of his lecture, redistributive taxation as a source for extra welfare finance is curtly dismissed. 'That the working class can achieve this shift painlessly by taxing the rich in order to pay for the social services is a fallacy . . .'[1] The point is made flatly and without supporting argument; Crossman obviously assumes that the proposition will be accepted as completely self-evident by his audience. Later I shall document in some detail the ways in which inequalities in income and wealth have been allowed to multiply during Labour's recent terms of office.

My basic proposition is that no adequate system of social security can be created without a serious redistribution of income. Most of the deficiencies of existing schemes for social security have arisen as a result of efforts by politicians and administrators to deal with poverty as if it were an isolated social problem, which could be attacked by diverting small flows of extra income to the poorest and by minimizing more radical changes in the overall distribution of privilege in society. The attempt to reduce poverty by multiplying inexpensive means-tested schemes has been largely self-defeating. The result has been to create a Welfare

11

State of such bewildering complexity that comparatively few working-class people on low incomes could possibly find out what they might be entitled to, or how to apply and to whom, for all of the benefits to which they might in theory be entitled.

The whole system is becoming increasingly irrational. Large numbers of people dependent on social security for an income are reduced to desperate poverty. Meanwhile the Government spends larger and larger sums of money on advertising campaigns to guide possible claimants through the maze of schemes, qualifying conditions, exceptions, application forms, means tests etc., which the attempt to run a Welfare State on the cheap has generated. An increasing array of social workers is employed, one of whose main functions is to offer guidance to citizens lost in the welfare jungle. In many cases the social workers themselves, despite expensive training, have a less than adequate grasp of the complexities of social security entitlement. Increasing amounts of money are devoted to the employment of highly paid administrators to organize the social workers into large, bureaucratic empires. Underlying all of these developments is a refusal to see poverty and social equality as issues which are, in reality, quite inseparable.

Poverty and Old Age

Two thirds of the total expenditure on national-insurance benefits goes to meet the cost of retirement pensions. The simplest test of the adequacy of the pension is to compare the level of the basic State pension with average earnings for full-time work. As illustrated in Table 1, the record is not inspiring.

For more than three decades, the relative purchasing power of the single-person pension has not risen above one fifth of the average industrial wage and the pension rate for a married couple has been continuously less than one third of the average wage. Thus increases in pension have barely matched improvements in working-class living standards. Since the mid 1930s, very approximately, the real purchasing power of the average wage has doubled. So too with the old-age pension. But *in relative terms*

Table 1: Old-age Pensions as Proportion of Average Wages

	Single-person pension (per week)	Average weekly earnings for manual work	Pension as % of earnings
1937	£ 0·50	£ 3·00	17
1948	£ 1·30	£ 7·05	18
1964	£ 3·37	£18·95	18
1966	£ 4·00	£20·65	19
1968	£ 4·50	£23·60	19
1970	£ 5·00	£28·90	17
1971	£ 6·00	£30·93	19
1972	£ 6·75	£36·20	19
1973	£ 7·75	£41·52	19
1974	£10·00	£49·12	20

the purchasing power of the basic pension has improved only very marginally.

Even the small gains registered during the 1970s are immensely vulnerable in a context of rapidly rising inflation. Until recently improvements in the cash value of pensions were made at irregular and widely spaced intervals. In 1971, 1972 and 1973 a pattern was established of pension increases each autumn. At the time of writing the practice is for pension increases to come roughly at nine-month intervals – i.e. there were increases in July 1974 and April 1975; a further review is promised for December 1975.

But already – and until the rate of inflation slows down – a shift to more frequent increases in all social security benefits has become very urgent. The improvement in benefits which the Wilson Government made in April 1975 left those dependent on national insurance worse off than they had been in July 1974. The April increase was 15·5 per cent for pensioners, 14 per cent for the sick and the unemployed. Yet retail prices rose by 17 per cent in the nine-month period ending in April 1975. More serious still, the Government were promising no further rise until December 1975, by which time on current trends pensions and benefits will have fallen more than 25 per cent behind the standard set in July 1974. Pensioners and other national-insurance dependants are

13

going to be in severe financial difficulties in the month or two before benefits are increased.

Since pre-war days old-age pensions have been continuously below the official poverty line, as currently defined by the Supplementary Benefit scale. This scale takes the form of a payment to cover rent and rates, and an additional payment in cash of 30–40p a week.

The official poverty line is one of the key elements in the whole structure of social security and will be discussed a good deal in this book – both the way it is operated and how it originated and developed historically. This minimum income system is now administered by the Supplementary Benefits Commission (SBC), which was created in 1966 to take over the functions of the old National Assistance Board.

Since the autumn of 1973, the SBC has run a two-tier system of rates. The long-term scale, which is higher, is paid to old-age pensioners and to those under retirement age who have been continuously dependent on supplementary benefit income for more than two years. However, the extra long-term benefit is restricted to adults; only the short-term rate is paid in respect of children, no matter how long their family has been on supplementary benefit. It should be noted that family allowances are *included* in the supplementary scales, not paid in addition. Of claimants under retirement age, over 60 per cent get only the short-term level of benefit, and a special regulation lays down that the unemployed and their families get only the short-term rate, however long they have been out of work.

The basic rates of supplementary benefit have been raised at roughly the same time as pensions. The kind of living standards available to people on supplementary benefit are indicated by the table on page 15.

The figures given in Table 2 were those operating in the autumn of 1974. The pattern shown is typical of the relationship between wages and supplementary benefits in the 1970s. Since supplementary benefit rates are changed no more frequently than pensions, it follows that the degree of poverty involved deepens considerably in the month or two before the new scales come into operation.

Table 2: SBC Payments as Proportion of Average Wages*

	Short term %	Long term %
Single person	22	26
Married couple	33	38
Married couple+2 children	46	—
Married couple+3 children	50	—

* Average rent payments are included in these rates. Assumed that 2 children are 5–10 years of age, and where 3 children the youngest is under 5. Family allowances added to wages, and are included anyway in SBC scales for children.

Not just retirement pensions, but most other long-term national-insurance benefits are currently so low that, if a person has no other income beyond the insurance benefit, he or she is automatically below the poverty line. Ever since the present system was set up in 1948 it has been the case that the main national-insurance benefits have provided less than a subsistence income to those dependent on them. As originally planned in 1948, national assistance was to be no more than the final safety net for a limited number of people who might slip through the fine meshes of the contributory national-insurance sector. It was expected and hoped by the Attlee Government that improvements in national insurance would eventually allow the means-tested supplementary system to be abolished altogether. But the outcome has been exactly the opposite. Year by year the number of people qualifying for supplementary assistance has increased. At the end of 1949 1·1 million weekly payments were being made by the National Assistance Board and the total of men and women provided for was 1·8 million. By the 1970s the corresponding number of supplementary pensions and allowances had risen to more than 2·7 million and the number of people catered for was over 4 million. The money handed out by the SBC goes overwhelmingly to supplement deficiencies in the level of benefits operating in the national-insurance scheme. Three out of four of all SBC allowances go to people with a pension or national-insurance benefit that has left them below the official poverty line. As Table 3 shows, a substantial proportion of people dependent on national insurance benefits are also obliged to apply for supplementary income.

Table 3: Dependent on National Insurance and
Also Getting Supplementary Benefit[2]

	%
Old-age pensioners	26
Widows	13
Sick and disabled	9
Unemployed	21

The Supplementary Benefits Commission is one of the most controversial institutions in the whole machinery of British Government. As portrayed in the more reactionary of the mass-circulation newspapers, its officers are sentimental fools, over-ready to fall for the plausible story and the soft touch. Correspondingly the typical claimant is assumed to be an unemployed man, feckless, disinclined to work, and with a large family for the State to support.

In fact the major function of the SBC is to supplement the inadequate State pensions of the elderly. In 1972, for example, 70 per cent of all allowances paid out by the SBC went to people over retirement age; of the remainder 10 per cent went to the sick and disabled, a further 11 per cent mainly to women with children to look after, widows, separated or deserted wives and unmarried women. Only 9 per cent of SBC allowances went to families where the bread-winner was unemployed.

Under the Poverty Line

Only very sketchy and out-of-date information is available about what sorts of individuals and families are below the poverty line, and why. Probably the largest group in poverty are those who, though entitled by the Ministry rules to supplementary assistance, nevertheless do not apply for it. The SBC does not go knocking on doors to find unmet need. It can advertise its willingness to help in newspapers, leaflets, and by posters on Post Office notice boards. The administrative rules allow its officers to go no further. The initiative to approach the Ministry must be taken by the prospective claimant.

Despite the importance of non-application as an immediate cause of poverty, only very limited information is available about the numbers and circumstances of those involved. It is, however, clear that non-application is particularly common among old-age pensioners. The only detailed official investigation was carried out as long ago as 1965 and indicated that some 850,000 pensioners could have received assistance had they applied.[3] One in ten of this group were living on an income more than 25 per cent below the poverty line. The main reasons given by pensioners for not applying were that they felt they could manage on what they had, or that they were not willing to accept charity, or that they did not realize they might be entitled to benefit.

More recently the Department of Health and Social Security has publicly conceded that non-application among the elderly is now even more extensive than in the mid 1960s. The Department estimates that at December 1972 there were 980,000 pensioners (in 760,000 households) whose incomes were below the supplementary benefit level, and who were not claiming a supplementary pension.[4]

A Government survey, *Circumstances of Families*,[5] carried out in 1966, had confirmed that non-application is by no means confined to the elderly. It was found, for example, that of the 135,000 men on unemployment or sickness benefit who had a family of at least two children, some 30,000 had incomes below the poverty line, but were not getting assistance from the Supplementary Benefits Commission. Some allowance must be made for income being understated in the interview, but over 19,000 of these families were more than £2 below the official poverty line. The same survey found that 7,000 fatherless families (7 per cent of this group) were also below the poverty line. It remained quite unclear whether such groups had in fact not applied, or whether a claim had been made and wrongly rejected.

In December 1972, it was officially estimated that there were 800,000 people (in 460,000 households) under retirement age whose incomes were below supplementary benefit level. Table 4 gives the details.

The SBC is not allowed by statute to give general financial

Table 4: Numbers with Income Below Supplementary
Benefit Level[6]

Family head or single person	Families	Persons
(a) normally in full-time work (including those sick and disabled for less than 3 months)	80,000	250,000
(b) sick and disabled for more than 3 months	70,000	110,000
(c) unemployed for more than 3 months	120,000	190,000
(d) others	190,000	250,000
	460,000	800,000

assistance to individuals in full-time employment, or to their
dependants. Yet the wages paid for a large number of jobs are so
low as to leave many families below the poverty line, particularly
if they have one or more children. In April 1974, nearly 1¼ million
men were earning less than £30 a week from full-time work,
including overtime.[7] Around 800,000 women in full-time work
were earning less than £17 a week. At that time a worker with
under £30 a week, after deduction of tax and national insurance,
would be taking home less than the poverty line standard for a
married couple with two children.

To try to fill the gap between low wages and the poverty line,
the Conservative Government in 1971 introduced the Family
Income Supplement (FIS), a special means-tested family allowance payable on application by parents in full-time work, and
with exceptionally low wages. This benefit has been exceptionally
ineffective in meeting its purpose. Although in its first two
years of operation, £783,000 was spent in advertising the
existence of FIS, one half of the families estimated to be
eligible did not claim the money to which they were theoretically
entitled.[6] Nor has there been any subsequent improvement in
take-up.

Thus, in summary, the immediate causes of poverty in Britain
can be reduced to three sorts of reasons. (1) That although
the national-insurance system provides benefits as of right, in
most cases those benefits leave an individual or family well below
the poverty line, unless they happen to have some other source of

income. (2) That the supplementary benefits system – which exists in theory to fill out the gaps and correct the inadequacies of national insurance – does not do an effective job. The SBC has no responsibility for actively seeking out cases of poverty. The nature of the 'help' offered by the SBC, and the terms on which it is given, are such as to deter many potential claimants from coming forward. (3) That for a substantial number of jobs the wages paid are so low that the family, especially where there are children, is automatically in poverty.

Exactly how many people are currently under the poverty line can only be a matter of guesswork – making projections from fragmentary and out-of-date evidence. The necessary large scale investigations could be carried out only by the Government, and in this critical area of policy recent Governments have preferred to let obscurity reign. In a study published in 1969 based on a careful assessment of the evidence, Professor Tony Atkinson concluded that 'around 5 million people are living below the income standard which the government feels to be the national minimum'.[8] It is unlikely that the position has greatly changed since this estimate was made.

In addition it is surely clear that the present SBC scale rate is too low to be acceptable as the line which defines poverty. In far too much current research it is assumed without question that as soon as income is above the SBC scale rate the family is no longer in poverty. That the problems of the poorest should take precedence over those of the less poor is reasonable enough. But it would be intolerably complacent to imply that the distribution of income in Britain would be quite satisfactory, provided that no one fell below what the SBC regards as a reasonable minimum income. The official minimum is far too low. In any case it is a curious definition of poverty which suggests that a family is not in poverty, although its income may be dependent on excessive hours of overtime work, or on the full-time work of a wife who has responsibility for young children, or on a husband working permanently away from home, or on bonuses earned by shift-work systems which disrupt family relationships.

Certainly the SBC scale rates can be used to define the poorest

19

– if not all of the poor – so that a start could be made by some radical reorganization of the social security system to ensure that no one falls below what the Government at present regards as a minimum tolerable income. From the point of view of the politician or the Government planner this need not appear as a completely impossible achievement – so long as the problem is posed only in strictly financial terms. The number of households living under the poverty line might be around two million. The average short-fall in their income might be of the order of £5 a week per household. A Government spending, in all, about £25,000 million a year should not be too pushed to find £500 million a year to eliminate the worst problems of financial poverty. Why is it not done?

For a great many reasons, some of which are strictly practical. It is one thing to use sample surveys to estimate the numbers of people whose incomes fall below some tolerable minimum, and by how much – although even that task has yet to be systematically carried out. It is quite another matter to identify and contact all of the actual families living throughout the country and to assess how much extra cash they should be paid. It should be remembered also that the two million households in question are not a fixed group of people who could be identified once and for all. It is a characteristic of life on the poverty line that household income tends to be irregular and fluctuating. The sums required to bring a family up to the poverty line will tend to vary, perhaps even from week to week. Any estimate of the numbers of people in poverty at a given time in fact conceals the real situation, which is of a much larger group of individuals or families, all of whom are under the minimum income line for some of the time. Thus the substantial costs of keeping millions of people under some kind of administrative surveillance would have to be added to the £500 million of additional benefit.

It has to be recognized that any serious attempt by the authorities to eliminate financial poverty would mean abandoning those assumptions and procedures which, in the present system, have the effect of penalizing and deterring so-called 'misuse' of the Welfare State. In practice this would mean the abolition of the

Supplementary Benefits Commission, since there would seem to be no way of reorganizing such a complex means-testing apparatus so as to ensure that people had not only formal rights, but the information and the power to enforce those rights. The gradual abandonment of the means-tested part of the social security system was a key objective of the Beveridge Plan, which formed the basis of the present social security system. And yet now – thirty years after the Beveridge Report – the abolition of means-testing is scarcely even mentioned in public discussion about welfare questions.

It is a quite widely held opinion that many of those dependent on social security are layabouts, who prefer a life of ease at public expense to doing an honest day's work. There is precious little evidence to support the layabout thesis. But that such doctrines should be generally accepted is convenient to any social group or Government which aims to defend the prevailing degree of social inequality. For people doing well out of the present social and economic system it is advantageous that inadequacies in the Welfare State should be blamed on the poor rather than on the privileged. Any serious attempt to abolish poverty endangers the whole structure of inequality in society – partly because money must then be found for the poor at the expense of the rich, but also because such an attempt threatens the values which underwrite social inequality and the whole existing structure of privilege. So long as society is organized on a deeply competitive basis, it appears indispensable that social failure should exist for individuals as a visible and possible fate. Poverty is such a fate, just as mental illness is another. Poverty cannot be considered as a residual, historically determined defect of an otherwise fair society, but as an integral element that helps support a competitive social order. It follows therefore that proposals to reduce poverty often involve very much more than technical and administrative problems. They tend rather to raise issues of principle about the whole structure of society.

Poverty and Equality in Britain

Rising Demand for Social Security

Senior politicians from both major parties have argued that the social security system is much more adequate than it was a decade ago because there have been substantial increases in the proportion of national resources spent in this area of welfare. It is clear from Table 5 that this claim is factually correct. For example, expenditure on social security benefits was 7·6 per cent of gross national product in 1966, and 8·6 per cent in 1973.

Table 5: Cost of Social Security Benefits[9]

	As percentage of total public expenditure	As percentage of gross national product
1964	17·3	7·1
1966	17·6	7·6
1968	18·0	8·8
1969	18·6	8·9
1970	18·7	9·0
1971	18·4	8·7
1972	19·2	9·3
1973	18·1	8·6

Unfortunately the evidence of Table 5 cannot be used to support the conclusion that there has been any improvement in the relative standard of living of individuals and families dependent on social security payments. Virtually all of the extra resources allocated to social security have been made necessary by increases in the numbers of people qualifying for benefits. These increases have arisen partly from changes in the demographic structure of the population, partly from a rise in rates of unemployment and sickness and partly from a trend towards earlier retirement.

Since about three quarters of Government expenditure on social security goes to old people, it follows that any increase in the numbers of the retired will have a disproportionately unfavourable effect on the finances of the system. In the period 1964 to 1973 the number of old-age pensioners rose by 25 per cent, from 6·3 to 7·9 millions. Compare, over the same period, a rise in the total population of Britain of only 9·3 per cent.

To some extent the numbers of the elderly are increasing because people, once retired, are living longer – but this is really only a minor factor, as Table 6 suggests.

Table 6: Expectation of Life at Age 60[10]

	Number of years		
	1901	*1961*	*1971*
Men	13·4	15·0	15·1
Women	14·9	19·0	19·7

Thus, in 1971 men at age sixty had an average expectation of further life of 15·1 years – an improvement of only 0·1 years as compared with their counterparts in 1961. Over the same decade, women did rather better, improving their expectation of life by 0·7 years. However, even the long-term comparison of life expectation of elderly people in 1901 and 1971 suggests that increased longevity among the old is not the most important reason for the recent rapid increase in the proportion of pensioners in the general population.

The major reason for rising numbers of old people is the high birth rate which prevailed in the early years of the century, combined with the lowering of death rates at all ages which has occurred progressively throughout the century. Thus the situation is not so much that the old are living longer, but that an increasing proportion of each generation has been surviving long enough to retire and claim a pension. Another factor increasing the proportion of the old in the population has been the gradual dying-off of the generation whose numbers were depleted during the First World War.

The second trend which has greatly influenced the numbers of the old reflects a change in customary behaviour, rather than in demographic structure. The number of old-age pensioners is rising faster than the number of people over the official age of retirement. People are tending less frequently to continue working after the age at which they become entitled to draw a State pension. In 1961 only 50 per cent of men actually retired at age sixty-five; by 1968 the proportion was 70 per cent.[11]

23

A rapid increase in the demand for retirement pensions has been matched, at the other end of the age scale, by an increase in the proportion of children in the population. This results largely from higher birth rates than in the fifties, with some small assistance from a further decrease in rates of infant mortality. Over the nine-year period up to 1969 the number of children for whom family allowances were paid rose by 1·1 million, to 6·8 million. This increase in the number of children reflects the continuing trend to an earlier age of marriage and of starting a family, an increase in the proportion of the population of child-bearing age who get married, and also an increase in the average number of children per family. Correspondingly there has been an increase in the demand for maternity allowances and grants. The demand for family allowances has also been increased, though this is a less significant factor, by a rise in the proportion of children staying at school after the minimum leaving age, since family allowances continue to be paid in such cases.

A simultaneous increase in the proportion of the population who are young or old does make for difficulties in social-service finance. It means increased pressure on virtually all sectors of the Welfare State (e.g. 30 per cent of all national-health expenditure goes to meet the needs of the 15 per cent of the population over retirement age). However, besides these changes in demographic composition, a number of other developments have increased costs in social security.

An increase in the rate of unemployment has to be substantial before it has much impact on the finance of social security. The reason for this is that the cost of unemployment benefit is not one of the larger items. For example, unemployment benefit cost about £50 million a year in 1964, plus perhaps another £25 million in national assistance to the unemployed. Compare, for the same year, over £1,000 million in old-age pensions and £200 million in sickness benefit. However, unemployment rates rose steeply in 1967, and continued to climb to a peak of nearly one million in the winter of 1971–2. After falling to around 600,000 in 1973, the trend in the two following years was a further persistent increase. On average the numbers of unemployed during the early

1970s have been more than twice as high as those in the early 1960s.

It is still the case, however, that sickness is more expensive than unemployment. During 1969 Ministry officials began to express concern about an apparent rise in the rate of claims for sickness benefit. In each year between 1966 and 1969 there had been a small but steady rise in the numbers of workers off sick. The official mind immediately assumed that the underlying reason must be increased laziness on the part of British workers, although to argue this also meant saying that British doctors who certify incapacity for work were becoming increasingly soft-hearted or careless. No one in the Ministry seemed to consider the possibility that conditions of work, in industry especially, might be becoming increasingly demanding and detrimental to health. The average length of the working week has shown little decline in recent years and, for men doing manual work, stands at an average of forty-five to forty-six hours per week. Meanwhile it is probably true that for many employees the time taken in travelling to and from work has lengthened. There is evidence, too, of an increase in the intensity of work in British industry. Productivity deals have been negotiated covering millions of workers in recent years, and such agreements generally involve more effort and concentration by workers. In 1954 12 per cent of all workers in manufacturing industries were on shift work; by 1960 the proportion had increased to 20 per cent, and by 1968 to 25 per cent.[12] The evidence is that shift work has an unfavourable effect on health and hence is likely to increase the incidence of absence from work because of sickness. Certainly there has been a considerable increase in the number of industrial accidents; the rate of new claims for industrial-injury benefit was running 20 per cent higher in the late 1960s as compared with a few years previously.

However, there has been a good deal of exaggeration about sickness in public discussion. Inevitably sickness rates fluctuate a good deal from year to year because they are heavily affected by outbreaks of influenza, which vary a lot in seriousness in different years.

Table 7: Days lost Through Sickness or Injury*[13]

(per worker per year – men only)

1967–8	16·4
1968–9	16·7
1969–70	17·6
1970–1	16·2
1971–2	16·0

*i.e. 'Certified Incapacity'.

The really expensive developments over the past few years have been the increase in the numbers of the retired, and the rise in unemployment. Between 1964 and 1973 there was a 1·5 per cent rise in the proportion of national resources devoted to social security. A very rough calculation suggests that about three quarters of this extra money would have been spent to meet the higher numbers of those retired or unemployed. A further smaller part of the extra costs was due to increased demand for family allowances, maternity benefits and industrial-injury benefits. The relative increase in the social security budget over the last decade arises from extra numbers in the categories who qualify for benefits, and is not due – as politicians often try to imply – to any relative improvement in the standard of living made available by the system to those dependent on it.

CHAPTER 2

The Social Security System

Despite many changes the social security system in Britain remains essentially the same as that created by the first post-war Labour Government in the years between 1946 and 1948. In designing this part of the Welfare State, the Attlee Government closely followed a detailed plan for the reform of social security, drawn up by Sir William Beveridge after the outbreak of war and published in 1942.

The system consists of four major sectors: the national-insurance scheme,* the supplementary benefits system, family allowances, and a variety of tax-relief schemes, offering tax exemptions, for example, to people with dependent children or to people contributing to private pension schemes. In each of these four sectors the basis of qualification for benefit is quite different. Entitlement to national insurance is based on a record of contributions previously paid into the scheme. Supplementary benefit on the other hand is officially known as the non-contributory sector. Here, in order to qualify for cash benefits, a person must be able to prove that his existing income is lower than the weekly scales operated by the Supplementary Benefits Commission. Thus the non-contributory sector is controlled by means-test procedures.

Family allowances are paid to anyone who has more than one dependent child. No record of contributions is required, nor is there any need to prove poverty. The effective value of a family allowance does, however, vary with the income of the recipient,

---

*The main national-insurance benefits are: retirement pension, widow's benefits, sickness, industrial-injury and unemployment benefit, maternity grants and benefits, the death grant, invalidity pensions and allowances.

since the family allowance is subject to tax as earned income. Thus people with an overall income which is too low to be taxed, in effect receive a larger family allowance than those with higher incomes.

The basic qualification for income-tax relief is that one is paying enough tax for a relief to be given on it. Thus this part of the social security system effectively offers benefits only to those with incomes large enough to be over the threshold points at which income tax begins to bite. The cash value of a tax relief is worth most to groups with very high incomes who are taxed at surtax rates.

National Insurance

Most of the Beveridge Report of 1942 was concerned with the reorganization of social insurance. By the end of the 1930s there were contributory schemes in operation covering a wide range of needs, old age, unemployment, widowhood, sickness, etc. These schemes, however, were generally run separately from each other and under a wide variety of rules and qualifying conditions. Beveridge proposed their amalgamation into a single comprehensive scheme of national insurance. What made his plan seem an important social advance was not the wide range of risks for which cover was to be provided, but rather the promise that adequate financial support was to be obtainable *as of right* and without a test of means. Beveridge proposed that non-contributory means-tested social security in the form of national assistance would continue even after the reconstruction of national insurance. But his intention was that there should be progressive improvements in national insurance, which over time would leave less and less of a role for the means-tested sector. In practical terms what this meant was that the level of national-insurance benefits would be increased year by year until a person whose sole income was the old-age pension or unemployment benefit would have an income above the official poverty line. Thus fewer and fewer people would need to have recourse to means-tested national assistance to supplement the national-insurance income which they had earned by earlier contributions to the national-insurance scheme.

Freedom from the hated means test which had been operated so ruthlessly in the inter-war period, particularly on the massive army of the unemployed – this was seen, especially by working-class people, as the supreme merit of the Beveridge Plan. The minimum income offered by Beveridge's proposals was scarcely generous. But that it should be paid as of right to the old, the unemployed and the sick, this seemed a wonderful thing. These were hopes which were to be sadly disappointed in the outcome.

The second major innovation of the Beveridge Report was that *all* employed persons were to contribute to and benefit from national insurance. Inter-war schemes of social insurance were selective in that only people earning less than a given income were required to contribute and able to benefit. For most of the period between the wars, social-insurance schemes were limited to manual workers earning less than £250 a year. White-collar workers were largely excluded by the provision that they could only get in if earning less than £160 a year. It was not until 1937 that the so-called Black Coated Workers Act was passed which allowed non-manual workers with less than £250 a year to join the scheme. In 1942 the upper income limit for all contributors was raised to £420 a year.

Beveridge proposed the abolition of all these distinctions and suggested that all employees, however highly paid, should be compulsorily enrolled as contributors. And, when the Attlee Government eventually legislated the Beveridge scheme into existence, this principle of universality was firmly embodied in national insurance.

In arguing the case for universality, Beveridge tended to assume that the admission of the higher income groups would involve some sacrifice on their part. Preparing his plan with only inter-war experience to go on, Beveridge made the assumption that it would once again be high rates of unemployment which would pose the most serious threat to the solvency of social-insurance schemes – as had been the case in the 1920s and 1930s. Since the middle classes are much less subject to unemployment than the working classes, Beveridge argued that the non-manual groups would be a relatively light charge on the finances of the scheme.

It has turned out quite differently. The growth in the cost of old-age pensions has easily outpaced any other charge on social insurance. Thus, the higher income groups have done well out of the system because of their longer expectation of life. Beveridge did try to allow for this by saying that people who had not been contributing to the earlier pension scheme, because they were above the income limit, should not be entitled to full new-scheme pensions unless they retired more than twenty years after the Beveridge scheme was started. The Labour Government, however, reduced the qualifying period to ten years and thus presented 400,000 mainly higher income people, retiring in 1958, with a remarkably good bargain – full pension rights after paying contributions for only ten years. For all other benefits apart from pensions, the higher income groups qualified as soon as the scheme started in 1948. They thus obtained a full share of the large reserve funds which had been accumulated in earlier schemes by mainly working-class contributors and, on their behalf, by employers. It was a substantial windfall for the middle class.

Since national-insurance benefits were to be paid as of right, it followed that wealth would be no disqualification. Provided he has paid his contributions, the rich man is as entitled to his old-age pension as the man who has nothing else to live on. Although, if the flat-rate benefit leaves anyone dependent on it in poverty, then the practice of paying welfare benefits to people who have ample other resources becomes difficult to justify.

The same applies to the contribution side. Beveridge proposed, and the post-war Labour Government agreed, that contributions should differ for men and women, and that boys and girls under eighteen should pay at a lower rate. But within these groups there should be absolute equality, irrespective of income. Once over eighteen the higher-paid man should contribute exactly the same as anyone else no matter how badly paid.

The flat-rate contribution principle had a number of important consequences. It very much limited the extent to which social security would redistribute income from richer to poorer. Certainly there was *some* provision for redistribution. The arrangement was, and is, that the money used to pay national-insurance benefits is raised in three ways: by contributions from those people who are employed; by contributions paid by employers on their behalf; and by a subsidy which is paid into the scheme out of general taxation. In theory the higher income groups, though they pay a flat-rate contribution like everyone else, nevertheless contribute more because they pay higher taxes. In fact, however, it has been a consistent aim of Government policy ever since 1948 to keep the Treasury contributions to national insurance out of general taxation as low as possible. For most years the Treasury share of total national-insurance expenditure has been kept down to about one sixth or less.

Throughout the history of post-war national insurance, the flat-rate contribution has been a straitjacket on the whole system. There is a limit to how high the cost of the national-insurance stamp can be raised without biting too severely into the wages of the lower-paid workers. This would mean hardship for individuals and electoral risks for the Government responsible. As it is, the cost of the national-insurance stamp has become a major item in the budget of any low-wage family. Between 1948 and 1968 the general level of retail prices a little more than doubled. But over the same period the cost of the employee's share of the national-insurance stamp rose by three and a half times. By 1970 any male worker with, say, £18 a week had to contribute £1·33 a week for national insurance. Thus the flat-rate contribution system, allied to a policy of tight control of the amount of the Treasury subsidy, placed strict limits on the total income of the national-insurance system. A contribution rate which imposed hardship on lower-wage earners was far lower than high income groups could comfortably have borne.

It was only in April 1975 that the flat-rate contribution for national insurance was finally abolished. In that month a new system was introduced whereby employees were to pay a contribution of 5·5 per cent on all earnings up to a maximum of £69 a week. Even this revised arrangement still carries some of the limitations of the previous flat-rate pattern. The ceiling of income on which earnings-related contributions are charged is not a high one – approximately 25 per cent above the average earnings of all male employees in industry. The effect is that managerial and professional categories, earning substantially more than the average income, will pay a much smaller proportion of that income in national-insurance contributions. So long as this remains the case, the flat-rate contribution system is not dead.

The flat-rate principle in Britain originated with the first national-insurance scheme, Lloyd George's Act of 1911, which introduced a scheme covering unemployment and sickness. Beveridge was happy to perpetuate it in his Plan because he intended the State scheme to provide nothing beyond a bare subsistence minimum. Beveridge was a lifelong Liberal, anxious that Government should interfere as little as possible with the play of market forces and with the opportunities for moral character building left available if the State scheme were limited. In the whole of a packed, 300-page report there is practically no discussion of the underlying rationale for the Beveridge scheme. However, tucked away in an obscure Appendix, one finds the following:

> Provision by compulsory insurance of a flat-rate of benefit up to subsistence level leaves untouched the freedom and responsibility of the individual citizen in making supplementary provision for himself above that level. This accords both with the condition of Britain, where voluntary insurance particularly against sickness is highly developed, and with British sentiment.[1]

Beveridge was not concerned with social equality as a general objective. He wanted a minimum limit to deprivation. It was no part of his intention that the cost of achieving this objective should be met by the very rich, any more than by other sections of the population.

Universalism versus Selectivity

In recent years there has been severe and mounting criticism of one of the essential pillars of the Beveridge structure. Increasingly the Conservative Party has begun to challenge Beveridge's universalism, the principle that all employed persons should be obliged to belong to, and be given equal rights under, the national-insurance scheme. Many Tories argue that the long-term objective in social security should be the dismantling of the present universal scheme. How absurd, they point out, to have a system which cannot provide an adequate standard of living to those in need, and yet which pays out money to other groups who are amply provided for by private insurance or in schemes run by their employers. It is recognized by most Tories that State provision is, and probably always will be, essential to meet the needs of people who are not able to earn a living, because of some kind of handicap or particular domestic responsibility. Similarly there must be provision for groups whose earnings are not sufficient to allow them to save for old age or widowhood. But the proper function of a State scheme, they argue, should be restricted to the provision of a substantial minimum income for the small group of people in real need.

Tory selectivists believe that the needs of the majority of the population would be better catered for by a further expansion of the private sector in insurance. They point out that the past two decades have seen considerable development of commercial insurance. There has also been a rapid growth in the field of occupational pensions and sick-pay schemes. More than half of the employed population is now contributing to such schemes, and men in the upper income groups derive retirement pensions and other forms of provision at a level which makes national-insurance benefits seem like a derisory supplement. Furthermore it is argued that national insurance with its compulsory contributions restricts the incentive and opportunities to save for people in the middle and lower income brackets.

Supplementary Benefit

Inevitably the supplementary benefit system must figure largely in any discussion about further extensions of the selective

33

principle in British social security. The Supplementary Benefits Commission, together with its predecessor from 1948 to 1966, the National Assistance Board, offers a major test case of the effectiveness and public acceptability of means-tested welfare.

A crucial feature of SBC procedure is that, whereas its officials have a statutory duty to help people in need of cash support, they are not under any duty to go looking for clients. The SBC machine only moves into action when an individual has made a personal application for financial assistance. Thus the effectiveness of the system in meeting need depends wholly on the extent to which people in poverty realize that they may be entitled to supplementary benefit and on their willingness to undergo the investigations of income which the SBC is required by law to carry out. A claimant must be able to display his poverty in the terms required by the rules operated by the SBC. At every stage the burden of proof rests with the claimant.

The scope of the SBC's operation is quite staggering. Between 1965 and 1971, the number of staff employed rose by 70 per cent, from 12,500 to 21,200.[2] In 1971 about twelve million interviews were carried out in SBC offices, and the number of separate claims totalled 6·5 million. In any one week, about 7 per cent (one in fourteen) of the population of Britain are wholly or partly dependent for their income on money handed out by the SBC. But, despite this immense effort, there is overwhelming evidence that the SBC has been ineffective in preventing the growth of poverty on an increasingly wide scale.

The surveys quoted in the last chapter indicated that by 1965 to 1966 substantial numbers of people, who would have qualified for national assistance because of low income, did not apply for the extra income which would have brought them up to the poverty line.

As a result of these and similar surveys the Government became concerned to make more people aware of their right to financial help and to try and rid the national assistance system of its tainted image of Poor Law charity. In 1966 the National Assistance Board was rebaptized as the Supplementary Benefits Commission, the application procedure was simplified and a massive publicity campaign invited claims. Advertisements appeared in the popular press. A television commercial was shown in which an attractive young lady with a seductive voice claimed that she was an SBC officer and implied that any viewer in need of cash would meet with a friendly reception at his local Ministry Office.

These efforts achieved only a very limited success – nowhere near the extravagant claims which were later made by Labour ministers. In the last months of 1966 some 300,000 new claimants appeared.[3] All but 5,000 of them were old people. However, at least 100,000 were not previous non-applicants, but became qualified in 1966 either because the poverty line was raised in that year or because the numbers of old people in the community were rising anyway. After careful study of the evidence, A. B. Atkinson concluded that:

the introduction of Supplementary Benefits had not had a major impact on the problem of people not applying for the assistance to which they are entitled. Even if we assume that it reduced the number not applying for assistance, this still represents only about one quarter of the number who were found by the Ministry enquiry to be not claiming in 1965. Moreover, the higher assistance scales themselves have increased the number eligible, so that the *proportion* of those eligible who claim may actually have fallen since 1965.[4]

The same conclusion would apply even more sharply for groups under pensionable age. The estimates were of about 42,000 non-applicants among the sick, the unemployed and the fatherless families; yet of these only 5,000 new applicants appeared in 1966.

Given the disappointing results of Labour's attempt to recast the image of the assistance system, it has to be asked whether it is in reality the 'image' of the SBC which is the key factor in non-application. Labour ministers proudly claimed that by the 1966 Ministry of Social Security Act the old National Assistance Board had been abolished. In name, it certainly was. Notice-boards outside Ministry offices were repainted, and the headings on stationery were changed. It was arranged that the supplementary benefits and the national-insurance sections of the Ministry of Social Security would be eventually housed in the same local office buildings up and down the country, instead of in separate premises as previously. This change has not yet been fully implemented, nor will it be for many years to come, because it depends on long-term building programmes. In any case, even when united under the same roof, supplementary benefits and national insurance would be run quite separately, by two different sets of officials, working according to completely different rules. The 1966 Act in fact provided that the National Assistance Board would continue to work in exactly the same way as it had since 1948, except that it was now to be called the Supplementary Benefits Commission. This method of 'reforming' social security had been subjected to withering criticism in 1962 by the Labour Party's leading welfare expert, Richard Crossman. He was explaining how a Labour Government would combat the humiliations inflicted by the NAB on its clients.

'Change the name,' they say. 'Make it look nicer in another Ministry.' I will change the name only when I have changed the system. Do not let us do any of this business of fiddling with names while there is any means test attached to the supplementary pension. While the means test is attached we had better be frank and honest and call it the National Assistance Board which it actually is. Our aim must be to raise these people above the level of the NAB and only after that . . . we will change the name.[5]

It is not surprising that the image of the SBC is by now no more wholesome than that of the old NAB. Some part of the explanation must lie in the conditions of work to which SBC officers are subjected.

SBC offices are the slummiest of all work places run by the Government. Even privacy for an interview is often not possible. According to a recent Report,

A review of 416 local offices dealing with supplementary benefit work showed that facilities were not up to accepted standards to the extent that 23 had no private interview room, 117 had open cubicles fronting public waiting space and 107 had a public waiting area which had not been acoustically treated.[6]

Most of the interviewing is carried out by officers in the poorly-paid clerical grade of the Civil Service. On present rates of pay, a married officer in his mid twenties and with children, may well find himself paying out more than his own take-home pay to a claimant in similar domestic circumstances.

As well as being underpaid the clerical staff are also over-worked. Since 1966, the increasing militancy of the Civil and Public Services Association has forced successive governments to take on more staff to cope with a rapidly growing work load. Yet it was reported recently that the *average* time an applicant has to wait for attention in an SBC office is two and a half hours.

There is a very high turnover of staff, and the current situation is unlikely to be very different from that revealed in a survey in 1968–9 of 22 supplementary benefit offices. Of the Executive Officers in post, 27 per cent had less than 18 months experience in the grade and 28 per cent of clerical officers less than 12 months.

Not unexpectedly, given this situation, the number of mistakes made by SBC officers in calculating claims is quite phenomenal. The Ministry runs an internal audit in which Inspectors double-check a sample of cases. The results for 1971 and 1972 were made public.[7] It appears, for example, that 9 per cent of the regular payments of benefit being made in March 1972 were wrongly calculated. In the case of one-off immediate payments of benefit, the error rate was 11 per cent. It was officially estimated that one half of these incorrect assessments of claims involved under-payment of benefit.

The defects of the SBC system are glaring but it is not a case that the usefulness of the SBC could be transformed merely by increasing the amount of money available for its administration.

The SBC is responsive to a widely publicized view which insists that many of the poor are wasters who deserve no sympathy or help. A critique of the system must be concerned not just with denouncing the notorious rudeness of SBC officers or seeking utopian vistas in bright, newly built offices, but by asking why certain influential newspapers are determined to define the poor as layabouts and parasites, and why politicians and administrators accept that the SBC must be run in a spirit of hostility and suspicion towards the poor.

It has been assumed too readily that large numbers of people in need keep well clear of the SBC, mainly because it runs means tests – and that these are resented because of an irrelevant historical folk memory. Certainly the means-test system operated by the Unemployment Assistance Board during the thirties deserves its evil reputation: the rule was that where the children in a family were at work their entire wages were considered as part of their parents' income. Thus the unemployed father would be refused assistance because of the earnings of the son or daughter and forced into financial dependence on their income. The only remedy was for the children to leave home. The system was hated because it destroyed family life, either by physical separation or by inverting the relationships of parent–child dependence, which people saw as natural and right. Since 1941 only the wages of a man and his wife are taken entirely into account in the assessment. A working son or daughter is assumed to contribute a part, rather than the whole, of his or her wages to the parents' income.

However, despite this change, it remains the case that in the means-test procedure the official still has enormous power over the applicant. This is partly because the claimant does not know in detail what he might be entitled to. The scale rates which are set out in SBC leaflets are only a very rough guide to entitlement. How they are applied in practice is determined by a complex set of rules, which try to take account of all sorts of special circumstances and contingencies. Only very general information about entitlement to benefit is made public. The detailed rules are contained in a series of confidential Code books used by Ministry officials. It is an offence against the Official Secrets Act for any material from these books of rules to be published, or for any unauthorized person to be told what they contain. The Codes are not available to MPs and cannot be discussed by Parliament or any of its committees. The penalties laid down in the Official Secrets Act are severe. Early in 1970, after a sustained campaign sponsored particularly by the Child Poverty Action Group, the Government brought out a pamphlet called the *Supplementary Benefits Handbook*. This certainly gave more information than was previously available about entitlement. The booklet costs 35p; it is obtainable from the Stationery Office or from its registered agencies; it is not sold or available for consultation in Supplementary Benefits Offices. The information provided falls far short of explaining the full criteria that govern assessment procedures. It is a helpful guide to researchers and social workers with the time and skill required to interpret bureaucratic prose. It is of little help to the claimant who wants to know what his rights are.

This unwillingness to let people know where they stand does not arise simply from a bureaucratic instinct to keep the customer at a disadvantage. It is the case that the rules laid out in the secret Code books do not determine the decisions taken in individual cases, but merely give guidance to the officers carrying out the means test. Generally these are Clerical Officers, i.e. people who, in the Civil Service, normally do very routine kinds of work under close supervision. In Supplementary Benefits, however, a quite different practice is followed. Here overworked Clerical Officers are required to take the initiative in making often complicated decisions that seriously affect the daily lives of their clients. It is very probable that the average SBC field officer has more power to make life on the poverty line tolerable or intolerable than the average social worker. Yet increasingly social work is becoming a profession, recruiting university graduates, generally with a one- or two-year diploma training in addition to their first degree. Field officers in the SBC will generally have five O-levels and a few weeks of scrappy in-service training. From a straightforward trade-union point of view, SBC officers are certainly entitled to consider themselves thoroughly exploited. Given the importance of their work, they are overworked, undertrained and underpaid.

It is possible for claimants to appeal against any decision by the Supplementary Benefits Commission which they feel to be unjust. However, an appeal against the SBC can only be to a local tribunal, and this body has the final say. Matters are quite different in the national-insurance sector where an appeal against a local tribunal can be taken to the National Insurance Commissioner, who is a full-time official of high legal standing. Local SBC appeals tribunals are not held in public (the claimant is allowed to take in two other persons to back him up) and the criteria on which appeals are decided are not publicly recorded in any way. Again, national insurance is run differently. The key judgements of the National Insurance Commissioner are regularly published, details of each case being given, together with the reasons why appeals were rejected or accepted. This means, of course, that in national-insurance matters someone with legal training or with trade-union experience can be of real assistance to a claimant. There is a published body of case law which can be read up and referred to in argument. In supplementary benefit cases the claimant has no such advantages, and the three members of the local tribunal are very likely to be at sea as well. It would be hard to devise a system more likely to end in arbitrary decision making. No action against the SBC can be raised in a court of law, unless there is a claim that the SBC have contravened an Act of Parliament. But the statutes governing the SBC are so vague that it is virtually impossible to imagine how the SBC *could* break the law.

Although the basic scale rates of the SBC have to be agreed by Parliament, this branch of the administration is more effectively sealed off from Parliamentary control and scrutiny than any other – except perhaps the secret security services. Since 1948 only one Act of Parliament has dealt specifically with the means-tested sector of social security, the 1966 Act which altered the name of the old National Assistance Board and made a number of other minor changes. Scale rates are increased from time to time to take account of any fall in the purchasing power of the currency over the previous period. This change is carried out by laying Regulations before Parliament. The House can accept or reject these Regulations; it is not allowed to amend them. The time taken to discuss these in the House of Commons is usually about ten minutes in each year. No individual case in which a person claims that the SBC has acted unjustly can be raised in Parliament. Again, what is involved is that a quite exceptional status is accorded the SBC. The fiction is elaborately maintained that the Minister of Health and Social Security is not actually in control of the SBC and therefore not answerable in Parliament for the action of its officers. From the official point of view the situation is thus that the Minister appoints eight people to be the Supplementary Benefits Commissioners. These Commissioners are paid out of public funds, but being part-timers they do not have the status of civil servants. The Commissioners then 'recommend' to the Minister the annual range of scale rates, which he somehow always agrees are just the ones the Government was prepared to pay anyway. The Commissioners next ask the Treasury for the necessary cash which by a coincidence is always the total the Cabinet had already decided would be available for this purpose in that year. Having got their funds, the Commissioners hand it on to the Post Office for distribution to clients. The latter get the money from the Post Office in exchange for orders which are issued by the SBC, and the issuing is done by about 25,000 civil servants whose status is exactly the same as any other civil servants, except that they do not really work for the Government but for a special set of part-time Government employees called Supplementary Benefits Commissioners.

All this elaborate make believe has only one purpose: to make sure that Parliament is not able to debate or question the Government on the work of the supplementary sector. The effect of all these legal and political arrangements is to isolate the system from any kind of democratic control and pressure. At the bottom of the pile, the claimant is generally left in the position of not even knowing whether his case has been dealt with fairly or not. Thus it is not an acceptable argument that hostility to the SBC and unwillingness to apply for financial help arise solely from public prejudice against means-testing. Most clients of course are not familiar with the legal and constitutional framework within which the SBC operates. But they are strongly aware of the day to day consequences of such a structure – arbitrariness, indifference, and bureaucratic complacency. In reality the SBC has two functions which are in contradiction. It has a statutory duty to help people in need. But it is also under pressure from the Government, from important newspapers, and from sections of the public, to distinguish in its help between 'deserving' and 'undeserving' cases, to make life tough for the unemployed, unmarried mothers and similar groups. Thus the SBC has what sociologists call a latent social function – to stigmatize the un-deserving. Such stigmatization arises not just from the indignity of the investigation of means, but from the whole administrative and political framework within which individual needs are assessed and benefit determined.

It is the argument of this book that stigmatization, and there-fore ineffectiveness in meeting need, will characterize any selective welfare system introduced into a society that is as deeply unequal in its structure as British society. Thus it will be argued that any reform of social security must begin by looking for ways of extending the universal sector of the system at the expense of the selective part – and not the other way round.

CHAPTER 3

The Subsistence Principle

The Beveridge Plan was designed to guarantee a national minimum income, and this was defined in terms of a subsistence standard of living. It is worth looking in some detail at Beveridge's reason for electing to plan a subsistence-based scheme and at the methods he used to define 'subsistence'. These questions are raised here not simply because of their historical interest, but because the standard of living provided today for those dependent on social security is in direct line of descent from the subsistence concept of Beveridge. The Labour Government of 1945 to 1950 confidently proclaimed the adequacy of the social security benefits it offered by invoking what it regarded as the 'scientific' authority of Beveridge's definition of subsistence. Subsequent Governments have defended their records and rationalized their complacency by arguing that the official poverty line provides a rather higher standard of living than Beveridge's subsistence income. It is certainly true that the purchasing power of benefits has improved over the past two decades. But there is a complete lack of any serious research into the adequacy of current benefits. No such research has in fact been carried out since the 1930s, and the investigations carried out in those years, because of their influence on Beveridge, continue to exercise a baleful influence on the social security system today. It is still relevant to stress just how extraordinarily pitiful was the standard of living which Beveridge labelled as a subsistence minimum.

Many of the assumptions which Beveridge brought to the task of redesigning the social-insurance system were based, not on considerations of social welfare, but on the prejudices of official economic opinion. All along, one of the most important of Beveridge's concerns was to limit the scope of the social-insurance schemes and to make the benefits paid out low enough to match contribution income. Repeatedly in his 1942 Report he refers to the overwhelming importance of 'financial soundness' in social insurance. What Beveridge meant by this was simply that at no point should the scheme require a large or increasing contribution from the State from general taxation. After protracted negotiations in 1941 and 1942 Beveridge won the support of Keynes and the Treasury chiefs for his scheme by arranging that during the early years of its operation the Treasury contribution to the national-insurance scheme would be stabilized at £100 million a year, or at 20 per cent of the total cost of benefits paid out. Necessarily, of course, this meant strict limits on the size of benefits. Thus before the Beveridge Report was made public it had already been tailored down to meet the notions of financial soundness which prevailed in Treasury circles.

Ever since the implementation of the Beveridge Report in 1948 the Labour Party have had a vested interest in maintaining the view that the scheme was a notable advance towards socialism. For many in Britain who lived through the period, the publication of the Beveridge Report, *Social Insurance and Allied Services*, remains one of the most memorable public events of the entire war. Of all State papers ever published only the 1963 Denning Report on the Profumo scandal could rival the immediate public impact of the Beveridge Report. It is still kept in print to this day and has sold something like 750,000 copies. For millions of people the Report was taken as a major expression of the social ideals for which the nation had gone to war – the more so since its proposals were definite and concrete, more meaningful than the empty phrases about freedom and democracy written into official definitions of war aims such as the Atlantic Charter. On publication day a queue a mile long formed outside the Government bookshop in Central London and 70,000 copies were sold within three hours. Three weeks after publication the Gallup Poll found that nineteen out of twenty adults had heard of the Report and most of them approved of its recommendations. The Education Service of the armed forces was overwhelmed with requests for lectures on the subject. The newspapers were enthusiastic. The

Archbishop of Canterbury pronounced that this was the first time that anyone had set out to embody the whole spirit of the Christian ethic in an Act of Parliament.

A close examination of the proposed scheme and of the role which Beveridge played in British politics gives very little support to the conception of national insurance as revolutionary. In the standard histories of the Welfare State Beveridge is presented as an idealistic and daring reformer – a kind of Prometheus of welfare provision. The truth is less inspiring and more interesting. From the outset Beveridge belonged impeccably to the governing class of the period. 'In India, at the age of four,' recounts his wife, 'William spoke English to his parents, Hindustani to his bearer and German to his governess.'[1] After an Imperialist childhood William attended Charterhouse and Balliol. He then did a stint as a social worker in a University Settlement in the East End of London. The objectives of University Settlements were memorably defined by Canon Barnett, founder of Toynbee Hall, where Beveridge worked after taking his degree. 'Vain will be sanitary (i.e. welfare) legislation, unless the outcasts are by friendly hands brought in one by one to habits of cleanliness and order, to thoughts of righteousness and peace.'[2]

However, Beveridge soon abandoned individual casework and took up social planning as his major concern, dividing his time between academic life and the higher reaches of the Civil Service.

The background to the Beveridge Plan was the social security experience of the inter-war period and, in particular, the events of the early 1930s. During that period, because of mass unemployment, the financial commitment of the State in meeting the needs of the unemployed increased heavily. Every effort was made to cut the level of benefit paid to the unemployed. But, even so, social security payments by the Government rose to 6·5 per cent of Net National Income in 1931. By the standards of today this level of expenditure was scarcely outrageous. But orthodox financial opinion at the time was deeply alarmed. The 'generosity' of the social security system was seen as a major element in the national emergency of 1931. When the May Committee was set up in February 1931 to devise solutions to the financial crisis, one of its chief recommendations was that unemployment benefit be cut. This proposal split the Labour Party and led to the installation in office of a Coalition Government under the Premiership of Ramsay MacDonald.

These events, and the acute social bitterness which accompanied them, made a profound impression on Beveridge and marked his subsequent thinking. Sir George May, the Chairman of the 1931 Committee on reducing State expenditure, had formerly been Secretary of the Prudential Assurance Company. The State social security system was defined then – and very largely still is – primarily on the model of the private insurance scheme. Beveridge was in substantial agreement with the conventional Establishment view that, apart from a limited contribution from general taxation, the same criteria of financial soundness should be applied to a State insurance scheme as to private commercial schemes. Beveridge became directly involved in the problem of social insurance when he became Chairman of the Unemployment Insurance Statutory Committee, established in 1934. This Committee, like the original forerunner of the National Assistance Board (the Unemployment Assistance Board also started in 1934), was explicitly designed to allow Governments to disclaim responsibility for their own policies. The Committee was supposed to be non-political, and its function was to see that the unemployment insurance fund remained solvent and to make recommendations to the Government about changes in benefits and contributions. As with the National Assistance Board, and later the Supplementary Benefits Commission, there was always an uncanny coincidence between what the Government thought should happen and what the non-political Committee was prepared to recommend. But the Minister could always blame it on the Committee.

In his Plan Beveridge gave expression to a broad section of hardheaded opinion in the ruling class of his period. He was for social reform, so long as the existing structure of society remained fundamentally the same. In fact he was for social reform precisely *because* it would allow the existing order to continue essentially unchanged. It is not as a visionary that Beveridge deserves to be remembered. Rather his particular distinction lay in an ability to translate the general objectives of ruling-class reformism into detailed and technically workable proposals.

Even had the Beveridge Plan been fully implemented (which it was not), the increase in the proportion of national resources to be devoted to social security would not have been very substantial. In 1938 to 1939, 5·3 per cent of Net National Income was paid out in cash benefits to individuals. Beveridge proposed to increase such transfer payments to 7·8 per cent of Net National Income, and to stabilize provision at that figure.[3] He made this decision although well aware that the proportion of the old in the population would rise quite rapidly in the late forties and in the fifties. In advocating a National Health Service, Beveridge allowed for an increase of only 20 per cent in health expenditure over the level prevailing in the immediate pre-war years.[4] Nor did Beveridge advocate any substantial increase in income redistribution. Indeed in a number of respects his proposals had the opposite effect. Had existing provision continued into the post-war period, without Beveridge's restructuring, then in 1945, for example, 61 per cent of the cost of social security and the health service would have been found from general taxation via the Exchequer. Beveridge estimated that were his scheme (including the National Health Service) in full operation in 1945, the Treasury would contribute only 50 per cent of the total cost of the scheme. Thus Beveridge contrived a swing in the financial burden away from general taxation and on to the more regressive contributions of employers and employees. He proposed a massive increase in the combined employer–employee contribution from £150 million to £330 million a year. Moreover, under the schemes existing before his Plan was adopted, the employers in 1945 would have paid 55 per cent of the combined employer–employee contribution. Beveridge proposed however that the employers' share be cut to 42 per cent, with the employees making up the difference.[5]

In essence, therefore, the Beveridge Report was largely aimed at preventing post-war social security schemes from biting too deeply into general taxation. Beveridge achieved this by allowing only for the most exiguous of benefit levels, by stepping up the employer contribution, and by a particularly sharp increase in employee contributions.* In making such proposals, Beveridge was partly inspired by the assumption that welfare schemes, except of the most limited sort, are dangerous to the economy. But equally the orthodox criteria of financial soundness matched comfortably with Beveridge's general social philosophy. Politically he was a lifelong Liberal and firmly committed to the principle of the least possible interference by Government with the freedom of individuals. Whole sections of the Beveridge Report read as if John Bunyan had lived long enough to write an allegorical apologia for British imperialism.

The Plan for Social Security is put forward as part of a general programme of social policy. It is part only of an attack upon five giant evils: upon the physical Want with which it is directly concerned, upon Disease which often causes that Want and brings many other troubles in its train, upon Ignorance which no democracy can afford among its citizens, upon the Squalor which arises mainly through haphazard distribution of industry and population, and upon the Idleness which destroys wealth and corrupts men, whether they are well fed or not, when they are idle. In seeking security not merely against physical want, but against all these evils in all their forms, and in showing that security can be obtained with freedom and enterprise and responsibility of the individual for his own life, the British community and those who in other lands have inherited the British tradition have a vital service to render to human progress.[6]

* As an example: Until the legislation based on Beveridge, no contributions were required from employees for the State scheme of Workman's Compensation for industrial injury, diseases or death. In 1946, for example, the employers paid the full cost of the scheme – £21 million. The post-1946 scheme certainly offered better protection to workers, but made them bear a substantial part of the cost. The new scheme began on the basis that the employers' contribution was reduced from £21 million to £10 million a year, and £10 million was raised from workers via a flat-rate levy paid as part of the national-insurance stamp. This shared arrangement has continued ever since.

That the social security system should make no provision above a minimum subsistence level was advanced, not regretfully, as a result of economic circumstances, but as a positive ideal and one of the chief merits of the whole scheme. 'Provision by compulsory insurance of a flat-rate of benefit up to subsistence level leaves untouched the freedom and responsibility of the individual citizen in making supplementary provision for himself above that level.'[7]

Writing in the months between the retreat from Dunkirk and the end of the Blitz, Beveridge felt that British sentiment might stand for the very mild degree of redistribution of income from rich to poor which his scheme would require. He was not in the least interested in increasing general social equality – only that a stringently defined minimum standard of living should be available to anyone incapable of work or unable to find a job.

The plan is one to secure income for subsistence on condition of service (i.e. paid employment) and contributions and in order to make and keep men fit for service ... the plan leaves room and encouragement to all individuals to win for themselves something above the national minimum, to find and to satisfy and to produce the means of satisfying new and higher needs than bare, physical needs ... But it must be realised that nothing materially below the scales of benefit here suggested can be justified on scientific grounds as adequate for human subsistence.[8]

Thus science was invoked in defence of the proposed definition of subsistence. What liberal principle suggested as desirable, science would justify as sufficient. For in preparing his scheme, Beveridge was obliged to do a great deal more than lay down the general principles by which the social security system could be reorganized. The Treasury wanted detailed calculations of the total cost of the various benefits to be provided, and this obliged Beveridge to state in precise terms of so many shillings a week what he thought should be a subsistence income for families of different sizes. In defining subsistence and in translating it into a cash equivalent, Beveridge relied heavily on calculations made by Seebohm Rowntree. In the course of research into poverty in York in 1936 Rowntree had found it necessary to establish the income levels below which a given family should be counted as in poverty. Later, while Beveridge was writing his Report, Rowntree became a member of the small sub-committee which advised Beveridge on what social security benefit levels should be recommended. In this period Rowntree was regarded as the leading British authority on poverty. Since the recommendations of the Beveridge Report about benefit levels have had an enormous influence on the subsequent history of social security and on the lives of millions depending on the system, it follows that Rowntree, just as much as Beveridge in fact, has to be regarded as one of the founding figures of the contemporary Welfare State.

Seebohm Rowntree (1871–1954) was a leading member of the Quaker family which built up the famous cocoa and confectionery firm based in York. Throughout his career Rowntree was deeply interested in questions of social reform, especially in the living and working conditions of the lower classes. His approach was partly practical. He was one of the leading British pioneers of the human-relations approach in industry, a tireless exponent of the blessings that would flow out to all concerned, if workers were treated as if they were people rather than so much labour power. Both as a Director at the Cocoa Works in York and as Head of the Welfare Department of the Ministry of Munitions during the First World War, Rowntree proved himself to be a fertile innovator. Quite a few minor amenities of welfare capitalism owe their original development to Rowntree's experiments and advocacy: works sports clubs, joint consultation, works canteens, employer-run pension schemes for manual workers, personnel officers, profit-sharing schemes, training schemes for management, and payments by results systems. In Rowntree's reformulation, philanthropy became not so much one of the leisure pursuits of the upper class but an integral, and profitable, part of everyday business activity. As Rowntree explained:

Real betterment of conditions springs in the last analysis from the conviction in the mind of the employer that here lies his plain duty, a duty which does not conflict with his business interests but promotes them, since it is obvious that workers who are in good health and are provided with the amenities of life are more efficient workers.[9]

One of Rowntree's more daring arguments was that employers should accept a responsibility for organizing production so that every one of their workers should be able to earn at least a subsistence wage.

At York most of the workers of the Cocoa Factory were paid on a piece-work basis. Their earnings were reviewed at the end of every three months to check whether or not they reached the minimum wage level, Rowntree himself taking part in the review. Men who had failed to reach the level were interviewed by the manager of their department. They were then either transferred to another department or given 'special attention' by the foreman in an effort to encourage them to increase their output. If it was clear that they were committed to work in the factory and were incapable of earning what 95 per cent of the workers earned, they might be dismissed, with long notice, and recommended to find a new job.[10]

The definition of a poverty line, specified in terms of so many shillings per week, thus became for Rowntree a necessary tool of managerial decision making. If workers earning less than a subsistence wage were to be sacked, some criterion of subsistence had to be devised.

More broadly, the definition of subsistence was also an important issue in the study of poverty. Rowntree's interests extended far beyond the factories under his control, and from an early age he devoted much of his leisure time to the investigation of living conditions and poverty among the working classes. Inspired by Charles Booth's monumental seventeen-volume report on *Life and Labour of the People of London*, published from 1889 onwards, Rowntree undertook a smaller-scale exercise in York in 1899. His aim was to establish the numbers of the poor in that city and the main factors underlying their poverty. He repeated his investigation in 1936 and in 1950. Rowntree's chief innovation in these studies was his attempt to measure poverty on a scale which had at least an appearance of scientific precision. Rowntree laid much emphasis on the distinction between what he called 'primary' and 'secondary' poverty. A family was classified as in primary poverty if its income was too low to provide for the barest physiological needs, even if that income was spent with the maximum budgetary efficiency. The term secondary poverty was applied to families whose income was so little above the line of primary poverty that physiological needs could not be met if the family spent any of its income on non-essentials or if there were any inefficiency in budgeting.

In the first two of his inquiries in York, Rowntree's central purpose was to show that there was a substantial proportion of families whose income was so low that, even with the greatest conceivable efficiency in budgeting, sheer physical efficiency could not be sustained. He was concerned, that is, to demolish the view that virtually all poverty could be blamed not on low wages but on careless housekeeping, improvidence, and luxury expenditure on tobacco, gambling and drink. Such a moralistic view of poverty, as caused principally by the dissolute habits and immorality of the lower classes, led to the comforting conclusion that the only true cure of poverty lay in the moral re-education of the poor. To hand out charity indiscriminately was to run the grave risk of confirming in the poor those careless habits which were the main cause of their poverty. The giving of money should be made conditional on an effort on the part of recipients to mend their ways.

Throughout his life Rowntree conducted a running battle with the exponents of the moralistic view about the causes and cure of poverty. His challenge was not exactly radical, since he was willing to grant the necessity of moral regeneration, if secondary poverty were to be abolished. But he argued that families in primary poverty needed more money as a first priority – and his studies found 15 per cent of the working-class population of York in primary poverty in 1899 and, with the same definition of poverty, 7 per cent in 1936. The polemical purposes of his investigations meant, however, that he felt obliged to adopt the most stringent possible definition of the line dividing those in primary from those in secondary poverty. He wanted no one to be able with any justification to accuse him of including any allowance in his minimum budget for expenditure on pleasure as opposed to necessities. Yet the outcome has been extraordinary. A definition of subsistence in the most stringent terms, adopted in the first place as a limiting case for the sake of an argument, subsequently became the administrative basis around which the post-war social security system was constructed.

In 1937 Rowntree published the second edition of a short book called *The Human Needs of Labour* and in this he explains how the primary poverty line used in the York study in 1936 was arrived at. According to this any married couple with three children and less than £2·65 a week would be counted as in primary poverty. The biggest item of expenditure allowed for was food, and the calculation was based on the contemporary state of research in dietetics.

As a student at the Quaker college in Manchester, Rowntree had devoted most of his time to chemistry, and his early years at the Cocoa Works had been spent mainly in chemical research in the field of gums and pastilles. Whether because of these early interests or more generally because of his involvement in the food-processing industry, Rowntree followed the contemporary development of dietetic science with close attention. For his poverty line Rowntree adopted the calorie and protein requirements formulated by a BMA committee reporting in 1933 on minimum diets to maintain health and working capacity. In this report a man doing moderate manual work was held to need 3,400 calories per day and 100 grams of protein, including 50 grams of first-class animal protein. As examples of what was meant by 'moderate work' we are offered bricklayers' labourers: 'These men have to do such heavy work as mixing concrete; they are climbing up and down ladders carrying mortar, or they have to dig, often in stiff clay, to prepare foundations and lay drains.'[11] No examples are given of what is meant by hard work! Rowntree defends his calorie and protein figures, rather oddly, by pointing out that convicts on anything more than light labour get less. The other cross-check offered is with the menus normally provided in two West End clubs. There, Rowntree established that members got 5,148 calories per day, including 202 grams of protein. In the calculation of minimum food requirements Rowntree allows a woman 85 per cent of the man's allowance, and children average 65 per cent of the man's allowance.

The next problem is to translate these minima into actual foodstuffs, and the argument from this point onwards becomes increasingly metaphysical. Rowntree is not concerned with what anyone actually buys, nor with whether his ideal minimum budget in any way reflects food preferences in the social groups he is discussing. The most he does is to make some allowance for what he calls 'national customs'. The concessions he explicitly makes to custom are very general indeed.

Even the poorest try to get a certain amount of meat; and though undoubtedly health can be maintained without it, we cannot, in selecting a dietary, ignore the fact that meat eating is an almost universal custom. So is the drinking of tea and coffee, and though these do not actually supply any nutriment, a certain amount must be included in the dietary.[12]

In choosing his dietary he is guided not by working-class food preferences but 'by certain menus worked out by teachers of domestic science, which were based on a list of foodstuffs supplied by the Nutrition Committee of the British Medical Association'.

Rowntree drew up a detailed shopping list of food and drink, calculated to provide a family of two adults and three children with the required calorie and protein content at the lowest possible cost.[13] It is an amazing catalogue. For example the family are required each week to eat $4\frac{1}{2}$ lb. of onions and 6 lb. of swedes. They are expected to bake all their own bread, although by 1936 this custom had practically died out. But the extra cost of the same amount of bought bread would be 5p to 10p a week, and Rowntree felt this extra could not be afforded. The family are expected to get through the whole week on 2 lb. of sugar. The dietary also includes the splendid allowance of one egg per week to be shared among the five members of the family – exactly how is not explained. The British Medical Association minimum diet which Rowntree uses as a basis had recommended 14 pints a week of fresh, unskimmed milk. Rowntree might have suggested instead that fresh skimmed milk would be appropriate for his model family. But by the 1930s fresh skimmed milk – which in earlier periods had been mainly consumed by lower-paid workers – was being increasingly used to feed pigs and poultry, rather than put on the market for domestic consumption. Thus Rowntree was led to make one of his silliest proposals; namely that in his ideal poverty dietary the family of five should be allowed 12 pints of *condensed* milk. Commenting on his scheme, the nutritionists took severe exception to the condensed-milk suggestion.

The other items in Rowntree's minimum budget can be quickly summarized. For rent he allowed 47½p a week – less than most Local Authorities charged for three-bedroom non-parlour houses – clothing for a family of five was 40p a week, 30p for fuel, light and household sundries, and finally 45p a week for 'personal sundries'. What was allowed under the last heading was broken down as follows.

Personal Sundries

	p
Unemployment and health insurance	8
Contribution to sick and burial clubs	5
Trade-union subscriptions	2½
Travel to and from work	5
Such necessities as stamps, writing-paper, haircutting etc. for the family	2½
A daily newspaper	3
Wireless	2½
All else: beer, tobacco, presents for the children, holidays, books, bus rides, cinema, football matches etc.	16½
Total	45

It is worth repeating that in those calculations Rowntree was less concerned to define what minimum wage levels or social security benefits should be than with showing irrefutably that primary poverty existed. He was concerned, that is, to show that certain groups of people were so far below his poverty line that no amount of moral improvement, careful budgeting, and abandonment of dissolute habits could bring them up to a standard of living which even the sternest critic of the sentimentality of sociologists could argue was over-generous. The real obscenity of such arguments about how cheaply the poor could be made to live came later, as research assumptions were translated into policy and built into the post-war Welfare State.

Rowntree's 'human needs' minimum for a family of five totalled the equivalent of £2·90 at 1938 prices. Yet in the Beveridge Report it is recommended that when the national insurance system is set up, the level of benefits was to be set at the equivalent, for a family of five, of only £2·65 at 1938 prices.[14] The main difference between the two scales is that Beveridge allows not a penny for the items listed above as 'personal sundries'. He argues that State insurance contributions would be waived when a man is out of work. He points out that a man out of work has no need of the 5p a week which Rowntree allowed for travel to and from work. He makes no allowance for travel in search of work. About the rest – the newspaper, postage stamps, radio, the presents for the children, the occasional entertainment, the haircut – Beveridge has nothing to say. It seems that these items must simply be done without.

In addition, since Beveridge is concerned with policy making, not research, he must make *some* allowance for the fact that working-class housewives do not prepare the family meals with reference to a BMA table of calorific values and with a committee of domestic science teachers available to advise. A margin has to be allowed over and above the maximum-efficiency diet. In discussing this, Beveridge makes no reference to the food conventions and preferences existing in actual social groups, nor to the social and psychological deprivation of having to miss out on accustomed items of diet. The scientific values of the nutritionists are presented as a realistic norm and deviations are patronizingly referred to as inefficiency.

The foregoing calculations, particularly that for food, assume complete efficiency in expenditure, i.e. that the unemployed or disabled person buys exactly the right food and cooks and uses it without waste. This assumption is clearly not likely to be realised. Some margin must be allowed for inefficiency in purchasing and also for the certainty that people in receipt of the minimum income will in fact spend some of it on things not absolutely necessary.[15]

But to counterbalance this inability of the poor to live scientifically the minimum weekly allowance for food is set only *one sixth* higher than absolute necessity demanded.

The second major modification which Beveridge made was the elaboration of a special scale for old people. First of all he argues that they need less food, about 75 per cent of the calories needed by adults of working age. However, Beveridge goes on to suggest that an allowance of 10 per cent must be made for the fact that 'the food of old people will be more expensive because of their failing mastication and digestion'.[16] Thus the old are allocated 85 per cent of the food budget of younger adults. Beveridge estimates the clothing requirements of old people at two thirds that of adults; however, he also makes a small allowance for the fact that the old are permanently poor and will need to replace clothing. They are allowed a little extra for fuel and the same margin as working-age adults for inefficiencies of spending. The rent allowance of old people is, however, 30p a week as compared with 50p for the standard family. Beveridge justifies the rent reduction with the delicate and enigmatic phrase, 'retired persons should be able to adjust their rents'.[17] What he means presumably is that they can move on retirement into a smaller and cheaper house. Even for 1942 such casual optimism about the ability of most old people to play the post-war housing market is amazing. The overall conclusion is that, whereas £1·60 a week at 1938 prices is allowed for a couple of working age, a retired couple is to manage on £1·43½. Again, even in retirement, no allowance is made for presents, entertainment, travel, beer, postage stamps, newspapers, radios or tobacco. When Beveridge says subsistence, he means it.

Many years after the implementation of the Plan, when Beveridge looked back on the reasons for the extraordinary enthusiasm which greeted its initial publication, he explained them as follows:

The central idea of the Beveridge Report is the subsistence principle, the guaranteeing to every citizen, in virtue of contributions and irrespective of need or means, of an income in unemployment, sickness, accidental injury, old age, or other vicissitudes, sufficient without further.

resources, to provide for his basic needs and those of his dependents. This central idea was that which most caught the public imagination; without this the report would have been no more than a rationalisation of existing services.[18]

The crucial point here is not so much the wide range of risks which are insured against, but that financial support is provided without a test of means. Freedom from the hated means test which was operated so ruthlessly in the inter-war period and especially on the massive army of the unemployed – this was seen by people as the strategic advance offered by the Beveridge Report. But whether the national-insurance scheme would lead to a dramatic reduction in the need for means-tested supplements to benefits claimed as rights entirely depended on the adequacy of basic national-insurance payments. We have discussed how the rigorous minimum standard of living defined by Rowntree was substantially reduced by Beveridge. It remains to compare the actual benefit levels set in 1948 when the scheme began to operate.

The Labour Government calculated its basic social security rates by adding 31 per cent to the weekly sums which Beveridge had worked out at 1938 prices. The extra 31 per cent was to compensate for the decrease in the purchasing power of the pound which had taken place between 1938 and the end of the War. The awkward fact, not mentioned by any of the Labour ministers responsible, was that the cost of living at the end of 1945 was already 45 per cent higher than in 1938. The Chancellor of the Exchequer in the new Government had promised to keep prices stable at only 31 per cent above the 1938 level, and this was considered a more reliable financial basis on which to found the new national-insurance scheme than the actual movement of prices.

By 1948, when benefits under the new scheme first began to be paid, the cost of living had risen still further and to achieve a Beveridge minimum would have required benefits at £1·70 a week for a single person and nearly £3 a week for a married couple. Instead, benefits were paid in 1948 at £1·30 for a single person and £2·10 for a married couple. Thus in terms of actual purchasing power the 1948 benefits paid to adults gave only three quarters of the standard of living regarded by Beveridge as an irreducible minimum. Beveridge in turn had set his scale at less than the level selected by Rowntree as a measure of primary poverty.

In one way, however, the Government did make an improvement on what Beveridge had proposed. In the Report he had made the extraordinary suggestion that the full rate of old-age pension should not be paid until twenty years after the inception of the scheme. Initially pensions should be paid at only 58 per cent of the full eventual rate and should be increased every second year over the twenty-year period. While this transitional process was taking place, the national-assistance scheme would supplement pensions and bring the income of applicants up to the poverty line. In 1944, when the Churchill Government pronounced on the Beveridge Report, they decided to pay the full pension from the start of the scheme, although at a much lower weekly rate than Beveridge had considered necessary. In this matter the Attlee Government followed the approach of the Coalition Government, rather than of Beveridge. However, immediate payment of the full-rate pension in 1948 was a much less dramatic improvement over the slow build-up which Beveridge had advocated than it may sound. In financial terms there would be little difference. Since the vast majority of pensioners would qualify for national assistance so long as pensions were kept well below subsistence, it would cost very little extra to give everyone the full rate of pension right away.

A very much more significant revision of the Beveridge scheme was decided on by the Coalition Government and accepted by the post-war Labour Government. Beveridge had proposed that unemployment benefit should continue to be paid no matter how long the period of unemployment.* This was one of the few adventurous proposals in the Beveridge Report, considering that Beveridge designed his scheme on the assumption of an average post-war unemployment rate of 8 per cent. Both Governments

* Subject to the condition that a person unemployed for a time might be required to attend a training centre.

accepted a drastic cut in the duration of unemployment benefit. They made it payable for only thirty weeks, and for a further limited period only where the claimant's record of employment was exceptionally good. This was a major reduction in the standards of coverage recommended in the Report. It has led to a situation in which only about one half of those who are unemployed at any one time are able to get unemployment benefit. This decision has never been reversed, even though it has turned out that unemployment rates have been vastly lower than those anticipated by Beveridge.

It was not for these reasons, however, that Beveridge eventually came to disown the scheme which was set up in his name. The level of subsistence which he had advocated was, as we have seen, the most stringent imaginable. But for Beveridge, in contrast to the politicians, it was absolutely fundamental to the whole conception of the scheme that national insurance should actually deliver this subsistence standard of living as of right and without recourse to means tests. National-insurance benefit levels were substantially below the Beveridge subsistence line when the schemes started in 1948, and in the succeeding years this gap widened impressively. Between 1947 and 1948 food prices rose by 8 per cent and between then and 1951 by a further 34 per cent. Apart from old-age pensions, national-insurance benefits were raised for the first time only in July 1952 – a 15 per cent increase. The next increases in the money value of national-insurance benefits were not awarded until 1955.

It was Beveridge himself who provided the fittest epitaph on the fate of the subsistence principle, which he considered the one fundamentally new element in his plan and the main justification for the popular aspirations which were evoked by his proposals. Speaking in 1953, shortly before his death, he insisted that,

either the Government will have to raise the benefit rates to adequacy for subsistence, or to say ... that they have formally abandoned security against want without a means test, and declare that they drop the Beveridge Report and the policy of 1946.[19]

The Government of course made no such declaration. But the

persistence of starvation levels of benefit spoke louder than words. In the most fundamental respect the Beveridge Report was never implemented. Politicians who report glowingly on advances made in social security provisions since the period of the late forties would speak more honestly if they recognized just how miserably inferior was the standard of the national-insurance schemes introduced by the post-war Labour Government.

CHAPTER 4

Social Security under Labour, 1964–70

In social security, as in so much else, Labour took office in 1964 with high aspirations and on the basis of a number of specific commitments. Prominent among these was an undertaking that the means test for national assistance would be superseded by what Labour leaders referred to as 'a form of guaranteed income'. This proposal gave rise to a great deal of public discussion during the 1964 election campaign and probably helped to bring the Labour Party to their narrow victory.

In the three years before the election the Labour Party had conducted a vigorous campaign against the humiliations of the means test, especially as applied to old-age pensioners. They pointed out, with justice, that the means test was inefficient in that many people in need were refusing to submit themselves to it. During the long period of Conservative Government the role of national assistance had been growing in the system, not withering away, as originally intended by Beveridge. The electorate were given to understand that under Labour the means test would be abolished. In the words of Mr Wilson, his Government would rule in the spirit that 'the fundamental inspiration of our social life should be the age-old socialist principle: from each according to his means, to each according to his needs'. How then were those in need to be identified, if not by the investigating officers of the National Assistance Board?

The solution Labour proposed was ingenious and had all the fatal neatness of the virtually unworkable. The income-tax return is one test of means which everyone must undergo. The obligation to submit a tax return may not be a cherished privilege, but it involves no special loss of self-respect for the individual concerned. The purpose of the return is to determine how much money a person must pay to the authorities. Why not extend its use to establish how much should be paid by the authorities to those whose incomes fell below some minimum figure laid down by the Government? In Labour's 1964 Election Manifesto, the undertaking was given in the following terms:

For those already retired and for widows an Income Guarantee will be introduced. This will lay down a new national minimum benefit. Those whose incomes fall below the new national minimum will receive as of right, and without recourse to National Assistance, an income supplement.[1]

Speaking on BBC television in a pre-election broadcast, Mr Wilson sounded an even more urgent note: 'What we are going to do now – we are going to do it early because it is urgent in the first weeks of a Labour Government – is to provide a guaranteed income below which no one will be allowed to fall.'

The Manifesto referred only to the retired and widows; Mr Wilson was more generous and included everyone. Many interested parties were left with the impression that the Income Guarantee was to be universal in application and would include people at work – the more so since, at that time, evidence was beginning to accumulate that large numbers of families with a bread-winner in full-time employment were still below the poverty line.

Once installed in office, the Government apparently felt the urgency of abolishing the means test rather less sharply than before the election. Mr Wilson's 'first weeks of a Labour Government' grew into the first year and a half. Eventually, after much studied vagueness on the part of the Minister responsible, Miss Margaret Herbison, it began to emerge that the Income Guarantee was to be much narrower in scope than many people had been given to understand. In February 1966 Miss Herbison explained to the Commons that the Income Guarantee 'certainly was not going to cover the unemployed man or the man in full-time work'.

Later in 1966 legislative proposals about National Assistance were put before Parliament, and it became clear that the system which had flourished under the wicked Tories was to survive virtually unchanged under Labour. Under the Ministry of Social Security Act the National Assistance Board was to be abolished – but in name only. Its personnel and functions were not altered, but henceforward it was to be called the Supplementary Benefits Commission. Furthermore this new title would not appear on the notice-boards outside the old NAB offices, but they would be renamed Ministry of Social Security, in common with the former national-insurance offices. It was hoped that some of the respectability of national insurance would rub off on the supplementary sector. As in the case of the NAB the fiction would be maintained that the Minister was not responsible for the operation of the Supplementary Benefits Commission. This would be run by the same Committee of part-timers. As with the NAB the operation of the SBC cannot be discussed in Parliament, nor any individual case debated, since in theory no one in the Government is responsible.

As to the Incomes Guarantee, the proposal to use the income-tax return to identify those in need was buried without a trace. In the key planning document of the new Government – the ill-starred *National Plan*, published in 1965 – the minimum-income guarantee was mentioned only once, and dismissed in a single brisk sentence. 'An Incomes Guarantee', it explained, 'would not contribute to economic growth.'[2] The reason why the Incomes Guarantee did not materialize was not at the time made public by the Government. There were strong rumours that the Inland Revenue refused point blank to have anything to do with such extra responsibilities. Certainly a negative-income-tax system would add enormously to the existing work of the Inland Revenue. For example there are several million people, mainly retired, whose incomes are too low to qualify them for the payment of income tax. It would be necessary to extend the machinery of the income-tax return to include this group. It was accepted that the negative income tax, like the supplementary allowance, would be tailored to take account of the capital of claimants, and also of the size of the rent they paid. This implied that the number of questions asked on the income-tax return would have to be greatly extended to include information on capital holdings and housing costs. This extra information would have to be obtained and processed for the entire tax population. It was never made clear, and perhaps was never considered, whether the Inland Revenue was to do the extra work on its existing complement of staff or whether the 20,000 employees of the National Assistance Board would be transmuted into Inland Revenue officials.

Probably the conclusive argument was the one recounted by Mr Crossman in a lecture delivered some three years after the demise of the Incomes Guarantee project. To a great extent the Inland Revenue operates retrospectively. There is a delay before changes in the income and family circumstances of an individual are noted by the Inland Revenue and are reflected in an increase in tax levied or in the return of tax overpaid. As Crossman explains:

Finally we discovered that our Incomes Guarantee might often have to be based on information for the previous year. With this kind of lag, in hundreds of thousands of cases, people's incomes and other circumstances would have changed, and since you cannot leave people to survive on an income which may have been sufficient a year before but which is totally inadequate today, we would still have had to keep a Supplementary Benefits Commission to look after all the people whose circumstances had changed. So having introduced an Incomes Guarantee in order to abolish the bulk of the work of the Supplementary Benefits Commission we would have been forced to retain the Supplementary Benefits Commission to look after the people the income tax machine cannot cope with.[3]

In the Ministry of Social Security Act of 1966 the Government tried to evade the embarrassment of their electoral pledge to introduce an Incomes Guarantee. An extra 45p a week was added to the supplementary pension and was also given to a limited group of those under the age of retirement, namely people who had been getting a supplementary allowance continuously for two years, provided only that this two-year period did not include any spells of unemployment. This 45p was not really a new payment, but rather a partial substitute for the previous system of discretionary allowances which NAB officers had been able to award to clients, if they felt that they deserved extra help. By 1964 such discretionary allowances were being paid to 72 per cent of all pensioners assisted by the NAB and the average amount paid was 47½p a week. Rather more individuals and families would get the long-term addition than had got discretionary allowances. But in any given case there would be no increase in the amount paid. All that would change would be that the new Supplementary Benefits Commission would save itself the expense, and its client the inconvenience, of special investigations into laundry books, needs for window cleaning or for a bit of extra coal in the winter etc. The 45p long-term addition was to be paid without regard to family circumstances; the large family received the same 45p as the single person living alone. It was this 45p long-term addition which the Government tried to pass off as what they had originally meant by a guaranteed income.

The Ministry of Social Security Act of 1966 was Labour's major contribution during their term of office to the abolition of poverty. It was largely an exercise in calling the same things by different names. The means test run by the National Assistance Board had been called 'a test of need'. Now the means test was to be referred to as 'a test of requirements'. A part of the 'discretionary allowance' was to be called in future a 'long-term addition'. But substantially the rules and procedures of the means test remained as before, except that two not very dramatic concessions were made in the case of old-age pensioners. Previously any candidate for assistance had to be interviewed in his or her own home. Now anyone over retiring age can elect to be interviewed in the local office of the Ministry. Previously people were re-investigated every six months. Now tests of means are only applied to the elderly once every twelve months.

One other problem was troubling the Minister of Pensions in 1966. People whose incomes are near to, but still below, the poverty line can find themselves being offered only a very small weekly sum to make up the difference. The Minister, Miss Margaret Herbison, reminded the Commons that:

Most of us have had experience of an old person making application to the NAB and getting a book of orders for 1s [5p] a week. Most of us know the resentment, and sometimes the bitterness which has been caused because of that. This will no longer obtain under the new rules.[4]

The solution she arrived at was certainly unexpected. By the 1966 Act, if a person's resources were under 10p a week below the official minimum income, then *no* supplementary benefit would be paid! This proposal aroused particular criticism from the Conservative side of the House. Dame Joan Vickers, at that time one of the leading welfare spokesmen for the Tories, vividly expounded the manifold possibilities of 5p a week.

It is an enormous benefit to people in a very low income category. It can mean more gas. It can mean another bottle of milk. It can mean a loaf of bread. It can mean some soup. An old person can get to the butchers and get some bones to make soup. It can mean potatoes. If 1s [5p] is put in the gas meter an old person can be warm an extra period during the day. It can give an old person sufficient hot water to fill up a hot water bottle.[5]

Despite the appearance of personal concern, Dame Joan Vickers was not of course suggesting that people entitled to only 5p a week should be treated more generously. Her solution was that the 5p should be saved up and handed out to claimants as a lump sum, 'either a monthly or a quarterly voucher. This would give them a nice nest egg'.[5]

Just like the old National Assistance Board, the new Supplementary Benefits Commission was forbidden by statute to provide financial assistance to families in which there is a bread-winner in full-time work. A survey carried out by the Government in 1966 had shown that wages in a whole range of jobs were so low as to leave large numbers of families below the poverty line. The official report of the survey (entitled *Circumstances of Families*) is one of the most unintelligible documents ever produced by a British Government. However, it was possible, with a good deal of labour, to elicit certain hard facts from the haze of contorted statistics. Around 125,000 families had a father in full-time work and a total income below the supplementary benefit scales introduced in November 1966. The total number of children in these families was 450,000. The Government promised an urgent remedy.

In July 1967, after months of internal disputation an increase of 35p in the family allowance was announced to take effect in April* of the following year. The second child in each family would get a family allowance of 75p a week and younger children would get 85p. As before, no family allowance would be paid for the eldest child.

This decision provoked the resignation of Miss Margaret Herbison, who had been the Minister of Pensions since 1964. Miss Herbison was too loyal a servant of the Labour Party leadership to explain her reasons clearly to the public, far less to attempt any kind of campaign against the family allowance decision. But the fact was that only a much more substantial increase in the family allowance would have met the main objective of the exercise, namely to bring all families with a breadwinner in full-time work up to the official poverty line. Mr Patrick Gordon Walker, the senior welfare minister at the time, was forced to admit to the Commons that the 35p improvement in the family allowance would still leave half of the wage-earning poor under the official minimum income. This arose because of the largeness of the gap between low wages and the supplementary benefit standard of living. As a final twist Gordon Walker simultaneously announced a 50 per cent increase in the price of the school dinner – raised to 7½p per meal – and an increase from 1½p to 2½p a pint in the price of welfare milk. Although, in theory, low income groups were supposed to get school meals and welfare milk free of charge, it was known that a great many eligible families were not qualifying. For example, the *Circumstances of Families* survey had shown that in 1966, 96 per cent of the families under the poverty line – although the father was in full-time work – were not getting welfare milk free of charge.

* Not everyone had to wait till the following April for a bigger family allowance. The fourth and subsequent children in large families were to get 5p of the 35p increase from November 1967. This did little to alleviate poverty among wage earners since 70 per cent of the children involved were in families of three or fewer children.

Family Allowance and Income Tax

Although it was the smallness of the family allowance increase which caused consternation on the left of the Labour Party, nevertheless the strategy adopted was one which had been enthusiastically canvassed by those who supported the retention of a universalistic framework in social security. The family allowance had been increased for everyone, but since this benefit is subject to income tax a proportion of the increase was drawn directly back into the Exchequer from millions of families paying income tax. When the 35p increase was announced in July 1967, the arrangement proposed by the Government was simply to continue the usual procedures for taxing family allowances. That is that the allowance would be counted as earned income, added to other income and taxed accordingly. For the vast majority of people this meant that the 35p increase in the family allowance would be subject to the standard rate of income tax – then about 33½p per pound per week. Only people with incomes too low to be subject to income tax would get the full 35p. This practice, whereby the Treasury presents money to people as a welfare benefit and then reclaims it from some of them in taxation, has become known as the clawback. Its effect in reducing the cost to the State of the family allowance increase was quite substantial. The 35p increase would cost £150 million gross, but of this £67 million would be clawed back, leaving a net cost of £83 million.

The clawback device was subject to a good deal of criticism in Conservative quarters. From the Opposition benches came pointed questions about the logic and the administrative costs involved in handing out money with one hand and taking it back with the other. The additions to personal income, resulting from increased family allowances, would have the effect of bringing some 300,000 households up into the income bands where income tax began to operate. A further 250,000 households would move up from the lower bands of income tax (20p and 30p in the pound) and become subject to tax at the full standard rate. Conservative policy at the time was that no one should get a bigger family allowance, unless a means test showed that their income was lower than the supplementary benefit scale. The Tories calculated that a means-tested family allowance would enable the Government to bring all wage earners up to the poverty line for a cost of only £13 million a year. Labour's proposals were denounced as a classic instance of the inefficiency, expensiveness and injustice of Beveridge-type universalism. Despite the clawback, most of Labour's £83 million family-allowance increase would go to people above the poverty line. The amount provided to those families under the poverty line would be sufficient to bring only half of them up to a supplementary benefit standard of living.

Long before the new family allowance actually began to be paid out the Labour Government shifted much further towards the Conservative position. In January 1968, as part of the post-devaluation programme of cuts in public expenditure, Labour announced that for people paying income tax the *whole* of the 35p increase would be taxed away. This would be done simply by reducing the tax-free personal allowance by exactly the amount of the family-allowance increase. The net cost to the Government of the increase in family allowances would be thus reduced from £83 million to £30 million a year.

One effect of the devaluation of sterling at the end of 1967 would be a sharp increase in the cost of living. To go some way to compensate for this, a further increase of 15p in the family allowance was awarded. Thus 1968 saw the rate of family allowance rather more than doubled, as compared with the level set in 1956. For people not paying income tax the effective rate became 90p a week for the second child and £1 a week for subsequent children. But, where a family paid income tax, 50p a week per child was to be paid back to the Government in extra income tax. The effect of the clawback system was that, although because of the two family allowance increases in 1968 the Government handed out an extra £180 million a year, no less than £133 million of this arrived straight back into the Treasury in the form of increased income taxes.

Even for the very poor, who received the full extra family allowance, the improvement this brought in their financial circumstances was limited and temporary. One half of the original group of wage earners in poverty still remained below the minimum official poverty line. And in the two years after 1968 the effects of inflation, combined with lower-than-average wage increases, were to restore the numbers of wage earners in poverty to at least the total which existed before 1968. In the period from 1968 to the end of 1970 the Retail Price Index rose by no less than 36 per cent. Surveys, carried out in 1970 by Incomes Data Services Ltd, showed that in the previous two years most categories of lower-paid worker had been getting less in the way of wage increases than average-paid workers and, moreover, that wage increases for the lower paid were being awarded at much less frequent intervals than was generally the case in industry.[6]

When family allowances were first introduced in 1945 by the war-time Coalition Government, a family of three children received in allowances the equivalent of 8·2 per cent of the average wage for manual work at that time. By 1967 the corresponding family allowance was only 4 per cent of the average wage. In the autumn of 1970, for those who paid enough income tax to experience the full impact of the clawback, the family allowance for a three-child family was 5 per cent of average industrial wages. Even for the very poorest, who received the full benefit of the 50p increase in 1968, the effect was only to restore the relative value of family allowances to the 1945 level. However, at the end of the Second World War family allowances had been set at only two thirds of the level recommended in the Beveridge Report.[7] The Coalition Government argued that the difference would be made up by the food subsidies together with free school meals and milk. But since 1945 successive Governments have whittled away most of the systems of subsidized nutrition which had been used to justify the original low level of family allowances. In 1956 the Tories abolished the subsidy for bread and reduced it for milk. After devaluation in 1967 Labour abolished free school milk for secondary-school children. In the spring of 1971 the Conservative Government followed the precedent set by Labour and abolished free school milk for all children over the age of seven; welfare milk for children under five was abolished at the same time.

Between 1968 and the spring of 1971 the price of a school meal was increased from 5p to 12p.

Income Tax and Poverty

It has to be noted also that the technique of clawback, if applied during a period of inflation, can mean rapid erosion of welfare benefits, affecting progressively poorer and poorer groups. In effect clawback involves the use of the income-tax threshold as a means-testing criterion. If income rises above the threshold at which income tax starts to be levied, then a substantial part of any family allowances the tax-payer is receiving begins to be taxed away. The level of income at which the tax threshold occurs is determined for any individual by the total of tax allowances he can claim. For people with below-average incomes the size of tax allowances is a much more important determinant of their income-tax burden than the size of the standard rate of income tax. The main tax allowances affecting lower-paid workers are the personal allowance for the tax-payer and his wife, children's allowances and the allowance made if income is earned rather than unearned.

One of the most inequalitarian achievements of the Labour Government of 1964–70 was that they allowed income tax to become a major cause of poverty, particularly in the two years ending in 1970. The income-tax threshold – the point of income at which people started to pay income tax – had been allowed to drop sharply downwards. The effect was that in the late sixties income tax was increasingly levied on incomes below the official poverty line. This situation arose because of a combination of factors.

If the size of tax allowances is held static during a period of rapid inflation, there are three consequences.

1. A higher and higher proportion of people find themselves paying income tax, and the new recruits to the tax-paying population are drawn from increasingly poorer sections of society.

2. For the whole tax-paying population, an increasing proportion of their income is subject to income tax.

3. The rate of increase in the proportion of income taken in tax is highest for people at the lower end of the income scale.

When inflation is rapid, these various trends can change the distribution of post-tax income with phenomenal speed, and always to the disadvantage of the lower income groups. This, in summary, is precisely what occurred in Britain during the late sixties and the fiscal policies adopted by the Labour Government only accentuated the unfavourable tax position of the lower income groups.

Anyone with dependent children gets a tax allowance for each child. Between 1963 and 1971 the child allowance remained unchanged at £115 a year clear of tax for a child under eleven, £140 for a child between eleven and sixteen, and £165 for a dependent child aged sixteen or over.

Given inflation, the effect of unchanged child allowances was that people with lower and lower incomes were having to pay standard rate on an increasing proportion of their income if they had children. As an example, three children aged between eleven and sixteen would attract tax-free children's allowances amounting to £420 a year, both in 1963 and 1970. This was half of the average wage for manual work in 1963, but less than one third of the corresponding average wage in 1970. In effect the purchasing power of the tax relief given in respect of children had been allowed to diminish sharply over the period.*

Much the same is true of the tax relief given in respect of a wife. In 1963 she was worth £120 a year of income exempt from tax. Not until the Budget of April 1970 was this increased, and then only by £20 a year, leaving the wife allowance at a level of £140 a year. By 1970, it would take nearly one and a half wives to achieve the same purchasing power in tax exemption which a

---

*Over a longer time span the fall in the relative purchasing power of children's allowances has been even sharper. Assume a family with two children under eleven and one child aged eleven to sixteen. Tax allowances for these children would have been 54 per cent of the average wage in 1952, but only 26 per cent of the average wage in 1970.

single wife generated in 1963.* As with children, the effect was that being married brought a man into the income-tax-paying bracket at a lower relative income than was the case in 1963.

The position was considerably worsened by changes made in the income-tax system in the last two Budgets of the Labour Government. From 1965 onwards the standard rate of income tax was 41·25 per cent in the pound. But in the years between 1965 and 1969 a person paid a lower rate of tax than the standard rate† on the first £300 of his income above the tax threshold.

The arrangement was that a person paid tax at only 20p in the pound on the first £100 band of income subject to tax, and 30p in the pound on the next £200. Only thereafter did the full standard rate begin to operate.

In the Budget of 1969 Roy Jenkins scrapped the 20p rate of tax and in the following year the 30p rate was also abolished. As a result the full standard rate in 1970 began to operate at a level of taxable income £300 lower than was the case in 1968 and earlier.

Partly to compensate for this abolition of the reduced rates, Jenkins made increases in the personal allowance given in respect of the tax-payer himself. It was raised to £220 a year by the 1969 Budget, and to £325 a year clear of tax in 1970. Jenkins did *not* improve the child allowances and, as pointed out above, raised the wife's allowance by only a minor £20 a year. As a result the single tax-payer reaped by far the largest benefit from the increase in personal allowance, which was given to compensate for introducing standard rate at an income level £300 a year lower than before. Married women got some benefit, but only if they earned an income by work. The change involved sharp discrimination against families in which the wife does not go out to work and in which there are children.

* Once again the contrast with the early 1950s is even more dramatic. In 1952 the wife allowance (then £90 a year) was 19 per cent of the average industrial wage, in 1970 only 10 per cent.

† Of course the standard rate on *earned* income was not 41·25 per cent, but a shade over 30 per cent. For the reduced rates of 20p and 30p in the pound, which operated until the late 1960s, the effective tax rate on *earned* income was correspondingly lower.

The consequences can be illustrated from the 1970 spring Budget. Jenkins claimed to have scored a victory for social justice, because he had freed two million tax-payers from any requirement to pay income tax. But 700,000 of them were single men and a further 800,000 were working wives. Only 400,000 of the two million were married men and many fewer of these would be men with families.[8] The latter suffered the full effects of the lowering of the standard-rate threshold; they got the same increase in personal allowance as the single man, but the value of this compensatory increase had to be spread out over all the members of the family.

Of itself this tax change increased the numbers of wage-earners whose post-tax incomes fell below the official poverty line. It meant that for family men the full standard rate began to bite at a much lower point of income than had been the case in earlier years. And this was in addition to the fact that inflation, plus static allowances for a wife or children, was in any case making standard rate reach further and further down the overall curve of income distribution. Thus the effect of both developments was to draw relatively lower and poorer groups into the population of income-tax payers.

As if this was not enough the Labour Government had compounded a disastrous situation when they increased family allowances in 1968. The extra 50p per child given from 1968 onwards was made subject to a progressive 100 per cent clawback as soon as total family income rose high enough for income tax to begin to operate. Thus, during the final two years of Labour rule, not only was there a rapid increase in the number of taxpayers who found themselves paying the standard rate of income tax, but, once they started paying income tax, families in receipt of family allowances were taxed at a 100 per cent rate on a band of income – the width of the band depending on the number of children for whom family allowances were paid. And, at time of writing (June 1975), the same arrangement still continued to function.

That a 100 per cent tax rate operates on groups with relatively low incomes is not generally appreciated. This is partly because the method used by the tax authorities to calculate how the 100 per cent rate will be paid tends to disguise what is happening. The clawback is not carried out by taxing family allowances directly, but rather by making an equivalent cut in the personal tax allowance of the father.

Table 1: Tax Thresholds on Weekly Income in 1970*

Married Couple with	Tax allowances Personal +wife	Child	Earned income	Total allowances i.e. tax thresholds
0 Children	£8·95	—	£2·55	£11·50
1 Child	£8·95	£2·20	£3·20	£14·35
2 Children	£8·15	£4·40	£3·60	£16·15
3 Children	£7·35	£6·60	£4·00	£17·95
4 Children	£6·55	£8·80	£4·40	£19·75

* All children assumed to be under age eleven. Weekly income here includes family allowances. Any income above the tax thresholds indicated here will be taxed at standard rate (i.e. 30·14 per cent on earned income).

The tax thresholds indicated in the right-hand column of Table 1 are those at which standard-rate tax begins to be levied. For each child for whom a family allowance is paid the 50p increase in family allowance awarded in 1968 has been fully clawed back by reduction of the father's personal allowance.

Notice how fantastically low these tax thresholds were. During 1970 the Trades Union Congress was campaigning (though without noticeable effect) for a minimum wage of £16·50. Yet a married man with no dependent children was paying in tax just over 30 per cent of all income above £11·50. Even a man with four dependent children started paying income tax at just under £20 a week. It was the case, in fact, that income tax came into operation at income levels below the official poverty line, and this is illustrated in Table 2. Supplementary benefit is not paid to families in which there is a bread-winner in full-time employment, and therefore there has to be some adjustment to establish an equivalent official poverty line where a man is working. This is done as shown in Table 2, by taking the supplementary benefit scales and adding an allowance for travel to and from work (here a modest 40p a week) as well as the employee's share of national-insurance contributions.

Table 2: Tax Thresholds and Poverty Line, 1970

Married Couple with	Minimum income provided by supplementary benefit	Extra expenses if at work	For wage earner – income equal to supplementary benefit	Income Tax thresholds	Tax threshold below poverty line by –
1	2	3	4	5	6
0 Children	£12·00	£1·40	£13·40	£11·50	£1·90
1 Child	£13·80	£1·50	£15·30	£14·30	£1·00
2 Children	£15·60	£1·60	£17·20	£16·15	£1·05
3 Children	£17·40	£1·70	£19·10	£18·00	£1·10
4 Children	£19·40	£1·80	£21·20	£19·80	£1·40

1. Family allowances are included in all incomes in Table 2. All children are assumed to be age five to ten, except for one child under five in the largest family.

2. Supplementary benefit includes £3 for rent and rates (£3·50 in a four child family); also included is a 50p long-term addition paid to families on supplementary benefit for more than one year. Supplementary benefit rates are those operating between autumn 1969 and autumn 1970.

3. Working expenses in column 3 are national insurance contributions plus 40p for travel to work.

As Table 2 indicates, for all of these family sizes the income-tax threshold was substantially below the official poverty line. The effect of this would be, for example, that if a man with two children had a gross family income of £17·20 a week – just on the poverty line – £1·05 of this would be subject to income tax at 30·14 per cent. Thus, after payment of income tax, total family income would be 32p short of the poverty line.

What is, if anything, more extraordinary is that none of the many pronouncements made by Labour Party leaders in 1970 on the subject of their record in office betrays the slightest awareness of the situation created by their fiscal policies. The same applies to the Opposition; it was not until the Conservatives had been in office for some months that they began to comment on the effects of Labour's taxation policies on poverty.[9]

Since 1970, both Conservative and Labour Governments have made some efforts to raise income-tax thresholds above the official poverty line, and these will be discussed and assessed in Chapter 5. However, there is one further point to be made here about the consequences of Labour's disastrous tax strategy in the late 1960s.

Very roughly the income limits above which a family loses entitlement to rent or rates rebates, or free school meals, and exemption from prescription charges, tend to be equivalent to the supplementary benefit scales. Thus the consequence of an increase in earnings above the poverty line may well be to leave a family worse off than before earnings were increased. The family is now paying tax on all extra income at 35 per cent in the pound. But to this marginal tax rate one has to add the loss of rent and rates rebates, and also the loss of exemption from the school-meals charge, which can mean a considerable addition to the necessary expenditure of any family with a number of children at school. Whether a family is entitled to free school meals is calculated on pre-tax rather than post-tax income. So an improvement in earnings can mean the loss of a school-meal-charge exemption, even if extra tax leaves the family no better off than they were before earnings increased.

The combination of all these factors means that for many

families whose incomes are around the poverty line any improvement in wages can leave them, after deduction, with a considerably lower income than they had before. Only exceptional improvements in wages can raise their standard of living. As one Labour M.P., Michael Meacher, explained in a graphic image:

Thus, getting out of poverty today is rather like getting out of a well. Unless one can jump right to the top one is all too likely to fall back precisely to the point from which one started. The accumulation of means tests, therefore, by building up further the side of the well, so far from assisting the poor, actually increasingly blocks the escape route from hard core poverty.[10]

If Labour ministers were aware of the effects of their fiscal policies – especially during 1969 and 1970 – in devastating the standard of living of low-wage earners, they certainly did not discuss the matter in public. A few months before the 1970 Election the Child Poverty Action Group published a pamphlet which carefully evaluated the whole range of Labour's policies in the field of social security. Its conclusions were that 'in many ways the plight of poor families is now worse than when the Government took office', and that 'poverty remains on a considerable and perhaps even greater scale than when the Government assumed office'.[11]

CHAPTER 5

Does Social Security Redistribute Income?

It is commonly assumed in middle-class circles that social security along with other sectors of the Welfare State is largely financed by high rates of taxation on the upper-income groups and operates mainly to the benefit of lower-income groups. Thus, on this view, the Welfare State is a huge funnel, redistributing resources and purchasing power from rich to poor. I shall try to show that this picture of social security is largely an illusion. In fact most of the financial arrangements which underpin social security have been carefully designed to minimize redistribution of income. Furthermore during the 1960s the original Beveridge scheme has been modified in a number of ways, which made the system as a whole even less redistributive than previously.

The Government finds the money for social security in two ways. (1) By contributions to the national-insurance scheme levied on employees, employers and the self-employed. (2) Out of general taxation – income tax, expenditure taxes etc. Family allowances are paid solely by the Exchequer out of general taxation, and so are the costs of the Supplementary Benefits Commission. The Exchequer also pays a part of the costs of the national-insurance schemes, in 1973 about 14 per cent of the total, the remainder coming from contributions.

At first sight it looks as though a large part of the cost of social security falls on employers, about one third in 1973, according to Table 1. It is agreed, however, by economists that there is not the slightest reason to believe that employers meet the social security charge by reducing profits or managerial salaries. When Beveridge's proposals were first published, a leading expert on the economics of taxation, Nicholas Kaldor, argued that the employers' contribution would in fact be passed on to wage earners

Table 1: Costs of Social Security (£ million) 1973

	Employees	Employers	Other* sources	Exch.	Total
National insurance	1570	1914	233	627	4344
Family allowances	—	—	—	360	360
Supplementary benefit	—	—	—	705	705
Totals				1692	5409

* e.g. from self-employed and from interest.

in the form of higher prices. He suggested that the whole notion of an employers' contribution was an unnecessary piece of obscurantism.

If it is intended that its incidence should fall on the employees, it would be better to charge it to the employees openly, and to abolish the employers' contribution altogether. If it is intended, on the other hand, that it should be a charge on the employers – that it should fall on profits not wages – it is no use levying a tax which enters into wage costs; it should be raised as a tax on profits, and not in the form of a tax on employment.[1]

Kaldor notes that the Parliamentary Liberal Party had urged Beveridge to propose just such a levy on profits. However such a step seemed far too radical to the post-war Labour Government.

For two decades the official position was maintained that the employers' contribution was not paid by consumers in the form of higher prices. But recently the light has dawned. The Government publish an annual report which shows the incidence of various sorts of taxation on households with varying income. In the 1969 report on 'The Incidence of Taxes and Social Service Benefits' the Central Statistical Office acknowledged that 'It has been decided that from 1969 onwards, for this analysis, the employers' contribution will no longer be regarded as part of the employees' income; instead it will be treated as an indirect tax included in the prices of goods and services produced in the United Kingdom.'[2]

Thus, at a stroke, it was officially recognized that more than £1,000 million a year of employers' contributions (one third of the total cost of social security) had to be regarded as a tax on consumers rather than as a free windfall presented to employees. This later view is certainly the correct one, and it enormously affects the final judgement about how far the social security system redistributes resources from rich to poor.

I have already mentioned that under the Beveridge system the redistributive possibilities of social security were severely limited by the fact that the contributions made by the employer and employee were at a flat rate. Until 1961 the national-insurance stamp cost the same for every employee irrespective of income. During the 1960s the flat-rate principle was breached by three important modifications of Beveridge's scheme.

The first occurred in 1961, when the Conservative Government introduced an additional graduated pension scheme which still operates alongside the main flat-rate scheme. For his graduated pension a man pays 4 per cent of whatever weekly earnings he has in the band between £9 and £18 a week. The employer matches this contribution. This is the celebrated scheme whereby every £7·50 paid in by an employee eventually earns him an extra 2½p a week on his pension. As a solution to the problem of poverty among the old the graduated pension scheme leaves practically everything to be desired. People who retired in 1971 after paying into the scheme for ten years, even if they had contributed at the maximum rate, got an addition to their basic flat-rate pension of less than 60p a week. For the two million old-age pensioners who depend on supplementary benefit to bring them up to the poverty line, the graduated pension scheme makes no net addition to their income. Any money from the graduated scheme is simply docked off their supplementary benefit. The maximum weekly pension that would *ever* be paid under the Tory graduated scheme would be £3·10 a week. This would only be achieved by people retiring in the year 2008 or after, and to get it they would have to have worked continuously for forty-seven years and paid continuously at the maximum rate for the scheme. (At the present rate of inflation – by 2008 £3·10 would be worth less than 20 pence of today's money.) The graduated pension scheme is such a small addendum to the main flat-rate scheme that, even if the Tories had built a serious redistributive element into their graduated scheme, the effect on the social security system as a whole would have been virtually nil. In fact the graduated scheme was arranged to keep redistribution at the barest minimum. From it people get a pension that exactly correlates with the amount they have contributed. There is no specially favourable rate for low-income contributors. No contributions are paid on earnings above £18 a week, which means that the higher a person's income the more lightly he escapes. Contributions are not levied on unearned income. The Treasury contribution to the scheme is strictly limited to one fifth of the total income of the scheme, so that, for example, the amount of money used to finance graduated pensions out of a redistributive tax like surtax is kept down to very minute proportions indeed.

When it was first introduced, the Labour Party used to refer to the graduated pension scheme as a bucket-shop swindle. There was much justice in this charge. The Tory scheme did nothing to alleviate poverty among the existing population of old people, virtually nothing for people retiring in the 1960s and 1970s, and precious little for generations beyond that. It was in fact purely a device to raise a lot of money by taxation of people currently at work. The pension rights given in return were small and subject to continual erosion because of inflation. From the Government's point of view the scheme was a wonderful device: a handy addition to revenue in the short term, but with no commitment to take account of inflation, when eventually paying out the pension. Note that, even after retirement, the graduated pension is not increased to compensate for decreases in its purchasing power.

While they were still in opposition before 1964, the Labour Party subjected the graduated scheme to a great deal of invective. Once installed in Government they seemed to undergo a change of heart. Six years passed, during which time not only was the 1961 pension scheme retained – it was not even modified. Eventually Labour decided that the graduated scheme would be superseded by the larger Crossman scheme. The 1970 Election, however, put paid to this intention, and the Tories returned to power to find their graduated scheme still flourishing. The rise in money wages over the six-year period meant that a much higher proportion of the labour force had weekly earnings of £18 or more and therefore paid a graduated contribution at the maximum rate. In 1963 Government income from graduated contributions was £177 million; by 1968 it was £405 million. Thus by the latter date the graduated scheme was providing the money to meet nearly one third of the cost of the basic flat-rate pensions paid out in 1968.

This last point may seem obscure. In a scheme which specifies exactly what future pension rights are built up by a given contribution in the present, it is natural to assume that the money you pay in will be accumulated into a fund from which your bit of graduated pension will eventually be paid. This does not of course happen in the main national-insurance scheme where, in effect, money drawn in from contributors during one week is paid out across the Post Office counter the next week to the old-age pensioners. However, ever since the Beveridge system started the Tories have criticized national insurance for not being properly funded – i.e. not having at every point in time a reserve fund big enough to meet all future obligations.

However, though they are enthusiastic about funding as a general principle, the Tories were careful in 1961 to make no commitment to accumulate a fund of graduated contributions. Instead the money levied each year in graduated contributions goes straight to help pay for current expenditure on the flat-rate pension. It has proved, moreover, an increasing part. In 1962 the graduated contribution paid 19 per cent of the current cost of old-age pensions; by 1968, 29 per cent. Thus, though the graduated pension scheme will make only a marginal difference to the eventual pensions of individual contributors, it has become a most significant support for the current financing of national insurance.

The graduated scheme was a swindle, because the Government offered so little in the way of pension rights to the people from whom it required contribution. Otherwise, however, there is nothing intrinsically wicked about the Government using current graduated income to meet its current obligations. The sting lies in the exact contribution arrangements, and how they determine which section of contributors foots the bill.

In the late 1950s the Conservative Government found itself in a spot about pensions. The proportion of the population over the age of retirement was increasing slowly but continuously. Since pensions are by far the biggest element of national-insurance expenditure, an increasing gap was opened between the costs of the scheme and the income drawn in from the flat-rate national-insurance stamp. It has been the rule that each year this deficit is made up by money paid into the national-insurance scheme by the Treasury, out of general taxation. Since income taxes are higher for the rich than the poor, the effect was that the higher income groups were paying an increasing part of the costs of the old-age pension. Not unexpectedly a Conservative Government regarded this as a most unsatisfactory state of affairs. It began to cast around for some fairly drastic solution.

The Tories squeezed the flat-rate lemon as much as they dared. Between 1957 and 1961 the employee part of the national-insurance stamp was raised on four separate occasions and ended up 40 per cent higher. This helped the finances of the national-insurance scheme to a certain extent – but not nearly enough. By 1959 the Exchequer found itself paying 27 per cent of the costs of the national-insurance scheme.

It was the graduated pension scheme, legislated in 1959 and in operation from 1961, which got the Government out of its difficulty and enabled it to reverse the tendency for national insurance to become increasingly redistributive of income from rich to poor. The graduated scheme made possible a substantial shift of the costs of pensions away from the higher-paid middle class and on to the shoulders of manual workers. The trick lay in the band of earnings on which graduated contributions were required. In 1959 average earnings for manual work were just under £16 a week. It was decided that no contributions would be required on earnings above £15 a week. Thus the average-paid worker would pay contributions on earnings below a ceiling which was equivalent to almost his total wages. The more a person earned above £15 the lower would be his graduated contribution as a proportion of his total income. On the other hand the floor was set fairly low; only the band of earnings up to £9 a week was exempt from the graduated contribution.

The implications of these arrangements have been clearly summarized by Tony Lynes.

The Government had succeeded in balancing the books of the National Insurance scheme by means of the new graduated contribution – essentially a regressive tax because it took as much from those earning £15 a week as from the highest-paid executive. The obligation accepted by previous governments, to meet the emerging deficits out of general taxation had been repudiated. It was more than a coincidence that in the same month in 1961 as the graduated contributions began, the Chancellor of the Exchequer announced the raising of the starting point for surtax on earned incomes from £2,000 a year to £5,000, at a cost of £83 million in a full year. Without the graduated pension scheme, that £83 million would have been needed to meet part of the deficit on the National Insurance Fund.[3]

In 1963, with a General Election imminent, the Conservative Government awarded increases in all national-insurance benefits. Again, unless the Exchequer contribution were to increase dramatically, an increase in the contribution of employers and employees would be necessary. The Government decided to raise one quarter of the extra £200 million required by raising the income ceiling on which graduated contributions were required from £15 to £18 a week. By 1963 the average industrial wage had gone up to just under £17 a week. The raising of the contribution ceiling meant that the group which paid the highest proportion of earnings in the form of graduated contributions continued to be employees with industrial wages a little above average. Thus after the changes in 1963 the graduated scheme required employers and employees each to pay in 4·25 per cent of earned income within the £9 to £18 band of weekly income.

Again Tony Lynes has provided a succinct interpretation of the political motives behind the 1963 amendments. Firstly, it would have been electorally unpopular to have raised all the money needed to finance the national-insurance increases by raising the flat-rate contribution. Flat-rate increases bear particularly heavily on the lowest-paid contributors, whereas graduated contributions put the main weight on the higher-paid section of manual workers.

Secondly, the Exchequer supplement is calculated as a proportion of the flat-rate minimum contributions. Any increase in flat-rate contributions therefore entails a corresponding increase in the Exchequer supplement. The graduated contributions, on the other hand, do not attract an Exchequer supplement. By raising £48 million of the £200 million through an increase in graduated contributions, the Exchequer was able to keep its share of the total about £10 million lower than it would otherwise have been. Thirdly, the yield of the graduated contributions rises automatically with average earnings. Thus, while the yield of the flat-rate increase is expected to rise very slowly from £130 million in 1964–5 to £144 million in 1981–2, that of the additional graduated contributions will shoot up from £46 million to £135 million, even on the Government's very conservative assumption of a 2 per cent annual increase in average earnings. Looking to the future, therefore, an increase in contribution which counts towards a higher pension for the individual contributor is an easier selling line than a flat-rate increase which only benefits existing pensioners and although a higher graduated contribution entails a higher pension bill, this does not have to be met in the early years of the scheme.[4]

These considerations proved equally irresistible to the 1964–70 Labour Government. The Tory graduated scheme was preserved intact. And in 1966 Labour introduced a scheme providing an earnings-related addition to flat-rate benefit during the first six months of any period of sickness, industrial injury or unemployment. This scheme was financed by a levy of 0·5 per cent of income on the band between £9 and £30 a week.

Later in 1969 Labour completely succumbed to the temptations of earnings-related financing. From the point of view of contributors the Tory graduated scheme did have at least one merit. A person's graduated contribution did create entitlement to an additional amount of future pension, however small that entitlement would be in fact. For example the raising of the contribution ceiling in 1963 was matched by an increase from £2·03 to £3·10 a week in the size of the maximum possible graduated pension. The Labour Government went one better. In 1969 they massively increased the graduated contribution without offering any corresponding improvement in graduated pension rights. Before 1969 only 0·5 per cent was taken on the £18 to £30 band of income, yet in that year the average manual wage reached £24·35 per week. Richard Crossman, who was then in charge of social security, needed a lot of cash to pay for the increase in flat-rate benefits awarded in 1969 and so a fresh raid was organized. At a stroke the earnings-related contribution on the £18 to £30 income band was stepped up from 0·5 per cent to 3·25 per cent. This particular increase produced an extra £260 million and took the total yield from the graduated contribution to over £700 million a year in 1970 to 1971 – not much less than half of the total expenditure on old-age pensions in that year. At the same time Crossman made no corresponding increase in graduated pension rights.

Labour having shown the way, the Tories in turn followed along the same path. In the 1971 Budget it was announced that there would be a further extension of the graduated contribution ceiling from £30 to £42 a week, and in addition that the percentage contribution would be put up from 3·25 per cent to 4·35 per cent on the whole income band from £18 to £42 a week.

What happened during the 1960s is that successive Governments were raising national-insurance contributions somewhat faster than benefits were being increased. The consequence was that there was a steady drop in the proportion of the costs of national insurance which were met by the Exchequer out of general taxation. In 1959 to 1961, 18 per cent of the receipts of the national-insurance scheme came from the Exchequer – but by 1970 only 15 per cent. Thus a substantial part of the extra money drawn in by contribution increases during the 1960s was not spent in improving pensions and other benefits. Rather, part of the extra cash was used to reduce the relative size of the Exchequer subsidy and hence limit the extent to which the scheme redistributed income from higher to lower income groups.

In this process there has been a happy collaboration between

Labour and Conservative administrations. Indeed in 1969 it was Labour who first introduced the convenient device of an increase in earnings-related contributions without the granting of any increase in future pension entitlement. Even more remarkable as an innovation was Labour's 1966 scheme for earnings-related sickness and unemployment benefit. This scheme provides an addition to flat-rate benefit during the first six months of sickness and unemployment.* Since national insurance began in this country in 1911, it has been axiomatic that part of the finance of each scheme should come from general taxation. In the 1966 earnings-related sickness and unemployment scheme, which still operates in 1975, the Exchequer contribution was eliminated altogether. The full costs of the scheme are met out of contributions made by employer and employee. The absence of any contribution from general taxation cancelled out one of the ways by which redistribution of income can be managed in such a scheme.

A second redistributive possibility lies in the relation established between contributions and benefits. It can be arranged that the higher-paid contributors get benefits which are lower than their contribution would justify. In Labour's scheme there was no such provision. The weekly benefit was calculated as one third of whatever earnings a person had been making above £9 a week, but not over £30 a week. What counted was average earnings over the previous year. Thus for example a person averaging £21 a week in 1970 would qualify in 1971 for one third of £12 – i.e. £4 a week – as an extra on his flat-rate sickness or unemployment benefit.

What Labour arranged was that within the scheme there would be no redistribution of income from higher-paid to lower-paid contributors. A person's benefits co-relate exactly with the level of his contributions in the previous year.

Viewed historically, the earnings-related scheme of 1966 was a unique invention. For the first time in the whole development of State welfare provision in Britain a scheme was introduced which

*The 1966 scheme also provides an earnings-related addition to the widow's pension during the first six months of widowhood.

was non-redistributive in design.* In one respect the scheme even worked in the opposite direction. The rule that benefits are exactly determined by contributions does not always apply in the case of lower-paid contributors. The wage-stop principle is built into the scheme. An earnings-related addition to flat-rate income is not paid if it would bring a man's income in sickness or unemployment above 85 per cent of his normal gross earnings at work. The same contribution is required irrespective of whether benefit will be paid or withheld. This arrangement was a further novel feature of the 1966 scheme. The wage stop had been operated since 1948 for supplementary assistance. Now, for the first time, the principle was introduced into a national-insurance scheme.

Anyone who has no income except flat-rate national-insurance benefit is underneath the official poverty line and so should qualify for supplementary benefit. Since 1966 – for the first six months of sickness or unemployment – the flat-rate benefit has been supplemented by earnings-related benefit. The effect is that for a great many contributors the earnings-related addition does not make them any better off when sick or unemployed. It merely cuts the amount they are able to claim from supplementary benefit. In such cases the only financial advantage of an earnings-related scheme is to the Government, which makes a saving on the costs of supplementary benefit. The loser is the contributor, who loses entitlement to supplementary benefit paid for out of general taxation and gets instead an earnings-related benefit half of which is financed out of his own pay packet.

There are some other features of the 1966 scheme which deserve comment. No earnings-related benefit is paid during the first fourteen days off work (Sundays included) and the benefit stops after six months. This means that a great deal of sickness and unemployment has to be endured on flat-rate benefit. For example a survey carried out in 1965 showed that of the eight million spells off work because of sickness, more than half (four and a half million) lasted less than two weeks. At the time the

* Except that there would of course be some measure of redistribution from groups with lower rates of sickness and unemployment to those with higher rates.

survey was taken 162,000 people had been off sick for *more* than six months. In the spring of 1971 nearly one third of those who were unemployed had been out of work for more than six months. At any one time only one in six of the unemployed are receiving earnings-related benefit.

The amount of earnings-related benefit which a person gets is determined by his earnings in the previous contribution year. No allowance is made for inflation in the period which separates contributions from payment of benefits. In the main flat-rate scheme an employee is credited with a contribution while sick or unemployed. But there is no crediting allowed in the earnings-related scheme. If a person should be sick or unemployed for a substantial part of one year, his earnings-related benefit during the succeeding year will be correspondingly reduced.

The final twist is that, since earnings-related benefits are determined purely by size of contribution (and therefore by amount of earnings), the benefits are paid without regard to need. A single man on a given wage will get exactly the same earnings-related benefit as someone with the same wage and a family. Nowhere else in the national-insurance scheme are family responsibilities discounted in this way.

Oddly enough the leadership of the Labour Party expressed great pride in their earnings-related scheme. Certainly, as the reader may have noticed, the scheme was so complicated that most contributors would not appreciate with what exactness they were getting only what they had individually paid for. For employees with incomes well clear of the poverty line the 1966 legislation amounted to no more than a scheme for compulsory saving. For low income groups it meant that more of them were brought above the poverty line in sickness and unemployment – but that this privilege was paid for by those same groups in terms of a lower standard of living while at work. For the poorest of all the scheme merely reduced the amount which the Government had to find in means-tested supplementary benefit. This legislation marks how far the Labour Party have retreated in practice from the ideals of equality and social justice which they still profess in theory.

In 1973, as part of a much wider reorganization of social security contributions, the Conservative Government announced the winding up of the whole graduated scheme, from April 1975: from that date no further contributions would be required. At the same time it was guaranteed that rights to graduated pensions accumulated during the fourteen-year history of the scheme would be preserved and paid over to pensioners on retirement. This was an insubstantial gesture given that preserved rights to graduated pension were not to be increased to compensate for inflation. Those retiring in the 1980s and 1990s would receive only a minute fraction of the extra pension rights which the Government had apparently promised them in return for substantial graduated contributions made in the 1960s.[5]

This, however, is a story with a happy ending. One of the very few benefits of the ultra-high rate of inflation which developed in Britain in the mid 1970s is that graduated pension rights – fixed in money terms, and small enough in the first place – were evaporating at a fantastic rate. The process was so devastating that Labour ministers decided to reverse all previous policy on the graduated scheme. In 1974, Barbara Castle announced that the graduated scheme would be wound up as the Tories had proposed, but that graduated pension rights would be protected against price increases. This guarantee was to apply both to graduated pensions in payment, and to those being preserved until those entitled came to retire. Thus, if only retrospectively, at least one of the more flagrant inequities of the graduated pension scheme was eliminated.

In general this chapter has been concerned with that part of social security finance which is raised by the levying of contributions on employees and their employers. I have argued that this contribution system remains highly regressive – i.e. the lower paid contribute a far higher proportion of their income to social security than do the high income groups. The employer's share of social security is paid for by the mass of consumers in the form of higher prices for the goods and services they buy. Whether the employer's contribution falls with more weight on the higher-paid than on lower-paid consumers has never been investigated, and to establish the true position would involve fearsome technical problems. There is, however, no strong reason for concluding that the employer's contribution is a progressive, equalizing tax in terms of its impact on different income groups in the population.

Much more information is available about which income groups pay most in the form of the employee's contribution. At the start of the 1960s the flat-rate contribution was the only one levied. I have traced in detail the increasing use of graduated contributions by successive Governments. In 1973 the long process of change-over from a flat-rate to an earnings-related contribution system was carried a stage further. In that year, the Conservative Government decided on a contribution from the employee of 5·25 per cent on all earnings up to a maximum of £48 a week. Their Labour successors accepted the same principle and as from April 1975 the contribution required was 5·5 per cent on all earnings up to a ceiling of £69 a week. As a mechanism for redistributing income, the type of earnings-related system is clearly more helpful than the earlier flat-rate pattern of the Beveridge scheme. Yet the level of the ceiling remains of decisive importance. The ceilings so far selected have been approximately equivalent to the *average* earnings for non-manual employees in the relevant years, and 25 per cent above the level of average earnings for manual work. The effect is that virtually all manual workers will pay the full contribution on all of their earnings, whereas a substantial number of professional and managerial employees will escape having to contribute on a substantial part of their income. In 1975, for example, around 5½ million people earned more than £69 a week. Very few of them were manual workers. Table 2 illustrates how the relative size of the social security contribution falls as income rises above the ceiling.

Table 2: National Insurance Contribution as % Income

Weekly income	%
Up to £69	5·5
£80	4·8
£100	3·8
£200	1·9

It should be noted too that national-insurance contributions are required only on income from employment. Yet in 1973 some £4,000 million flowed into the personal sector of the economy from rent, dividend and interest.

Thus the introduction of the earnings-related principle has merely transferred the heaviest weight of national-insurance finance on to the middle income groups, the higher-paid section of manual workers, and the lower paid among white-collar and professional workers. The graduated principle has increased the extent to which social security transfers income from one income group to another, but not from people with high incomes to those with low incomes. Rather, insofar as the poorest are subsidized via social security, it is the income groups at or just above the average wage level who contribute most heavily to that subsidy. Only about one sixth of the cost of national insurance is met from general taxation, as opposed to contributions. But the full costs of family allowances and of supplementary benefit are paid for out of general taxation. The net effect is that something like one third of the finance for the social security system as a whole comes from income tax, purchase tax etc. It remains to discuss how far the pattern of general taxation helps to make social security more or less equalizing in its effect on income distribution. This question is taken up in the next chapter.

CHAPTER 6

Taxation, Equality and Social Security

It is not possible to decide whether social security leads to greater or less equality in British society, without at some point discussing the impact of general taxation. There are three reasons for this. Firstly, those who believe that the social security system lessens the gap between rich and poor attach particular importance to the role of general taxation in the financing of social security. They would concede, as anyone must, that the contribution principle used in national insurance – and discussed in the last chapter – is highly regressive in its impact. The lower the income, the higher the percentage of that income which is absorbed by national-insurance contributions. However, it is the case that one third of the total cost of social security is met, not out of employer and employee contributions, but from the general run of Government taxation. In particular, the Exchequer pays the full cost of family allowances and of supplementary benefit, as well as one sixth of the cost of the national-insurance scheme. Surely, runs the standard argument, it is through the mechanism of general taxation that the higher income groups finance a disproportionate share of the costs of social security.

The second reason for discussing taxation as part of an account of social security in Britain is that the tax system is in itself an important cause of poverty. Official figures suggest for example that the average old-age pensioner pays about 20 per cent of his or her income in various forms of taxation. The overall proportion of personal income taken in tax has risen quite sharply in Britain since the early 1960s. More important, there is clear evidence that the taxation of lower-paid workers has risen much more rapidly than for the higher income groups. In particular there have been massive increases in the amount paid in income

95

tax by wage earners. By the time the last Labour Government lost office in 1970 the income level at which wage earners began to pay income tax was actually below the equivalent poverty line operated by the Supplementary Benefits Commission.

Thirdly, there is no good reason why social security should be defined solely as a series of schemes whereby people in danger of poverty are given cash to meet their essential needs. A very large part of social security is in fact managed through the tax system by the mechanism of giving people tax relief. There is no essential difference between a family allowance obtained in cash from the Post Office and a children's allowance by which a person is allowed exemption from income tax which he otherwise would have to pay. In either case the effect is the same: the Government makes special financial concessions to people with children. Thus the notion of social security can legitimately be extended to include all kinds of tax reliefs – the personal allowance for a wife, tax relief on interest paid on a mortgage, tax relief on life-insurance policies, tax relief on contributions paid into an occupational pension scheme and on the unearned investment income accumulated by savings in an occupational pension scheme. To define social security in this broad way profoundly affects any conclusion about the influence of social security on the overall pattern of income distribution.

On the first issue – the extent to which the British tax system is progressive – the Central Statistical Office regularly makes public some very useful evidence. Each year a fairly large sample of households is asked to keep a detailed record of all expenditure during a two-week period. The Government statisticians supplement these expenditure diaries with estimates of types of spending which occur at wider intervals and which may not figure in a two-week period. The result is a series of tables showing in detail the spending patterns of households with various incomes, numbers of children etc. These tables are published annually by the Department of Employment and Productivity in a volume called the *Household Expenditure Survey.**

* For further details of this survey, see the discussion of cost-of-living indices in Chapter 9.

This information is used for a number of purposes, and notably in the construction of the Retail Price Index. The point of such an index is that it should reflect increases in the actual cost of living for an average family, by taking account of price increases in particular items to the extent that such items figure in household budgeting. A second important use made of the household expenditure survey is in estimating the amount paid in taxation of all sorts by households at differing income levels. Thus for example the statisticians can estimate the proportion of income taken in taxation by purchase tax or the tax on tobacco, because they have estimates of the amount of income which households are actually spending on tobacco or on the sorts of consumer goods which are subject to purchase tax.

Table 1 summarizes the results of these studies. It shows the proportion of income taken in tax by households with various incomes. The definition of income is a broad one, and includes the income of wives and of children as well as of the head of the household. Family allowances are included as income, as are old-age pensions and other types of social security benefit. Similarly the definition of taxation is a comprehensive one and includes, for example, local rates, national-insurance contributions, purchase tax, T.V. licences, as well as income tax and surtax.

Table 1: **Proportion of Income Paid in Taxation[1]**

Weekly income	1971 %	1973 %	Difference between 1971 and 1973
£13–	30	27	−3%
£16–	32	30	−2%
£19–	33	30	−3%
£23–	35	33	−2%
£28–	36	32	−4%
£34–	36	33	−3%
£41–	35	33	−2%
£49–	36	33	−3%
£60–	36	33	−3%
£72 & over	37	33	−4%
All incomes	35	32	−3%

Table 1 shows first that, contrary to the strongly held popular impression, the tax bite diminished slightly as a proportion of income in the early 1970s. Taking all incomes together, 35 per cent was paid in taxation in 1971, and 32 per cent in 1973.

Secondly, in 1973, over the whole income range from £23 a week there is no difference in the proportion of income taken in taxation. Separate figures are not available for groups with a household income of £10,000 or £20,000 a year. Presumably these would experience a somewhat higher-than-average rate of taxation. But it should not be assumed for example that the higher rates of income tax (which used to be called surtax) make much of an impact on income levels below the astronomic. It is true that surtax takes £5,000 out of an earned income of £20,000. But a married man with one child pays only £200 in surtax out of an earned income of £7,000 a year and only £69 out of earnings of £6,000 a year.[2] It is also the case that the very rich have at their disposal a wide range of tax-avoidance techniques, some of which are discussed later in this chapter.

At incomes below £23 a week the incidence of taxation is very little less than for much higher income groups. For example, in 1973, households with between £16 and £19 a week paid 30 per cent of that income in tax, and the lowest income group in the Table (£13–£16 a week) paid 27 per cent of it in taxation.

According to popular mythology the tax system in Britain is progressive – i.e. the higher a person's income the higher the proportion of that income which will be removed in taxation. The reality is quite different, namely that taxation in this country is virtually non-progressive.

It is also apparent from the right-hand column in Table 1 that the system was becoming somewhat less egalitarian in the early 1970s. Two out of the four lowest income groups saw their taxation reduced by only 2 per cent during this period. The highest income group enjoyed a drop of 4 per cent.

It has to be added that the trend had already been well established under the previous Labour administration. Table 2 shows the position as established during 1969, the last full year of the second Wilson Government.

Table 2: Proportion of Income Paid in Taxation[3]

Weekly income	1969 %	Change from 1964 to 1969
£5–	31	+9%
£6–	26	+2%
£7–	30	−1%
£9–	30	+2%
£11–	31	+2%
£13–	33	+3%
£16–	35	+5%
£19–	35	+5%
£23–	36	+6%
£28–	36	+5%
£34–	36	+4%
£40–	36	+4%
£50–	36	+3%
£60 & over	39	+1%
All incomes	36	+5%

Table 2 shows that the lowest income group, with £5, experienced a massive 9 per cent increase in taxation from 1964 to 1969, compared with only a 1 per cent rise for the highest income group. The position of some of the other low income groups showed some relative improvement, but the £16 to £34 groups fared worse than those with higher incomes.

Notice too that Table 2 seriously under-represents the massive swing of taxation to the disadvantage of the poorer groups, because no allowance is made for inflation in the way the data are presented. Thus for example a household with two thirds of the average manual wage in 1964 would have lost 29 per cent of it in tax – but the same relative income in 1969 would have lost 35 per cent. If the tax system were seriously progressive, one would expect a *drop* in the percentage of income taken in tax when comparing households with the same income over a five-year period during which average wages rose by about a third.

Behind the non-progressive pattern of British taxation lies a whole number of factors. Newspaper comment is much impressed with the tax tables which the Government publishes at Budget time, and which appear to show, for example, that in 1975 a man with £10,000 a year would lose £4,000 in income tax. But such

Poverty and Equality in Britain

tables refer to *taxable* income, i.e. what remains after the multitude of possible tax allowances has been claimed. The typical taxpayer with £10,000 a year, provided he furnishes himself with an imaginative and persuasive accountant, will be doing badly if he ends up paying tax on more than half of his earnings. Given this, it is not surprising to find that in 1973 surtax raised only £342 million – less than 5 per cent of the total charged in income tax.

In any case the contribution of income tax to total Government revenue is a lot smaller than is often imagined. Regressive taxes such as local authority rates, national insurance and expenditure taxes raise, in total, far more money than income tax.

Table 3: Main Types of Personal Taxation, 1973[4]

	£ million	%
Income tax	7,271	34
Expenditure taxes	6,457	31
National insurance	3,636	17
Local authority rates	2,617	12
Taxes on dividends, interest and trading income	1,224	6
Total	21,205	100

The bare bones of the system are illustrated in Table 4 which refers to only one family size, namely two adults and three children. It shows that the progressiveness of income tax is virtually nullified by the fact that the other main forms of taxation take a much higher proportion of low incomes than of high incomes.

Table 4: Proportion of Income Taken by Major Taxes[5]
(1969 – household of 2 adults, 3 children)

Weekly income	Income tax %	National insurance %	Expenditure taxes and rates %	Total %
£16–£19	—	4·0	24·2	28·2
£23–£28	7·0	4·0	18·8	29·8
£60 and over	17·0	1·0	12·6	30·6

Expenditure taxes are very various, but in general bear down more heavily on the lower income groups.

Value Added Tax at 8 per cent (in 1975) is levied on a wide range of household necessities, such as soap, detergents, disinfectants, prams, toothbrushes, writing paper, lamps, razor blades. And from May 1975 a 25 per cent rate of VAT was charged on items such as refrigerators, washing-machines, electric irons and kettles. The taxation of motor vehicles and of oil and petrol enters into the prices of many goods and services – wherever road transport is part of the cost of production. Tobacco and alcohol may be officially designated as luxuries, but in taxation terms they lean hard on low income groups. It is also the case that local authority rates have a heavier incidence on lower than on higher income groups. This is partly because the criteria used to establish the rateable value of houses tend to undervalue many of the superior features of houses occupied by the wealthy. And, contrary to the myths cherished by embattled owner-occupiers, it is the case that people who live in council houses have to pay rates on them. The rateable values for newer council houses are often impressively high. Finally it has to be recognized that many of the taxes which are ostensibly paid by business companies, are fully passed on to consumers as additions to prices. These are officially known as 'intermediate taxes' and, on the evidence given in Table 5, are seriously regressive in their impact.

Table 5: Percentage of Income Taken by
Rates and Expenditure Taxes, 1973[6]

| | Weekly income | |
	£16–19 %	£72 and over %
Local authority rates	3·8	1·2
Intermediate taxes	5·2	3·3
Tobacco tax	3·3	1·2
Alcohol taxes	2·3	2·2
VAT	3·1	3·3
Oil, petrol	1·0	1·6
Total	18·7	12·8

Table 5 shows that households with what would be in most cases a poverty level income of £16–19 a week in 1973 were losing 18·7 per cent of their income as a result of the taxes indicated – compared with a loss of only 12·8 per cent by households with over £72 a week. Even taxes such as VAT – supposedly levied on luxuries – and the oil and petrol taxes, popularly regarded as the scourge of the higher income motorist, had only a slightly progressive effect. All the others were regressive in their impact. Note that local authority rates bore much more heavily on the lower income group despite the existence of a means-tested rate rebate scheme introduced in 1967 by Labour, which was intended to reduce the gross inequity of this form of taxation. The figures in the Table take account of the meagre benefits of rates relief.[7]

The general conclusion must be, then, that the British tax system is on the whole a non-progressive one. The higher income groups certainly hand over more money in taxation; but as a proportion of income the incidence of taxation remains pretty even over a very wide band of income from poor to rich.

Taxation of the Very Rich

How far would this conclusion be modified if we could look separately at the tax position of the very rich? There is no satisfactory answer to this question. Nothing about British society remains more obscure than the degree of inequality in holdings of wealth. Virtually no serious research has been done on the matter. The only official figures on the distribution of wealth are those provided by the Inland Revenue. These are thoroughly misleading since they do not measure the actual distribution of wealth as between rich and poor. All that the Inland Revenue does is take note of the size of estates of people dying in each year, and then only of that part of wealth being transferred at death which is subject to Death Duty. There are plenty of devices, discretionary trusts, settlements etc. whereby the payment of Estate Duties can be avoided, even when transfer of wealth occurs at death. Thus the official figures reflect only the distribution of such wealth as has not escaped through the myriad loopholes left open by the tax system.[8]

There is little doubt that the avoidance and evasion of taxes on wealth is an increasing phenomenon in this country. For example Estate Duty is now contributing a lower proportion of Government income than at any point in the past eighty years, as Table 6 illustrates.

Table 6: Estate Duties as
Percentage of Total Government Income[9]

1888–97	12·6
1898–07	14·4
1908–15	16·1
1916–19	6·4
1920–22	5·0
1923–32	9·8
1933–38	11·3
1939–42	6·7
1943–46	3·7
1947–48	4·9
1949–58	4·2
1959–64	4·1
1965–69	3·5

Thus, to take the extremes, in the period 1908 to 1915 one sixth of Government revenue was derived from Estate Duty. But by the late 1960s, this tax was providing only one twenty-ninth of total revenue. Since these calculations were made, the relative size of death duties has fallen still further. In the four years 1970–73, only 2·1 per cent of Government revenue was derived from this tax. Between 1972 and 1973, the amount paid in death duties fell by 13 per cent, whereas revenue from all taxes rose by 11 per cent.

It could be argued of course that the declining contribution of taxes on wealth to Government income merely reflects a reduction in the numbers of the very rich, who are taxed at the highest rates. This is unlikely, to say the least. There are a number of factors which tend to increase the value of the wealth holdings of the very rich more rapidly than the average. For example the richer a person is, the higher the proportion of his wealth that will be devoted to the sorts of investment which expand most rapidly in value. In general equity shares are an exceptionally attractive form of investment. They can attract substantial dividend payments and offer scope for speculative gains by buying and selling on the market. But, most important of all, improvements in economic productivity are directly reflected in the capital value of equity holdings. Few forms of wealth are more unequally distributed. The latest available study shows that the richest 1 per cent of wealth holders owned 81 per cent of all stocks and shares in companies, and that the richest 5 per cent held 96 per cent of the available total of equity shares.[10]

In a Fabian Society study Michael Meacher has attempted to calculate the overall amount of personal wealth in Britain and to put a figure on the cost of tax avoidance.[11] The Inland Revenue estimates total personal wealth in 1968 at £88 thousand million. Meacher's calculations suggest that in reality the total is now three times as great as this, at £267 thousand million. The implication is that £179 thousand million is not subject to *any* form of taxation of wealth. The main wealth tax which operates is Estate Duty, which currently raises about £380 million a year. If Meacher is right about the total amount of personal wealth being held in Britain, this means that only one seven hundredth part of existing capital is being taxed away each year by Estate Duty. Meacher argues that improvements in productivity in Britain over the past sixty years have chiefly accrued to capital rather than labour, and estimates such gains at a little under 2 per cent per annum. Thus increasing economic growth is inflating the total of personal wealth fourteen times faster than Estate Duty is reducing it. And the rates of growth are highest for the forms of wealth which figure most heavily in the largest holdings of wealth.

Over the past two decades there has been an explosive growth in the value of equity shares. This has been generated not just by the increasing productivity of the British economy, but by a number of other factors in addition. The fact that taxation of income has been more severe than taxation of capital has encouraged a tendency for profits to be retained by companies rather than distributed as dividends to shareholders The latter lose nothing by this, since retained profits tend to increase the capital value of their share holdings. Partly as a result of increased retention of profits, there was during the 1960s a sharp decline in the proportion of company finance which has been raised by the issue of new shares for sale on the market. The result has been an acute shortage in the supply of equities. The resulting competition among those who wish to hold wealth in the form of equities has been greatly to the advantage of existing holders – overwhelmingly, as suggested above, the exceptionally rich. The effect of greater profit retention is to confine future profits and the return from long-term growth very largely to existing holders of equities. All of these trends have been particularly to the advantage of the largest holders of wealth.

Michael Meacher estimates that even if Estate Duty were applied with no greater effectiveness than was the case in 1908 to 1915, then an extra £650 million a year would be drawn into the Treasury each year. This extra sum would be enough, for example, to finance an immediate increase of £2 a week in the old-age pension of every retired person in the country.

Tax avoidance is now a major industry and gives lucrative employment to a vast army of highly skilled accountants and lawyers. 'Tax planning', as it is politely called, can be seen as a minor art form. Much of it is concerned with creating a fantastic world of shifting appearances beneath which reality is carefully concealed. For example, a good deal of tax avoidance is managed by making it appear that capital is not really owned by those who enjoy the fruits. The basic method here is to vest control of a chunk of capital in the hands of trustees who are paid fees for their work of management, but otherwise do not benefit directly from the capital. The trustees pass investment income and capital gains back to the beneficiary. Thus in legal terms no one actually owns the assets in question, which are left hovering in a kind of tax-free limbo, since Estate Duty is levied only on what a person actually owns at the point of death.

Virtually no research has been carried out on trusts, so that no one has the slightest idea how many trusts are in existence, or how much capital is salted away in them. But it is clear that they constitute an enormous loophole for the avoidance of Death

Duty. In 1971 in his spring Budget Anthony Barber gave a further boost to tax-avoidance trusts, by freeing them from the obligation to pay capital gains tax periodically.

There are a variety of devices which exploit the fact that personal taxation is to a great extent levied on individuals, whereas wealth is enjoyed by family units. By a careful distribution of wealth among its various members, one rich family can be presented to the tax authorities as a collection of less rich individuals, to be taxed at appropriately lower rates on the progressive tax scale. This process of redistribution of wealth within the family was encouraged by the fact that until recently gifts of capital escaped death duties if they were made more than seven years before the death of the original owner. Gifts made within seven years of death were taxed at appropriately lower rates. In 1974, the Labour Government made an attempt to close off this widely used channel for tax avoidance by introducing Capital Transfer Tax.

At first sight the new CTT looks an impressive instrument of redistribution. Gifts of wealth made over a lifetime will be cumulated by the tax authorities, and as the total rises so will the rate of taxation. Much has been made of the fact that after someone has made gifts of wealth totalling more than £2 million, all subsequent gifts are taxed at a rate of 75 per cent. But the top rate which may in theory be charged is a misleading guide to the general effect of the whole tax. Thus for example the first £100,000 of gifts will require a CTT payment of only £9,000, which is very modest compared with the kinds of rates which are charged in income tax.

In any case, a capital transfer tax is easily avoidable by not making gifts of wealth, at any rate until a Conservative Government is returned to power and the tax is abolished or its rates reduced. Labour admit this point, and do not expect their CTT to produce much revenue or to have any more than a marginal impact on the distribution of wealth. But they argue that if the flow of gifts of wealth is blocked off for ten or fifteen years by the existence of the CTT, then over a time estates which previously would have avoided death duties (because of the operation of the gift system) will be subject to the full rigour of death duties as their owners die off. Thus, it is claimed, the point of Labour's strategy lies in a *combination* of gift and death taxation of wealth.

At best this is likely to be a very slow process, and for its effectiveness seems to rest on the unlikely assumption that there will be no Conservative Governments over the next decade or two. It is not the case that the larger holdings of wealth are at present concentrated in the hands of the very old. The very extensive use of gift techniques of wealth transfer prior to the 1974 legislation means that there is little difference in the distribution of wealth ownership at different ages.

Moreover when they introduced CTT in 1974, Labour made two changes in death duties which considerably weakened the effectiveness of their fiscal attack on inequalities in wealth. The rates of Death Duty were substantially reduced. Before the Budget of November 1974 the Death Duty on an estate of £100,000 was £37,250. Mr Healey cut it to £28,250. On estates valued at £1 million, he reduced the Death Duty by £87,000. The Chancellor estimated that as a result of these reductions the Exchequer would lose £25 million in tax in the year 1975–6.

More important still, Mr Healey opened one of the biggest loopholes ever to appear in the British tax system by announcing that in future gifts and legacies between husband and wife would be free from all forms of capital taxation, *including death duties*. The consequence is that by a succession of marriages, specially arranged if necessary, rich families will be able to keep their wealth intact for ever. The game will operate like musical chairs. So long as a person manages to avoid dying without a husband or wife to inherit, an estate can be passed down the generations without payment of capital taxes.

Around the world a rich variety of tax havens are available for the rich. Substantial tax concessions can be obtained by anyone who cares to invest in agricultural land or forests in Britain. Many wealthy people find it convenient to convert themselves into private companies. This allows a person to issue tax-free bonus and debenture shares to himself, and a great many living expenses can be made to appear as legitimate business expenses. The standard of living of many managerial personnel depends as much on tax-free fringe benefits as on directly earned income.

Even when people are caught defrauding the Inland Revenue, their treatment by the tax authorities is notoriously indulgent. For example, in 1972, the Inland Revenue recovered about £1 million in 250 cases where profits had been under-reported by at least £10,000. Virtually none of those involved was taken to court, and no one was jailed. Compare, in the same year, the 12,000 prosecutions for social security fraud, mostly involving small amounts of money. In extreme cases the Inland Revenue can charge penalties, without taking the matter to court, but these rarely amount to more than 40 per cent of the amount defrauded. The tax authorities can also charge interest on back tax but the rates are modest. For amounts rising since before 1970 the rate is 3 per cent, thereafter 4 per cent.

The Inland Revenue Staff Federation, which has been running a campaign calling for tougher rules on tax frauds, believes that the scale of evasion may run as high as 10 per cent of the total revenue raised annually – about £1,500 million in 1975. The Federation points out, for example, that around five million people in Britain claim to be their own employers, but the Inland Revenue has only 3½ million self-employed on its books. Even stranger, 86 per cent of these claimed (in 1973) that they were earning less than £30 a week. Some of these, maybe as many as half a million, would be building workers on the Lump, and in their case the Government has been attempting to eliminate tax evasion. But little is known about other categories of the self-employed. The Inland Revenue Staff Federation reports

When we inquire into the reasonableness of the profits of the self employed, we find that they don't smoke, don't drink, that they never take their wives out, that they never take a holiday, that they wear second hand suits and that they never drive their Jaguars more than a few miles of private motoring.[12]

The general conclusions of this brief examination of the tax system can be easily summarized: that there is in Britain a tremendous inequality in the distribution of wealth; that the taxation of wealth is inconsiderable, and easily avoided; and that over most of the income scale the tax system is not progressive.

It follows that the commonly-held view that British taxation is generally egalitarian in its effects is based on myth. Insofar as the social security system and other parts of the Welfare State are financed out of general taxation, there is no reason to believe that the social services modify existing social class differences in any really thorough-going way.

Taxation as a Cause of Poverty

Taxation causes poverty in the obvious sense that expenditure taxes figure as part of the price of a great many goods and services. What is not generally realized is just how deeply such taxes bite into the budget of people on low incomes. Official figures are available only for old-age pensioners, and the information is tucked away in an obscure corner of a complicated official report on the incidence of various sorts of taxation. The Central Statistical Office studied the expenditure patterns of 528 single retired pensioners in 1969 with an average weekly income of £7·30 each. It was found that the average which each pensioner paid in taxation was £1·60 – i.e. 22 per cent of total income.[13]

In a further sample of retired married couples the average weekly income was found to be £10·80 per week, and average tax paid was £2·73 – 25 per cent of income. Since retired people do not pay national-insurance contributions and since income tax scarcely affects incomes as low as these, what is showing up is quite simply the enormous weighting of expenditure taxes in the British fiscal system.

I have already discussed in Chapter 3 the reasons why the income-tax threshold dropped sharply down in the late 1960s to income levels below the official minimum. In 1971, the Conservative Government attempted to restore the situation by introducing the Family Income Supplement, which is a tax-free benefit paid to low-wage earners with children. When this benefit was first made available, the Government set itself the target of achieving an 85 per cent take-up rate among those eligible. By

September 1973 Ministers were reporting that £785,000 had been spent on advertising FIS. Despite this the proportion of those claiming has never risen above 50 per cent of the eligible.

In addition, since 1970, as the rate of inflation has accelerated, the personal tax allowances have been increased on a number of occasions. However, the pattern has been that improvements in tax allowances have no more than kept up with the increase in the money value of earnings. Average wages have doubled between 1970 and 1975. Over the same period, the tax allowance for a non-working wife rose from £140 to £280 a year. In 1970, the allowance for a child aged 11–16 was £140; in 1975, £275. It follows therefore that for the majority of wage earners the tax threshold in 1975 operates at roughly the same proportion of earnings as five years earlier. Since FIS is a tax-free allowance, for the 50 per cent of those eligible who actually get it, there will have been an improvement in the tax threshold, but not for the remainder.

The wage-poverty trap continues to operate with scarcely diminished severity. Thus for a family with earnings and family allowances totalling between £25 and £27 a week in 1975, the whole of an extra £1 of income would be lost in taxation and reduction in benefits. Income tax would take 35p and national insurance 6p. If the family were getting FIS, then this would be reduced by 50p on an extra £1 of income. Council rent rebate would be cut by 17p if earnings rose by £1. There might also be a loss of rates rebate and free school meals, if the family were in receipt of these benefits.

It thus remains the case that many families in the lower income bands can experience a marginal rate of taxation/benefit loss that is greater than the highest rate of surtax charged on the rich.

There are two conclusions which can be drawn from the facts about what some commentators have referred to as a surtax on the poor. The first is the matter of incentives. It is conventionally assumed that a tax system should always encourage people to work harder, to look for overtime or to seek promotion to a better-paid job. From this point of view the present pattern of taxation and welfare benefits is disastrous over a broad range of low-income categories. The second conclusion is less frequently drawn in middle-class discussion of the tax system. That is that any trade union representing groups of workers on below average earnings will scarcely improve the financial position of the family men among its members, if it seeks only modest improvements in pay. In a great many cases only very substantial pay increases will make any appreciable difference to the standard of living of lower-paid workers.

Tax Relief as Social Security

There is a further important connection between the tax system and the Welfare State: namely the fact that a good deal of social security provision is made via the mechanism of tax relief. In money terms the tax reliefs given for dependent children are exceedingly expensive for the Government. The total annual cost of child allowances is about £700 million. This is twice as much as the £350 million a year paid out in family allowances.

In social security terms child allowances offer far better coverage than family allowances. Tax exemption is allowed on every dependent child; no family allowance is paid for the first child except in one-parent families. Child allowances are graduated according to the age of the child, and thus extra provision is made to meet the extra costs of older children. Finally, and most importantly, child allowances are in effect a means-tested social security benefit. They are available only to those with a large enough income to be paying income tax. The result is that families with a large number of children and a low income tend to get less help from child allowances than the same size family on a higher income. Thus the effect of the child allowance system is emphatically regressive.

At high levels of income, where surtax comes into operation, the child allowance system offers very large benefits indeed. The higher the rate of tax which a person pays, the more a child allowance is worth to him in terms of hard cash. The child allowance was worth £228 a year in 1970 to a standard-rate tax-payer with four children* but £415 a year to the same man, if he

* Assuming two children under eleven, and two children between eleven and sixteen.

had an income of over £8,000 a year and were paying surtax at 62 per cent on the top band of his income. The wealthy man will also of course pay surtax on his family allowances, but this extra payment will be very much less than the gain he will make from his child allowances.

Child allowances are only one part of an elaborate system of welfare payments made through the mechanism of tax relief. The valuable tax privileges allowed to people with life-insurance policies, and to contributors to occupational pension schemes will be discussed in Chapter 7. A further example is the tax relief allowed to owner-occupiers buying their house on a mortgage. Tax relief is allowed on the interest charged on money borrowed against a mortgage. In 1972–3 owner-occupiers received £340 million in tax relief – more than the £320 million paid in council house subsidies in the same year.[14] Among owner-occupiers it is those who can afford the bigger houses and the bigger mortgages who benefit most from tax relief. And, as with all tax allowances, the higher the income and the higher the rate of tax paid, the more valuable a privilege is tax exemption.

No adequate research has been carried out into the incidence of tax-relief benefits. But it is clear that social security managed through the mechanism of tax relief is a very expensive part of the Welfare State and very inegalitarian in the sense that tax relief offers no benefits to the poor and exceptional benefits to the wealthy.

Tax Credits

There has been much discussion in recent years about proposals for amalgamating the currently separate systems of tax relief and social security benefits. In Chapter 4 I described the fate of Labour's 1964 scheme for a guaranteed minimum income, which, as originally envisaged, would have involved a very thorough integration of the income and social security benefit mechanisms. A much more modest tax credit scheme was unveiled in October 1972 in a Green Paper published by the Heath Government.[15]

Further study in Whitehall had confirmed the view that the

type of comprehensive negative income-tax scheme which the previous Labour Government had sought to introduce was administratively unworkable. What Labour had wanted was a scheme which would be based on an adaptation of the existing PAYE system for collecting income tax, and which could, therefore, be introduced without having to wait for the whole mechanism for collecting direct taxes to be overhauled. Secondly, Labour ministers had hoped for a scheme which would include the entire population, and which, in particular, would cater for all of the three million households currently supported by the supplementary benefit system. Finally, the Labour Government's aim was a scheme which would operate as a substitute for a broad range of means-tested benefits, and which would include, for example, rent and rates rebates and provision for free school meals.

When examined against such a target, the Conservative tax credit scheme appeared rather diminutive and unenterprising. It required a reorganization of the tax system which apparently would take five years to carry through. It excluded 10 per cent of the population – those not in employment or not in receipt of one of the main national-insurance benefits – and among those to be left out were substantial numbers of the poorest, most vulnerable and most insecure. Personal and tax allowances, the family allowance and the family income supplement were to be replaced by a tax credit. But most sectors of the tangled means-test jungle were left unaffected by the new scheme – rent and rates rebate, exemption from prescription, dental and ophthalmic charges, free school meals, educational maintenance and clothing allowances and many others.

For that section of the population who would qualify for entry, the scheme would work as follows. All earnings and national-insurance benefits would be subject to income tax at 30p in the pound. Against the tax bill of each household would be set a tax credit, fixed provisionally at £4 for the tax-payer himself, £2 for his wife, and £2 for each child.

Thus, for example, if the scheme had been operating in 1971 a single old-age pensioner would pay tax of £2·02 on his weekly pension of £6·75. This tax payment would be offset by a tax credit of £4. The pensioner would end up £1·98 better off than at present. In effect, the scheme would mean an increase in the minimum State pension to £8·73 a week for a single person.

A man with earnings of £30 a week would face a tax bill of £9 a week. If single he would pay tax of £5 a week, and if married, £3. If he had two dependent children he would pay no tax and would be entitled to a credit of one pound a week; three children would produce a weekly credit in this case of £3 a week.

According to the Green Paper, this tax credit scheme would provide benefits in addition to the existing provision of £1,300 million a year. A major objective of the scheme was the reduction of poverty among low-wage earners and sections of the population dependent on social security benefits. Yet when the scheme was sent to a Select Committee of the Commons for further discussion, it began to emerge that the scheme would in fact pay much more substantial benefits to higher income groups. The Report of the Select Committee published estimates of the extra income the scheme would have provided to households at various income levels, had it been in operation in 1972–3.[16]

Table 7: Extra Income from Tax Credits

Weekly income	Extra tax credit income
Under £20	29p
£20–40	72p
£40–100	83p
Over £100	£1·33p

The ineffectiveness of the scheme as a mechanism for redistributing income arises for two reasons – because the personal and child credits are set at a uniform rate irrespective of income, and because the scheme is devised to produce a uniform marginal rate of extra tax/loss of credits of 30 per cent right up to the high income level at which surtax comes into operation.

In 1974 the Labour Government decided that, for the time being, no tax credit scheme would be introduced. Except in the remote future, Labour has produced no alternative to the present heavy reliance on means tests in social security.

CHAPTER 7

Pension Plans and Social Equality

When they took office in 1964 the Labour Government gave the widest publicity to the fact that they were carrying out an urgent and comprehensive review of the whole structure of social security in this country. Their intention was to introduce the earnings-related principle into all sectors of the national-insurance system, and they had undertaken to do this within their first two or three years of office. In effect the 1966 National Insurance Act was concerned not just to extend the earnings-related principle in contributions and benefits, but also to develop a new principle in post-war British social security – the principle that groups experiencing short periods of unemployment and sickness would be much better provided for than those whose sickness or unemployment ran for more than six months. Thus began the erosion of one of the key principles built into the Beveridge scheme, namely that there should be a pooling of risks – that those fortunate enough to escape unemployment or sickness should be required to contribute towards provision for *all* of those less fortunate in this respect, and certainly not that the most unlucky should be excluded from any part of such a system of mutual insurance.

So far as intentions went, the core of Labour's earnings-related strategy was to be a scheme to introduce such a principle into the field of old-age pensions and other long-term social-insurance benefits. These plans were developed in the most leisurely way imaginable. Not until 1969 were details of the proposed schemes made public in a series of White Papers. The delays and postponements which characterized the pensions policy of the late Labour Government were aptly summarized by Douglas Houghton, the Minister originally responsible for the

'Major Review'. In 1966 he told the Commons that: 'We are now engaged in an urgent study of the whole problem and have been for a long time.' In the event the General Election of June 1970 interrupted the passage of the earnings-related pensions Bill through Parliament, and the Conservatives scrapped the whole thing as soon as they took power.

The Labour Party have never clearly explained why it took them no less than five years after 1964 to gestate an earnings-related pension scheme. After all, as long ago as 1957 detailed proposals for such a scheme had been submitted to the Annual Conference of the Labour Party, in the form of a document called *National Superannuation*. This scheme was greeted with acclaim by the Party, and formed the centre-piece of Labour's Manifesto in the 1959 General Election.

Unlike many proposals which the Labour Party has put before the British electorate, the National Superannuation scheme was not an exercise in hopeful speculation. The economic, fiscal and actuarial implications of the scheme had been thoroughly worked out. The soundness and workability of earnings-related national superannuation had been carefully explored by three leading experts on national-insurance finance, Richard Titmuss, Brian Abel-Smith and Peter Townsend – all, at that time, teachers of social administration at the London School of Economics. The political coordinator of their labours was Richard Crossman, one of the few professional politicians in Britain with sufficient stamina and agility of mind to grasp the more esoteric complexities of national insurance. The report produced by this team is still worth reading, not just as an historical document, but as an exceptionally lucid guide to the financial implications of national pension schemes.

Labour lost the General Election of 1959, but, with only minor modifications, the 1957 National Superannuation scheme was again offered to the electorate in 1964. Yet when Labour took office, the scheme was promptly buried. The task of designing an earnings-related pension scheme was begun again from the beginning. This time the planners were civil servants rather than academics with Labour Party sympathies. When Mr Wilson formed his first administration, the Minister appointed in charge of pensions planning was Mr Douglas Houghton. Two and a half years later Houghton was removed from the post, without having made public any evidence of progress in redesigning the existing pension scheme. Houghton's replacement was Patrick Gordon Walker, who had some reputation as a foreign affairs expert, but had never displayed the slightest interest in or knowledge of old-age pensions. Eventually, early in 1968, Richard Crossman took over from Gordon Walker as Minister of Social Security, and in 1969 the new National Superannuation scheme was unveiled. It turned out to be profoundly different from the scheme which had provoked enthusiasm at Labour Party Conferences from 1957 onwards.

This was remarkably strange, for the earlier pension scheme had been a very significant milestone in the political career of Richard Crossman. To it he owed his first recognition as a politician of real stature and his rise into the top leadership of the Labour Party. Crossman expounded his first superannuation scheme to the Brighton Conference of 1957 in a masterly speech which was received with prolonged and fervent applause. From that moment onwards Crossman was clearly marked for glory.

None of those responsible has ever explained why the 1957 scheme was scrapped as soon as Labour took office in 1964, so any reason offered here must be speculative. It is true that in a number of respects Crossman Mark II was superior to his Mark I version. In particular it was arranged that in Mark II, a person, once retired, would have the money value of his pension upvalued from time to time, to match any increases which had taken place in the average earnings of manual workers. Thus any improvement in the standard of living of manual workers would, after a delay, be extended to pensioners as well. This provision was distinctly better than the proposal made in 1957, that after retirement, pensions would be increased only enough to protect the pensioner's standard of living against increases in retail prices. Thus in the Mark I scheme the pensioner would not share in any improvement in the standard of living of workers generally.

This was an important difference. But on the fundamental

117

point – how generous would the eventual pension be as compared with a person's previous standard of living while at work – there was nothing to choose between the two schemes. The earlier scheme had been sold to the electorate as giving half pay on retirement to a man who had earned the equivalent of the average manual wage throughout his working life. But in fact the arrangement was that pensions at this level would not begin to be paid until the scheme had been going for forty years. The average earner retiring in the twentieth year of the scheme would, if single, get a pension of only 42 per cent of his average life earnings. This size of pension was identical with the one proposed for the twentieth year of the 1969 scheme.

Nor could the long delay in producing legislation to introduce earnings-related pensions be blamed on the succession of economic crises which rocked the Wilson Government. Neither the earlier nor the later scheme was concerned with providing a better standard of living for existing old-age pensioners. Both schemes involved a sharp increase in the amount of money taken from people at work, in the form of higher national-insurance contributions. But for the first ten years of each scheme expenditure on higher pensions would rise very much more slowly than the increase in contributions. Thus both schemes were really a device for increasing the level of compulsory saving by the working population. All through the 1960s it was a prominent part of the official diagnosis of Britain's economic crisis that the public were spending too much on current consumption and not saving enough of their income to sustain a higher rate of national investment. A pension scheme in which contributions rose in the short-term, but pensions only in the long-term, would be a handy device for increasing the amount of available investment capital. The consequent dissatisfaction of people from whom higher contributions would be required would be limited by promising higher pensions in the future to current contributors. The real sacrifice would be made by existing generations of old-age pensioners. However, pensioners, though a large block of the electorate, are relatively ineffective politically. They are weakly organized, contain a high proportion of non-voters and tend as a group to vote consistently and as a matter of habit for one particular Party ticket.

From the point of view of generating extra investment capital both the earlier and the later of the Crossman schemes were equally attractive. Why then was Mark I abandoned in favour of Mark II? The most convincing explanation is that the 1957 version was torpedoed, because it suddenly dawned on Labour Ministers in 1964 that this scheme committed them to a greater degree of redistribution of income from higher to lower income groups than they were prepared to entertain. This was the fundamental difference between the 1969 pensions plan and the earlier one that was scrapped; the later scheme involved a much lighter transfer of purchasing power from richer to poorer groups in the population.

To see why, it is necessary to look briefly at the mechanics of an earnings-related pension scheme. The basis is simple enough. People pay in a percentage of their earnings; eventually they qualify for a pension that is bigger or smaller depending on the amount they have contributed. However, if everyone got a pension which was exactly the same percentage of his earnings while at work, then large numbers of pensioners would still remain under the poverty line, just as is the case with the present flat-rate scheme. For example, half pay on retirement would give only £8 a week in pension to anyone who had been earning the equivalent of £16 a week in 1970. One objective of both of Labour's earnings-related pension plans was to allow – at least in the future – for a serious reduction in the role of the Supplementary Benefits Commission. This would only be achieved by allowing lower-paid contributors an eventual pension which would be higher than half of their earnings while at work. The principle arrived at was that the lower paid would be allowed a somewhat higher pension than the level of their contribution would strictly justify, and that this would be financed by giving higher-paid contributors a lower pension than their contributions would strictly warrant. Thus in the arrangement linking contributions to pensions a measure of income redistribution would be introduced.

In both schemes a person was not required to pay a percentage contribution on his entire income, but only on income up to a certain ceiling. In the 1969 scheme the ceiling was to be one and a half times the national average earnings for manual work in a given year. Thus, if the scheme had been operating in 1969 to 1970, when average manual earnings were £24 a week, a person would pay contributions on any earnings he made up to £36 a year. On earnings above £36 no contribution would be required. This is a low ceiling and has the effect of minimizing redistribution from higher to lower income groups. By comparison the contribution ceiling proposed in the 1957 plan was very much higher – four times average manual earnings in a given year, i.e. up to nearly £100 a week in 1970.

This difference in contribution ceiling had marked effects on the pension rights offered to lower income groups. In both schemes a person who throughout his working life had earned the equivalent of £15 a week in 1970 would eventually qualify for a pension (if single) of £8 a week. But under the 1969 scheme the contribution would be just over £1 a week, whereas under the 1957 scheme the contribution would be much less, at 61p a week.* Such a large difference in weekly contributions continued throughout a working lifetime would make an enormous difference to the total amounts which lower-paid contributors would eventually have paid into the two schemes. Under the 1969 scheme they would pay not far off twice as much as under the 1957 scheme, in order to qualify for the same ultimate pension. Crossman Mark II was much less favourable to the lower-paid contributor, and correspondingly to the advantage of the higher income groups. Redistribution *within* the scheme was minimized in the 1969 version.

The other way in which redistribution of income can be effected via a pension scheme is through the Treasury contribution to the scheme from general taxation. The more the tax system takes

* These examples of pensions and contributions in the two schemes are given in terms of 1970 money values. In both schemes the money values of contributions and pensions were to be scaled up from time to time to match changes in average earnings. However the ratio of the contributions to the eventual pension would remain the same.

money from higher income groups rather than from lower, the greater the size of the Treasury contribution to a pension scheme, the greater is the extent to which that scheme will transfer income from richer to poorer. Here again there was an important difference between Labour's earlier and later pension plans. In the 1957 version the Exchequer was to provide a subsidy to the scheme, equal to 24 per cent of the combined contribution of employers and employees; but in the 1969 scheme the Exchequer contribution was reduced to 18 per cent. Once again Crossman's Mark II pension plan was much less redistributive of income.

The rejection of the earlier pension plan thus marked a major retreat from the politics of social equality, which has been an important part of the traditional philosophy of the Labour movement. By 1964 the degree of redistribution built into the earlier pension scheme had become a quite anachronistic element in Labour's ideology. The two years previous to 1964 witnessed a profound change in the attitude of the Labour Party leadership towards the question of social equality. Until this period the Party leaders accepted, like everyone else, that a Labour Government would see as one of its major goals the reduction of disparities in income between rich and poor. During the inter-war period and until the early sixties, the idea of an incomes policy – direct Government influence on the relative size of incomes paid – formed no part of Labour's philosophy. Even the development of legislation to govern *minimum* wages had attracted little attention within the party since the late thirties. It was accepted without question that greater financial equality was to be achieved by redistribution managed through the taxation system and in the financing of the social services. Indeed it was assumed that reforms and improvements in the social services could not be achieved except on the basis of higher rates of redistributive taxation.

The programme which Labour put forward at the General Election of 1959 marked the first break with these assumptions. It was suggested for the first time that welfare expenditure could be dramatically increased, without requiring the higher income groups to pay more in taxation. True, as described above, the pensions section of Labour's 1959 Election Manifesto promised a scheme containing a significant degree of income redistribution. But it was proposed that in all other areas of the Welfare State the extra resources needed were to be found out of the proceeds of an increase in the rate of economic growth. Mr Gaitskell assured the electorate that under a Labour Government rates of taxation would not be put up.

It was in this period in the late fifties that British politicians began to identify the management of a high rate of economic growth as the overriding objective of economic policy. In the years previously the politicians had been just as concerned to restrict inflation as to achieve increasing prosperity. Also prosperity had been defined in terms of a low rate of unemployment and steady, if moderate, expansion rather than the period of economic miracle which it later became fashionable to promise. But by 1959 there had developed a great deal of anxiety in Establishment circles about the obstinate refusal of the British economy to grow as rapidly as its nearest Continental rivals, and in particular West Germany. The Labour Party responded fully to this concern and since the early 1960s, for the dominant factions within the Party, the problem of attaining a more just and humane society has become quite subordinate and is seen as contingent on the obtaining of a higher growth rate.

The downgrading of social equality in Labour's scale of priorities was fairly skilfully disguised. Many loyal Labour supporters are under the impression that the manifest failure of the Wilson Governments to reverse the trend to greater inequality of income in Britain is to be attributed to the economic difficulties since 1964, rather than to any change in the social philosophy and political intentions of the Party leadership. What has confused the issue has been the Party's continued adherence to the view that the social services are in urgent need of a lot of extra resources. There has been less appreciation of the consequences of making increased welfare expenditure dependent on a more rapid rate of growth – especially if such growth is not then forthcoming. However, the attractions of such a strategy in welfare have proved irresistible to politicians in recent years. Since incomes and consumption rise with economic growth, there is a corresponding increase in the amount of taxation drawn in by the Exchequer, even if tax rates remain constant. Indeed the amount of money paid over in taxation will increase faster than the general rise in incomes. Sections of the population move up into more highly taxed income brackets or will spend more money on heavily taxed 'luxury' goods, especially tobacco, drink and motor transport. Thus in 1959 Gaitskell felt able to offer the electorate an apparently seductive package: improved social services (at an eventual extra cost estimated by the Tories at many hundreds of millions a year) and no increase in tax rates. Labour's Election Manifesto explained that:

> If in the past three years industrial production had gone up as fast as it did under the last Labour government, our national income would today be £1,700 million a year higher. The Chancellor of the Exchequer would be collecting £450 million in extra revenue without adding a farthing to existing tax rates.[1]

This argument quite understandably produced a certain mystification in the electorate. The fine distinction between tax rates and the total revenue levied in taxation was not clearly appreciated. Labour seemed to be denying the obvious – that they intended to take more money from tax-payers. Public suspicion was further sharpened by the fact that it was not until the middle of the 1959 election campaign that the Labour Party began giving undertakings that income-tax rates would not be increased and that purchase tax would be abolished. One authoritative study of the campaign argues that these promises, and their timing, cost Labour the election.

> Journalistic enterprise and Conservative eloquence consolidated the picture of Labour leaders bidding for votes with a succession of wild fiscal promises ... In retrospect the two tax pledges appear as the turning point of the campaign itself. All the opinion polls indicate that about ten days before the vote the tide which had been flowing so strongly to Labour was checked and then reversed.[2]

This diagnosis, however, figured very little in the argumentative post mortem in which the Party debated why they had been rejected by the electorate for the third successive time in 1959.

The backfiring of the taxation issue was seen as a tactical error of timing and presentation, not as based on an incorrect strategy.

Nevertheless most of the influential voices calling for a fundamental restructuring of Labour's political priorities and Party image argued that social equality should continue to be central. Oddly enough it was the Party's right wing which was particularly insistent. However, the particular type of inequality which they said they wanted to see reduced was in the ownership of wealth, rather than the differences in income which had been steadily widening throughout the 1950s. The Party leadership judged that an undertaking to attack inherited wealth and privilege would appeal to the white-collar groups, whose support a refurbished Labour Party should try to attract. And they hoped that a continued emphasis on reducing inequalities in wealth would make the dropping of further nationalization more palatable to the broad mass of Party adherents. Anthony Crosland and Douglas Jay, key members of the group around Gaitskell, both wrote extensively in favour of such a package deal – nationalization to be dropped, but a crusade to be mounted against wealth.

In 1963 the accession of Wilson to leadership of the Labour Party meant that the goal of economic growth became if anything even more paramount in Labour's scale of priorities. The crusade against wealth and privilege was quietly forgotten amidst a blaze of rhetoric about a dynamic new Britain and a revival of the abrasive buccaneering spirit of the merchant adventurers.[3] There were undertakings to attack the huge profits being made by land speculation and takeover bids, etc. However, these measures were not rooted in any doctrine of social justice, but were rather proposed in the interests of greater economic efficiency. As in 1959, and again with the exception of pensions, the election of 1964 was fought by Labour on the policy that extra resources for welfare would be found not by redistribution but by increasing the rate of economic growth. On the subject of national insurance the 1964 Labour Manifesto said: 'the key factor in determining the speed at which new and better levels of benefit can be introduced will be the rate at which the British economy can expand'.

The Government hoped for a growth rate of 3·8 per cent per annum, and the ill-starred National Plan of 1965 was shaped in terms of this objective. Income distribution was not directly discussed in the National Plan, but, in the section of the document in which predictions were made about trends in consumption patterns up to 1970, it was assumed that income would continue to be distributed much as in 1964. It was laid down in the National Plan that between 1964 and 1970 there would be a 25 per cent increase in Gross National Product. As it turned out the growth rate achieved in this six-year period was less than 2 per cent per annum, the provision of extra resources for social security and other welfare sectors being correspondingly restricted. Even in the original terms of the National Plan, social security had been treated as something of a Cinderella. Writing in 1966, Brian Abel-Smith pointed out that during the six years up to 1970,

The allocation for higher social security benefits is to be an increase of 15 per cent after allowance has been made for the natural increase in persons entitled to benefits – more aged persons entitled to pensions, more children entitled to family allowances, etc. As the plan provides for wages to increase by 21 per cent, it is apparently intended, even without any extension in the scope of social security, that the level of living of social security beneficiaries will fall behind that of wage earners.[4]

It is extraordinary, in retrospect, that the leadership of the Labour Party was able to convince itself or anyone else that the 1969 Crossman scheme would mean a revolution, however distant in the future, in the living standards of the elderly. During the first ten years in which the scheme operated the extra transfer of resources to the elderly would be very small indeed. Even after thirty years, when the scheme was in full operation, the net improvement in the position of the elderly would be inconsiderable, as the White Paper made quite plain. Pensioners, who currently make up about 15 per cent of the population,

account at present for 10 per cent of total personal consumption, and the rest of the population for 90 per cent. The projected increase in the living standards of pensioners might raise this share of personal consumption to about 12 per cent by the turn of the century, thus reducing the share available to the rest of the population by about 2 per cent of the total.[5]

An extra 2 per cent after 30 years!

This cold assessment accurately summarizes the very limited scope of the much discussed National Superannuation plan. Even had the scheme been legislated into existence, it would have been a meagre return for fourteen years of thought and planning by the Labour Party's pensions experts and by their academic advisers. It represents a milestone in the evolution of the Labour Party away from any serious concern to increase equality in British society.

The more recent period in the history of State pensions planning in Britain has been dominated by the problems of the private sector in pensions, and especially by the schemes run by employers. It is to these that we now turn.

CHAPTER 8

Occupational versus State Pensions

Until recently Conservative thinking about pensions has started from the premise that occupational pension schemes offer a more desirable method of provision for old age than any type of universal State scheme. They argue thus that the first object of Government policy on pensions should be to encourage the development of occupational schemes and that the role of the State scheme should be progressively reduced to a residual one, catering for people who have, for one reason or another, missed out on an occupational scheme.

Certainly, in recent years there has been explosive growth in the occupational pension sector. In the period 1956 to 1967 the number of separate occupational schemes almost doubled – from 37,000 to 65,000 – and the number of employees belonging to a scheme rose from eight million to twelve million. Approximately one half of the employed population now belongs to an occupational scheme and this total includes two thirds of all male employees.

However, there is no automatic process at work leading to universal occupational pension coverage. Indeed between 1967 and 1971 there was a drop from 52 per cent to 49 per cent in the proportion of employees belonging to schemes. There are a variety of factors which operate to limit further growth in the occupational sector. For example a great many of the people who have no occupation-based pension scheme work for the small employers. There are in fact around one million employers in Britain, and a surprising number of people work for small businesses. Out of the one million separate employing concerns only 65,000 have pension schemes. In hundreds of thousands of cases employers will not consider starting a pension scheme because their labour force is too small. In other cases an employer will not set up a pension scheme because the business is not solidly enough established to justify the long-term financial commitment involved. Even the largest companies are often loath to provide a pension scheme for workers in job categories which have a rapid turnover of labour.

It cannot therefore be expected that the occupational pension sector could ever become large enough to include all workers, and thus some kind of State scheme would continue to be necessary for those left out. Even in businesses where superannuation schemes exist, not all workers are allowed to join. In a great many types of job a person must work for a particular employer for a year or more before becoming eligible to join the superannuation scheme. In 1971 it was found in an official survey that nearly two million people were currently being excluded from occupational schemes run by their employers because they had not yet completed the qualifying period.[1] (This total is in addition to a further two million workers who were too young to be given entry to schemes.) It is thus very difficult for those who make frequent changes of employer to accumulate much in the way of pension rights.

The 1971 survey also turned up almost three million people whose employers ran pension schemes, but who were not admitted to those schemes because of the sort of job they did. Generally they were the more routine or less skilled sort of jobs, non-manual as well as manual. After all, for employers a pension scheme is a business proposition, to be used to attract and retain types of labour that are in short supply. For many skilled jobs there has been a scarcity of labour in Britain over the past decade. This has not been so much the case for less skilled and more routine types of work. High turnover, no shortage of people capable of doing the job – these are also the sorts of reasons which make it difficult for less skilled workers to organize in defence of their wages and conditions. And such effective militancy as can be developed tends to be absorbed in a struggle for an adequate wage rather than in pursuit of longer-term demands, such as for a superannuation scheme.

All of these factors tend to operate particularly to the detriment of women. As a group women tend more often to work for smaller employers (in small-scale manufacture, or in distribution), to enter and leave jobs more frequently, to do less skilled work, to be paid lower wages and more often to work in jobs without effective union organization. Thus, whereas at any one time women make up one third of the labour force, they provide only one fifth of the membership of occupational pension schemes. Or, to put the point another way, although two thirds of employed men are in schemes, only one third of employed women have any occupational pension provision.

Government experts estimate that though there will be some further expansion of the occupational pension sector, nevertheless the limitations on this expansion are such that even by the turn of the century fully one third of all retirement pensioner households would have no occupational pension of any sort.[2]

Next we have to consider the sort of provision made for the twelve million people who are accumulating pension rights in a work-based scheme. Certainly the provision being currently made by such schemes is a good deal short of spectacular.

In 1971 it was found that some three million retired workers, or their widows, were receiving an occupational pension. Effectively this meant that there were about two million pensioner households who derived no income from the occupational schemes. The lack of coverage was most heavily concentrated among widows. By 1971 only one in five of widows over age 60 was receiving occupational benefits.

In a great many cases the amounts of pension involved were extremely small. In 1971, at a time when the State pension was £9·70 for a married couple, 10 per cent of occupational pensioners were getting less than £1 a week from their employer's scheme, and a further 21 per cent were getting between £1 and £2 a week. For something like one half of current occupational pensioners, what they get from their employer's scheme is only enough to disqualify them from a supplementary pension and thus adds nothing to their total income. An occupational pension is better than supplementary pension, because it is paid as of right and without a means test; but in a great many cases it offers no more cash.

At the other end of the scale, some 20 per cent of occupational pensioners in 1971 were getting more from an occupational scheme than from the State. The occupational sector is marked by deep inequality in the level of provision made.

For the majority of pensioners there has been a tendency over the years for the benefits paid to fall behind increases in the cost of living. On the whole, pensioners who have worked in the public sector do rather better in that once retired they have from the State a guarantee to maintain the purchasing power of their pensions – this undertaking was given statutory force by the Pensions Increase Act of 1971. Within the private sector, the situation is far from satisfactory. Some employer-run schemes will not increase pensions after retirement to compensate for inflation. According to studies carried out by the Government Actuary, even in cases where post-retirement increases had been granted, the average annual increase in the ten years up to 1971 was $2\frac{1}{2}$ per cent a year. Yet during this period prices rose by an average of $4\frac{1}{2}$ per cent a year.

It can be argued that the pensions paid to those now retired provide no reliable guide to the prospects of younger generations contributing to occupational schemes. The bulk of those currently receiving occupational pensions will have belonged to schemes instituted a long time ago, or, if the schemes are newer, the contribution record of people now retired will be limited. Possibly the newer schemes offer better terms to their younger members. The one thing certain is that it is very hard to say. The 65,000 separate pension schemes are bewilderingly various. The information provided to the ordinary member of such a scheme is usually enigmatic and incomplete. It is hard to think of any area of comparable personal importance to millions of people which has been accorded so little systematic and independent research. The Government has carried out four surveys of occupational pension schemes, but has published no information about how much money per week people can expect from their occupational scheme when they come to retire. What can be said with more confidence is that the general run of employer-run schemes have suffered from three crucial drawbacks: (1) inadequate provision for widows, (2) inadequate protection against post-retirement inflation, and (3) loss of pension rights when changing employers.

Of the occupational pensions now in payment, something like two thirds make no provision for surviving widows. In such cases all payments cease when the husband dies. Newer schemes make better provision for widows, but still about a third of men at work today are in schemes that give no permanent widow-cover once retirement has taken place. This is a serious defect, given that in the majority of marriages it is the husband who dies first. In the section of the population aged over 65, widows outnumber widowers by four to one. Lack of provision for women made widows by the death of a retired husband is a particularly serious drawback, since few wives spend sufficiently long at work to earn an adequate occupational pension of their own.

A further major drawback of occupational schemes has been that in the vast majority of cases pension rights are lost when the individual changes employer. On this point, the findings of the Government Actuary's 1971 survey were widely regarded as a damning indictment of the effectiveness of the occupational sector in providing for a long-term accumulation of pension rights. It was apparent, moreover, that there had been little serious progress in this crucial area since a previous inquiry in 1963.

The total number of employees leaving schemes in 1971 – other than by death or retirement – was one million. There was thus an annual turnover rate of members amounting to 9 per cent. For 20 per cent of those leaving, no benefits were paid or preserved; even their own contributions were not returned. In a further 38 per cent of cases, the rules of the scheme required the member to accept a refund of his own contribution; and in such cases the employer retained his part of the total contributed. In another 31 per cent of cases, the employer chose to withhold his contribution.

For only 3 per cent of leavers the accrued benefit was preserved by transfer to the new employer, and for 5 per cent of leavers the accrued benefit was preserved by the original employer.

Thus no form of preservation was allowed for a total of 58 per cent of leavers, and this was exactly the comparable proportion established in the 1963 inquiry. The proportion of leavers who chose a contribution refund was again, at 31 per cent, identical with the 1963 figure. In 1971, as in 1963, only 8 per cent of leavers were awarded transfer or deferred benefits.

The benefit of the employer's contribution was only available in 50 per cent of cases, and even then this was frequently only at the discretion of the employer, or only after certain conditions as to age and service had been fulfilled. The report adds that 'On the whole, for private and public sector schemes alike, the rules of manual schemes allow benefit of the employer's contribution less frequently than for staff schemes'.[3]

What is involved here is a straight conflict of interest between employees and employers. From the employer's point of view his contribution to the pension scheme is a reward for service and loyalty, not a deferred wage. He sees pension rights as a useful adjunct to discipline and a way of discouraging the movement of scarce labour. The employee on the other hand would wish the employer's contribution to be treated simply as wages paid in retrospect, together with whatever interest has been earned by that contribution in the meantime. In Britain employers have been in an exceptionally strong position to enforce their definition of the purpose of pension schemes. Until recently, the Government has played little or no part in supervising or setting standards for occupational schemes. And trade unions are usually presented with a pension scheme on a take it or leave it basis. Employers make every effort to avoid negotiation over the details of schemes and to remain in sole control of the running of schemes. In many cases even the size of the employer's contribution is not made known to the employee membership. In France, by comparison, it is normal for pension schemes – both the State schemes and private-sector schemes – to be run by committees containing representatives of both management and unions. The effect is that:

Social security is not regarded as marginal to the main interests of the union, as has tended to be the case in Britain, but as one of their most important fields of action. Their concern even extends to the drafting of detailed proposals for the reform of the whole security system . . .[4]

These various defects of the occupational pension sector were so glaring that during the 1970s both Conservative and Labour Governments have been moved to lay down and enforce certain minimum standards for recognized occupational schemes. However the nature of their decisions has been deeply influenced by well directed lobbying by the employers' organizations and by that section of the insurance industry which runs the occupational pension sector.

Over the past two decades, the occupational pension schemes have developed into a force of major importance in the financial landscape. In 1971 total contribution income was £1,870 million – not greatly less than the £2,530 million paid in contributions to the national-insurance scheme, which covers a broad range of social security needs for the whole employed population. In addition the occupational schemes derived a further £750 million in the form of investment income. The funds controlled by pension schemes are gigantic. In 1974 alone, £1,300 million were added to reserves, after paying the pensions and administrative expenses due in that year. No less than one quarter of total personal savings in Britain each year are now made via the pension schemes – and they provide 10 per cent of all investment capital absorbed in Britain. Thus, apart from the enormous resources which the pension interests can deploy in propaganda and lobbying, they are armed also with the powerful argument that the continued survival of British capitalism rests partly on the volume of new investment capital which they provide.

These resources are not, of course, invested with any consideration of the overall public interest, but strictly on business criteria, namely that investments should be safe and as profitable as possible. Control of investment is vested in insurance companies, trustees or professional pension-fund managers, employed by the parent companies, but with autonomous responsibility for managing the schemes. The occupational pension funds have become, in short, a classic institution of what Richard Titmuss once called 'The Irresponsible Society', since at no point are their activities subjected to any form of democratic control and scrutiny.

Those who believe that the occupational schemes should be encouraged to spread at the expense of the State scheme usually base their case on one particular virtue which they attribute to the occupational sector – actuarial soundness. They argue that, since occupational schemes are funded, they offer greater security for the individual than is provided by the pay-as-you-go financial basis of social insurance. It is certainly true that the State scheme works on a hand-to-mouth basis; the contributions paid in are immediately spent on meeting the cost of current pensions. There is no accumulation of a reserve fund large enough to discharge all current obligations. One cannot, however, conclude from this that the State scheme is built on foundations of sand. The rights of the future State pensioner rest on the willingness of future generations of voters to demand adequate provision for the elderly; given that willingness, only some kind of total national economic collapse would imperil the future rights of current contributors. On the other hand the occupational pension schemes, despite their accumulation of reserves, cannot be regarded as providing copper-bottomed security. As the President of the Institute of Actuaries explained in 1958:

I do not know a completely satisfactory definition of solvency, but even if one is assumed to exist then many schemes which are solvent on that definition at one point of time would immediately be rendered insolvent by an increase in the level of wages ... What is crucial is the ability of the employer to fulfil his obligations and to increase his contributions wherever necessary. Solvency is therefore often inextricably bound up with the resources of the employer.[5]

As we shall see later, the appearance in 1974 of high levels of inflation, combined with an undermining of profit levels, had a very damaging effect on the financial position of many private-sector pension schemes.

Another common argument used to defend the occupational schemes is that they provide flexible cover adapted to meet differing personal needs. Tony Lynes comments as follows:

Top hat pension schemes for a few wealthy individuals may do this – the main 'personal need' catered for by them being the need to avoid income tax. But the average employee in a firm which runs an occupational scheme is obliged to join in and offered little or no choice as to the level or type of benefits for which he is covered. Why compulsory membership of the ICI pension scheme, for example, should 'give the citizen the feeling of providing for his own future' is a profound mystery.[6]

Given the very rapid development of the occupational pension sector over the past fifteen years, it is remarkable how little public discussion there has been about the need for greater public control of the schemes, or, on a more radical view, about the possibility of assimilating these private schemes with the State social security system. The case for doing so is a strong one, and it is surprising that such a proposal has received virtually no discussion within the Labour Party in recent years. Yet it was only in the early 1950s that the Labour Party dropped its long-standing traditional commitment to nationalize the insurance industry, or at least those companies whose main business was the provision of industrial assurance.

The term 'industrial assurance' refers to policies paid for by weekly contributions and providing in particular a lump-sum death benefit, such policies being sold mainly to working-class customers by techniques of high-pressure salesmanship. This is a type of business which still flourishes mightily and still forms the basic bread and butter of one of the giants of the British business world, the Prudential. In 1967 there were over sixty-four million industrial insurance policies in force. The total funds held as backing for these policies was over £1,700 million.[7]

Traditionally, in the Labour movement, industrial insurance was regarded as a way of exploiting the working class. A vast army of persuasive salesmen induce people to take out a policy whether or not they can afford it. The financial stability of the schemes is guaranteed only by a high rate of lapsed policies. In 1967, for example, four million new industrial insurance policies were taken out, but in the same year 700,000 policies were forfeited without any compensation paid by the companies to the customer. The other argument which, historically, the Left have made against industrial assurance is that the expensive selling techniques used mean that a high proportion of the premiums paid by people insuring themselves are absorbed in running expenses. The result is a far higher expense ratio than in any other form of insurance. In commercial terms industrial assurance must rank as one of the 'Worst Buys' in consumer history. In 1967 expenses of management were £80 million – i.e. 36 per cent of a total premium income of £224 million. Compare in the public sector a total expenditure of £147 million on the administration of the social security system, only 5 per cent out of a budget of £3,000 million.

It is still the case that nationalization of industrial insurance ought to be on the agenda of the Labour Party, even if its pretensions to be a socialist party have now to be accepted as fairly minimal. But some of the traditional arguments used in the Labour movement about industrial insurance apply to the occupational pension sectors. No information is publicly available about the administrative costs of these schemes, but they are bound to be substantial. This is not because of their sales techniques, but simply because of the very large number of schemes, 65,000 of them, each requiring a separate structure of management. There must be enormous scope here for economies of scale – i.e. the lowering of adminstrative costs when operations are conducted on a large scale.

Secondly there can be very few of the millions who belong to work-based superannuation schemes who understand, even in an approximate way, how their scheme works. A booklet of rules is generally provided, but anyone who spends a few hours studying a range of such rule books will know that the information provided is highly selective and limited. In any case fuller information would leave most people none the wiser. Such schemes are immensely complex and the jargon used by the experts who design them is pretty well impenetrable without a great deal of study. Short of some kind of direct workers' control over social security, there is little incentive for an employee to go deeply into these matters, since he is excluded from any influence on the design of his scheme. Some of these arguments also apply to the trade unions, for whom a thorough evaluation of 65,000 separate schemes would constitute an overwhelming task. In any case, as I argue elsewhere in this book, effective bargaining power over wages and conditions has in recent years rested much more with the shop stewards on the factory floor, rather than with the national union negotiators in their London offices. Shop stewards are even less in a position to become amateur actuaries than full-time trade-union officials.

The occupational schemes are often referred to as the private pensions sector. Strictly the term is a misnomer because the occupational schemes are heavily subsidized by the State. The mechanism of subsidy is tax relief. The employer's contribution counts as an ordinary business expense and escapes corporation tax. An occupational pension fund is not subject to capital gains tax, nor is any tax levied on its income from investments. The contributions made by employees are deducted from their earnings before income tax is levied. In effect the employee's contribution is not treated as part of his taxable income.

The total cost of these exemptions is one of the best kept secrets of British public life, and no comprehensive estimates have been forthcoming from any recent Government. But the sum involved must be enormous. Back in 1954 the Phillips Committee found that the annual sacrifice of revenue arising from tax relief for occupational pension schemes was of the order of £100 million a year.[8] At that time the total income of pension schemes was £271 million a year. In 1971 the total income of the schemes approached £2,700 million – more than one quarter of this being derived from interest. There is no reason to suppose that tax exemption adds up to a lower proportion of total pension-fund income at the present time than was the case in 1954. Indeed, since rates of taxation tend to be higher now than in the early fifties, the privilege of tax exemption has become correspondingly more valuable. Thus we can be fairly sure that State subsidies to the occupational sector in 1971 were running at £1000 million – more than twice as much as the total £494 million subsidy paid by the Exchequer in 1971 into the national-insurance scheme.

Thus the State is giving double the subsidy to pension funds catering for only half the population as it gives to the whole national-insurance system which covers the whole employed population.

It should be remembered, too, that the national-insurance scheme covers unemployment and sickness as well as old-age pensions and widows' benefit – whereas the occupational schemes are limited to pensions only, together with a degree of patchy coverage of widowhood. Yet the occupational schemes get more generous subsidization from general taxation.

It is remarkable how little public discussion there has been about the State subsidy to the occupational schemes. Very few people seem aware of its existence. Yet it is a massive and major item of Government expenditure. At £1000 million in 1971 the occupational pension subsidy cost the Treasury half the amount of money spent on the entire health service, three times the cost of family allowances, over four times the cost of council house subsidies. A sum of £1000 million would be enough to give an immediate increase of £2·40 a week to every retired person in the country.

Since most of the income of occupational schemes derives from contributions which are charged as a proportion of wages and salaries, it follows that the flow of money into the schemes increases as inflation pushes up incomes. The cost of the relief rises correspondingly. Thus the subsidy benefits of scheme membership are effectively made inflation proof. Earnings roughly doubled in money terms between 1971 and 1975, and therefore it is likely that by the latter date the subsidization of occupational pensions was costing something like £2000 million.

Serious questions have to be raised about the fairness of arrangements whereby half the population gets its future pension generously subsidized by the other half. What is even less defensible is that this subsidy is heavily concentrated in favour of people belonging to the higher managerial and professional groups. This is an effect of the method used to allocate the subsidy – tax exemption. The bigger the contribution made by the employer, or by the employee himself, the greater the financial

138

advantage of exemption from taxes on capital gains and investment income.

Within the field of occupational pensions there are fantastic inequalities between the sorts of schemes provided for manual workers and those designed for the high-salaried classes. The higher up the income scale the more likely it is that the employer will pay full contribution and the employee be exempt from contributions. The higher a person's earnings, the bigger, as a proportion of earnings, is the contribution being salted away on his behalf in a pension fund. The higher the rate of tax which a person pays, the more valuable to him is a tax exemption. A tax exemption will allow a person rich enough to pay surtax to hang on to correspondingly more money than the person with a lower income who only pays income tax at the standard rate. All this is very well known to those familiar with the employment conditions of the upper middle classes in this country. And yet it is extraordinarily difficult to provide up-to-date statistical evidence in support. The necessary research has not been done by anyone or, if done, has not been made public. The two possible sources of information would be either the Government or the National Association of Pension Funds, which acts as a spokesman and public-relations service for private pension interests. The latter organization puts out a good deal of material, but this, naturally enough, is designed to suggest the increasing numbers of employees who are gaining some kind of occupational pension coverage and to prove that there is no need for any extension of the State scheme. The National Association of Pension Funds is not interested in providing evidence of the extraordinary variations in the value of pension rights accumulating in the occupational pension sector.

If you study the comprehensive statistics provided by the Inland Revenue on income, wealth, and taxation, you will stumble on an even more remarkable mystery. Occupational pension schemes seem to have no real existence. Every year the Inland Revenue publishes elaborate tables indicating the distribution of income and wealth as between richer and poorer income groups. Yet the contributions made in a given year to pension schemes are not included in the statistics of personal income, nor in the tables indicating the distribution of wealth. To explain this, it is not necessary to postulate a deep conspiracy linking the Inland Revenue authorities with the pension-fund interests. The reasons are more technical in nature. The Inland Revenue is not in business to provide accurate research about the distribution of wealth in Britain – but rather to collect taxes. The statistics they publish are shaped by this primary purpose. It follows that a great many of the forms of income or wealth which are exempt from taxation are omitted from Inland Revenue statistics, or at best figure only in a shadowy and fleeting way. This is exactly the case with pension-fund income from contributions, capital gains, and interest. There is also the fact that for tax purposes, personal financial resources are classified by the Inland Revenue into two distinct categories – income and wealth. These categories are defined in such a way that private pension rights cannot be included with one or the other. Pension-fund rights only become income at the time when the pension comes to be paid. Nor do such rights count as personal wealth, since they are not controlled by the individual member of a pension scheme, but are held and administered on his behalf by the employers or by trustees in whose care the management of the scheme has been vested.

A few glimmerings, however, penetrate the general obscurity. The Inland Revenue has a table showing the distribution of tax relief on life-insurance premiums according to size of income. There is a connection between life insurance and occupational pension provision via a series of technical devices, whereby the employer can obtain special tax privileges for a favoured employee, by, in effect, buying him life insurance. The table, however, relates to life insurance in general, whether arranged by an employer or by a private individual. Table 1 illustrates the way in which State subsidies awarded via tax relief rise sharply with income and much faster than income. The inequalities involved can be illustrated in a different way: it is the case that the 2 per cent of people with the highest incomes get 17 per cent of all money handed out by the Government in the form of tax relief on life-insurance premiums. It is likely that the value of tax relief will

Table 1: Life-insurance Tax Relief[9]

Annual income of beneficiary	Average annual value of tax relief
Under £1,000	£11
£1,000–	£13
£2,000–	£44
£5,000 and over	£149

rise just as sharply with income in the case of occupational pension schemes as it does for life insurance.

The reason which is put forward officially to justify these tax exemptions is that people will one day pay income tax on their pension when they start to receive it. There is a principle built into the income-tax system that the same bit of income should not be taxed twice. But, as applied to pension-fund contributions and interest, this justification of tax exemption is very thin indeed. The block of income paid into a pension scheme does not lie there, as if preserved in aspic, until retirement. Rather these contributions are savings which grow at a compound rate by the accretion of interest and capital gains. The tax system, however, conveniently ignores this fact, and the fiction is solemnly maintained that all of the income which eventually makes up the pension is *earned* income. That the whole of the eventual pension counts as earned income is to the great advantage of the pensioner, since earned income as compared with unearned qualifies for a special tax exemption currently running at about 9p in each pound. Thus occupational schemes operate as a useful tax-avoidance device, whereby a person can acquire investment income and benefit from capital gains, which are taxed at the lower rate for earned income rather than at the higher rate which normally applies to unearned income from investment.

A superannuation scheme confers two further privileges on its members, both involving tax avoidance. In most cases, and even in the most generous of occupational schemes, people have a higher income during their working life than when retired. Once into the surtax range of earnings, the higher the income the higher the rate of taxation. By being able to spread out income more evenly over his lifetime, a person can lower the overall rate of taxation that he will pay on his total lifetime income. An example may make the point clearer. Currently a married man with no children and £10,000 a year will lose 42 per cent of those earnings in income tax and surtax. He would do much better to accept a salary of £7,500 (tax loss only 36 per cent) and take the rest in the form of a pension say of £3,000 a year (tax loss only 26 per cent). His overall average rate of taxation is thus considerably reduced and, into the bargain, while his money is sealed away in the pension fund, it is attracting tax-free interest and capital gains.

A second advantage is that normally a person on retirement with an occupational pension has the option of taking part of that pension in the form of a lump sum rather than in monthly payments. Such a lump sum is completely exempt from payment of tax. In a report on Top Management Salaries the Prices and Incomes Board give an example. Normally the superannuation schemes designed for higher management personnel provide a pension of two thirds of final salary – e.g. £6,000 a year on a salary of £9,000 a year. But instead,

an executive retiring after 40 years with a salary of £9,000 a year could receive an annual pension of £4,500 a year and commute the remainder of £1,500 into a lump sum, usually 10 times the value of the commuted pension, i.e. in this case £15,000. The advantage of a lump sum payment is that it is not liable to tax.[10]

Incidentally the tax treatment of occupational pension contributions contrasts sharply with that of national-insurance contributions. The latter contributions are not exempt from tax. Thus a man draws his wages, has income tax deducted, and has to pay for the national insurance out of what remains of his wage. The contribution to an occupational pension scheme is deducted from earnings *before* income tax is calculated. The effect is that it costs a good deal more to contribute one pound to the national-insurance scheme than to an occupational scheme.

In their recent plans for the redesign of the State pensions scheme both the Labour and the Conservative parties started from one crucial and shared assumption: that the occupational sector could not and should not be compelled to extend its schemes to make adequate provision for lower-paid employees. Thus in one way or another the requirements of several millions of mainly manual workers could only be met by the creation of a substantial new earnings-related State scheme. Both parties, however, declared it their sincere intention that the occupational sector should receive every encouragement and protection from the State. The Labour Party was put under strong pressure to adopt this position by the large white-collar unions which are affiliated to the Party, and provide a major source of its finance. Effectively, the principle of partnership between State and occupational schemes meant allowing members of such schemes to pay a much reduced contribution to the State scheme. This in turn posed difficult problems in raising finance for the new earnings-related scheme. It would be catering for the overwhelming majority of lower-paid workers, yet the withdrawal of higher-paid employees into the occupational schemes would limit the extent to which the pensions eventually to be paid to lower income workers could be financed on a basis of vertical redistribution within the new State scheme. Yet, without some degree of internal redistribution, the contribution income from the lower paid would be insufficient to provide pensions above poverty line levels. It would not then be possible to plan for an eventual phasing out of supplementary benefit – one of the key objectives of the replanned scheme. The preservation of the occupational sector limited the possible extent to which resources could be transferred from higher- to lower-paid contributors within the new State scheme.

The Joseph Plan

The pensions plan produced by the Conservative Government in 1971 proposed that there should be a new earnings-related State scheme, into which employers would be able to put all those of their workers for whom no adequate occupational provision was available. It was reckoned by the Conservative administration that about seven million workers would become members of this State Reserve scheme. They thus envisaged, and hoped to encourage, the expansion of the occupational sector from the level of eleven million employees current in 1971, to around fourteen million.

In structure the State Reserve Scheme would closely resemble the occupational schemes which it would supplement. Contributions and returns from investment would be accumulated into a fund from which benefits would be paid according to strict actuarial principles. The scheme would be kept entirely separate from existing systems of State social insurance. The management of the Reserve Scheme would be devolved on to a Board of Trustees, appointed by the Government, but required to manage the funds and regulate the flows of contribution and benefit in accordance with commercial criteria. The Government would not in any special way underwrite the financial viability of the Reserve Scheme, and no subsidy from general taxation would be paid into it. In this respect, therefore, it would be quite unlike the national-insurance scheme, to which the Government contributes a subsidy from taxation, amounting generally to about 18 per cent of the contribution income derived from employers and their employees. The decision not to subsidize the Reserve Scheme was justified by the Government in the following terms:

If there were any element of subsidy from the taxpayer, employers well able to run their own schemes would be tempted to use the reserve scheme instead, at the taxpayer's expense.[11]

Although, in this way, the standard of provision in the Reserve Scheme was limited so as not to threaten the occupational sector with competitive pressure, there were to be some new conditions for Government recognition of an occupational scheme. (The rule was to be that all employees would have to be enrolled in either a recognized occupational scheme or in the Reserve Scheme.) To secure recognition, an occupational scheme would have to provide a pension for men at a rate of not less than 1 per cent of earnings up to a level of $1\frac{1}{2}$ times average national earnings; and, in addition, offer a widow's pension representing half of the husband's pension rate. Employer-run pension schemes would be obliged to protect the value of the pension, after award, by linking it to the cost of living index. And the Government would insist on either the preservation or transfer of pension rights accumulated by any employee leaving his job.

These proposals were open to criticism on a number of grounds. First, for people retiring over the next ten or twenty years the extra pension rights to be provided by the Reserve Scheme would be very small indeed. The following Table shows the size of the Reserve pension which would be paid to a man retiring in 1971, if the scheme had been in operation during his working life.

Weekly Pensions in Reserve Scheme[12]

Retired after paying into scheme for	Men with average earnings of	
	£20 per week	£30 per week
10 years	90p	£1·30
20 years	£2·20	£3·30
30 years	£4·10	£6·10

Effectively this meant a very slow reduction in the level of reliance on supplementary benefit. Only if a person with below average wages had been contributing to the Reserve Scheme for more than twenty years would his total pension (including the flat-rate element) be higher than the official poverty line. Reserve pensions only *half* of the above levels would be paid to surviving widows.

Women employees would be worse off. As at present they would not be compelled to contribute to the basic flat-rate scheme, but they would be obliged to pay into either an occupational scheme or into the Reserve Scheme. Women in the Reserve Scheme would contribute at the same rate as men. But because women retire at 60 and tend to live longer than men, they were to be given correspondingly lower pensions.

Weekly Pensions in Reserve Scheme[13]

Retired after paying into scheme for	Women with average earnings of	
	£10 per week	£20 per week
10 years	40p	70p
20 years	90p	£1·80
30 years	£1·70	£3·30

What was disastrous both in the Reserve Scheme, and in the minimum qualifying conditions for occupational schemes, was the lack of effective provision for inflation occurring *before* retirement. In the occupational sector the minimum was to be £1 week of pension for every £5000 earned during his working life. A period of rapid inflation would profoundly undermine the value of future pension rights, given that the indexation guarantee was to apply only to post-retirement pensions.

It seemed to many critics that the Conservative Reserve Scheme was designed more to increase the level of funds available for national investment, than to assure the standard of living of future pensioners. It was anticipated that the funds of the Reserve Scheme would increase at an annual rate of £250 million, and that by the end of the century the fund would stand at about £5,000 million.

The Castle Scheme

The most recent Labour Party scheme – and the one which now seems certain to come into operation – attempts to meet some of the criticisms made of the Conservative plan.

The expanded State earnings-related scheme will not be funded. Rather, it will operate, as does national insurance, on a pay-as-you-go basis. Pensions will be financed by a direct transfer of resources from the economically active to the retired section of the population. However, so far as the individual contributor is concerned, the new scheme will operate *as if* there were funding. His eventual pension will be determined by the length and size of his contribution record. And fully matured new scheme pensions will not be paid until twenty years have elapsed from the inception of the scheme – currently expected to be in 1978.

Although the Labour Government's maturity period of twenty years is half that required by the Conservative scheme, many observers have been puzzled as to why such a considerable maturity period should still be required. For, although rights to a new scheme pension depend on accumulated contributions, it does not appear to be Labour's intention to hold the cash derived

146

from the extra contributions in a separate and sacrosanct fund. It would appear that this money would be available for the financing of the general insurance scheme, which provides not only for pensions, but for a whole range of other benefits in addition. Certainly the estimates so far published of the extra money to be spent on national insurance benefits in the early years of the new scheme do not seem to justify a large increase in contributions, unless perhaps there is to be a considerable accumulation of reserve funds.

Estimated Cost of Benefits[14]
(at July 1974 earnings levels) £ million

	1978–9 £m	1983–4 £m	1988–9 £m	1993–4 £m	1998–9 £m
Retirement pensions					
Present scheme	4,040	4,128	4,148	4,158	4,067
New scheme extra cost*	5	82	230	443	725
Other benefits					
Present scheme	1,560	1,574	1,576	1,571	1,599
New scheme extra cost*	22	107	176	258	333

* Assuming 8 million contracted out by occupational schemes.

Thus, for example, in the tenth year of the new scheme, the extra benefits to be paid out, as compared with levels due under existing legislation, represent an increase of only 5·5 per cent in the case of retirement pensions and 11·2 per cent for other benefits. The present Government have not yet published projections of the expected total of contribution income under their new scheme.

In its handling of inflation proofing, the Labour scheme is clearly superior to the Conservative plan. When a person's pension comes to be fixed his contributions will be related to the level of average industrial earnings in the year in which the contribution was made, and revalued in the light of average industrial earnings in the year of retirement. The earnings-related State pension will be considered as the guaranteed minimum pension, and all occupational schemes must deliver pension rights at this level or better. The State will take over full responsibility for proofing pensions against post-retirement inflation, both in the State and the occupational sectors.

The other area in which Labour's scheme is regarded as being especially innovative is in its provision for women. Widows without pensions on their own contribution record will be entitled to inherit the whole of the earnings-related pension of their husbands. Women will benefit particularly from the rule that pensions will be calculated not on the complete contribution record but only on the basis of those twenty years of working life in which the individual's earnings were highest in relation to average national earnings. Furthermore,

membership of the scheme will continue, without any requirement to pay contributions, for a person who is at home looking after children, or who in specified circumstances has to stay at home to care for an adult receiving an invalidity or retirement pension or an attendance allowance.[15]

On the other hand, however, the levels of contribution required from women are to be sharply increased. At present roughly four million of the five million married women who work have elected to opt out of the main national-insurance scheme. This choice will not be available under the new scheme, and the contributions of women will rise from 2 per cent to 4·75 per cent of relevant earnings.

In two respects the Labour Government's proposed scheme is more egalitarian in its structure than the previous Conservative scheme. I mentioned above that the Conservative State Reserve Scheme was to receive no Exchequer strictly from general taxation. Labour have arranged that their earnings-related State scheme will enjoy a taxation subsidy equivalent to 18 per cent of total contribution income.

Second, the ratio of contributions to eventual pensions will be higher for lower-paid contributors and vice versa. There will thus be a measure of vertical redistribution within the scheme. The variation in ratio can be illustrated as follows:

Single-person Pension as % Earnings-contributions over[16]

Weekly earnings	5 years	10 years	20 years
	%	%	%
£20	53	56	62
£30	37	42	50
£40	30	34	44
£50	25	30	40
£60	22	27	38
£70	20	25	36

These are impressively steep gradients, implying a sharp discrimination against higher-paid workers. Yet when expressed in cash terms at 1974 earnings levels the extra benefits accruing to lower income groups under the new system are quite marginal.

Earnings-related Pension, Single Person
(Additional to £10 basic pension, 1974)

Weekly earnings	After 5 years contributing	After 10 years contributing	After 20 years contributing (maximum)
	£	£	£
£20	0·62	1·25	2·50
£30	1·25	2·50	5·00
£40	1·87	3·75	7·50
£50	2·50	5·00	10·00
£60	3·12	6·25	12·50
£70	3·75	7·50	15·00

It is apparent that for lower-paid contributors, a great many years must pass before the new scheme pension, combined with flat-rate provision, can deliver a standard of living much superior to the current combination of flat-rate pension and supplementary benefit. Not before 1998 will average-paid contributors retire with a pension of £20 at 1974 earnings levels – i.e. twice the current flat-rate level of £10 – and for a single person this will amount to no more than the equivalent of 40 per cent of his earnings during working life.

The addition of pension rights derived from the earnings and contributions of a working wife will somewhat improve the position. For a man earning £20 and a wife earning £15 (at 1974 values) the fully matured new scheme provision will be £7·75 a week above existing provision; and £10·25 if the husband has earned a steady £30 a week.

Even so, despite the many virtues of Labour's latest scheme, this remains the central and dismal fact about it. For millions of lower-paid workers, it implies a painfully delayed, and rather inconsiderable, rise in income above the kind of poverty line current today. And yet the mechanics of the scheme apparently allow a generous degree of internal redistribution from higher- to lower-paid contributors! It should be remembered, in addition, that for many workers in occupational schemes, pension levels may not be much in excess of those indicated above – since provision under the State scheme is to be the minimum for the occupational sector.

The information currently available does not allow for any accurate analysis of the structure of the new State schemes. The Government has not published estimates of the numbers of employees of different income levels which it expects to be put by their employers into the State earnings-related scheme, rather than contracted out into an occupational scheme. We may suspect that the Government reckons that comparatively small numbers of higher-paid employees will be enrolled in the State earnings-related scheme. Such an expectation has meant that a limited number of higher-paid workers will be available to help subsidize the pensions of the lower paid. To compensate for the imbalance in numbers between higher- and lower-paid contributors, the former are to be rather severely stung – to an extent which will turn the prediction of few higher-paid members into a self-fulfilling prophecy. It is apparent that Labour have produced a scheme which provides extra financial assistance for lower-paid workers at the expense primarily of the higher-paid sections of manual workers, rather than of the upper income groups.

Two further points can be made to substantiate this conclusion. First, the Labour Government have followed their Conservative predecessors in selecting a remarkably low ceiling of earnings to be subject to earnings-related contribution. Employees, and employers, will be required to pay a percentage contribution on earned income equivalent to only one and a half times national average earnings. Secondly, no social security contributions are required on unearned investment income. This decision has clearly been arrived at in order to protect the viability of the occupational sector. Yet the effect is to limit enormously the amount of resources flowing into the State scheme, part of which would have been available for redistribution to those down the income scale.

Thus in summary, both Labour and Conservative Governments in recent years have accepted as permanent the incapacity of employer-run schemes to make pension provision for lower-paid workers. But their anxiety to preserve the highly subsidized privileges offered by the occupational schemes has severely limited the provision they have been able to build in to the new earnings-related State sector.

Indeed, in its latest plan, the Labour Government proposes to extend still further the level of subsidy fed into the occupational schemes. For example, the State will take over the enormous and open-ended commitment to proof occupational pensions against post-retirement inflation. In addition the State will take over some responsibility – to an extent not yet clearly specified – for inflation proofing the accumulated contributions of employees who leave occupational schemes after less than five years of membership.

These undertakings that State assistance will be provided to protect occupational benefits from erosion by inflation have been warmly welcomed by employers and by the occupational pensions interest. In recent months there has been considerable anxiety about the soaring costs of pension provision in the occupational pension sector as the overall level of inflation has risen to an annual rate of 20 per cent. The crucial area of concern has been the relationship between the rate of increase in the cost of living and the rate of return which occupational pension funds can expect from their investments. The generally accepted view is that the financial viability of occupational schemes depends on their being able to secure an investment return approximately 15 per cent higher than the going rate of price inflation. Over the past year, rates of return on investments have fallen well behind increases in the cost of living.

As a consequence many companies have found it necessary to make special uncovenanted payments into their pension schemes. The Chairman of Barclays, one of the major British banks, has recently reported that in 1974, the bank had to pay into its pension fund a sum equivalent to 43 per cent of its annual salary payments.[17] One of the largest insurance companies, the Commercial Union, contributed to its pension scheme the equivalent of 10 per cent of total salaries in 1970; by 1975 the expected contribution has risen to 30 per cent. And, on present trends, the company predicts that its pension fund will cost as much as its total salary bill by 1980.[17]

Given this situation, Labour's new legislation – which initially was received with some hostility by the occupational pension industry – is now being viewed with considerable enthusiasm. The Conservative Party have withdrawn their opposition to the overall structure which Labour are introducing,[18] and instead are attempting to secure a series of amendments which would still further increase the level of State subsidy for the occupational schemes. Moreover, the Conservatives have announced that when they return to office they will make no fundamental alterations to the pension system which Labour has designed. This unexpected consensus, very uncommon in the history of British welfare legislation, is the product of fears that inflation will continue at a high rate, that the rate of return on investments will lag behind, and that in consequence the occupational schemes cannot remain financially self-sufficient without an intolerable level of expenditure by employers. From this fate, and at unlimited State expense, the Labour Government has saved them.

CHAPTER 9

Measuring Poverty

It is a common practice for Governments to defend their record in social security by comparing increases in money benefits with the movement of the Retail Price Index. Real improvements are claimed wherever the money value of benefits has risen faster than the level of consumer prices. By this standard the record seems not unimpressive over the past twelve years. Between 1962 and the end of 1974 benefits increased by just under three and a half times. In the same period the Retail Price Index rose by two and a quarter times. It looks as if there has been about a 50 per cent improvement in the purchasing power and standard of living of people dependent for an income on the national-insurance system. Wages also rose by about three and a half times during these twelve years. It would thus appear that, while pensioners and other social security groups did not improve in their relative economic position, they shared in the general improvement in living standards over these years.

On closer inspection, however, doubts begin to arise. There are good reasons for challenging the assumption that changes in the cost of living of groups around the poverty line are in fact accurately measured by the Retail Price Index. To understand why, it is necessary to look a little more closely at the procedures used in calculating changes in retail prices. The official Retail Price Index is not designed to measure the changes in the level of prices in general, but rather to reflect changes in the cost of living of an average household. This means that a change in the retail price of carrots, for example, only affects the Index to the extent that the average household spends money on carrots. A sudden rise, however astronomical, in the price of snuff will not affect the Index because the money spent by the average household on snuff is virtually nil. On the other hand even a small increase in major items of household expenditure such as rents, or the cost of electricity or coal, is likely to push up the Index.

It follows therefore that to calculate such a cost-of-living index it is necessary to have accurate information about how people spend their money, so that the Index can be correctly weighted. For this reason, among others, the Government carries out regularly a survey of household expenditure. Each year a fairly large sample of households (10,400 in 1968) are asked by the Government Social Survey to keep a detailed record of all income and expenditure over a two-week period. Each member of the household over the age of fifteen is asked to keep a diary of all financial transactions, however minute. Allowance is made for spending at longer intervals such as on local-authority rates, or household equipment. The results of this survey are published annually in the *Family Expenditure Survey*.

The level of detail in which household budgets are analysed is quite astounding. In the reports one finds picturesque details such as that the average household spends 5p a week on fish and chips, $4\frac{1}{2}$p on ice cream and $37\frac{1}{2}$p on 'undefined vegetables'. Such apparent precision however rests on shaky foundations and there are many deficiencies in the information obtained in expenditure surveys. The demands made on respondents are heavy – a two-week record of every bus fare, box of matches or bag of jelly babies. The Government gives two pounds to everyone keeping a diary, but this is a small return for the effort involved. Not surprisingly, only seven in ten of the sample approached agree to collaborate. As in all such surveys there is a higher rate of non-response at the lower end of the income scale. Thus the information gathered is likely to provide a poor guide to spending patterns at low income levels.

Secondly the household expenditure survey is plagued by a tendency for people to under-report spending on certain kinds of 'luxury' items. It is reckoned that respondents spend twice as much on alcohol as they put down in the diary and that only four fifths of spending on tobacco is recorded. This type of bias is known as the 'halo-effect', a tendency for people to represent themselves to interviewers as more angelic than they are. It also appears that respondents in these budgetary surveys manage to spend more money each week than they claim to have, and this, too, perplexes the statisticians.

The pattern of expenditure that is reflected in the Retail Price Index is that of the *average* household submitting diary record of spending. Thus the Index is calculated from a highly abstract weighting of goods and services bought by families. No one is likely to have an average spending pattern, any more than 0·9 of a wife and 2·8 children. The Index is particularly unreliable as a guide to the cost of living of groups with low incomes, given that their pattern of consumption is an exceptional one.

A number of studies have shown a clear tendency over the past two decades for prices of basic necessities to rise faster than the general run of prices. For the period 1948 to 1961 Tony Lynes found that whereas the Index for all retail prices rose by 61 per cent, food prices went up by 87 per cent and the cost of fuel by 104 per cent.[1] Excluding housing, the cost of living for single pensioners rose by 88 per cent, for pensioner couples by 76 per cent and for widowed mothers by 84 per cent – as compared with a 59 per cent price rise for the average consumer. The widowed-mother group, for example, spent over half their total income on food and so were particularly hit by the sharp rise in food prices.

A recent official study has shown that the same trend continued in the 1960s, and at the same time indicates how far the spending patterns of lower-income households diverge from the average. Table 1 gives some illustrations.

Pensioners spend, relatively, far more on basic necessities such as food, housing and heating and much less on travel, clothing, drink and cigarettes. The large family group was less deviant, except that they spend a great deal extra on food. If it happens that the prices of basic necessities such as food are rising more rapidly than prices in general, it will follow that the Retail Price Index will not reflect the actual deterioration in the standard of living of low-income groups. The expenditure pattern of the elderly in particular is so exceptional that this group is simply ignored in the calculation of the monthly Retail Price Index.

Table 1: Expenditure Patterns of Low-income Households[2]

	Pensioners % of income	Large families* £10–£20 a week % of income	Average† household % of income
Housing	18·8	11·1	11·4
Food	35·2	39·0	28·4
Fuel, light, power	14·1	7·9	6·3
Tobacco, alcohol	5·5	11·1	10·1
Transport, vehicles	5·1	7·8	12·9
Clothing, footwear	3·0	7·2	9·1
Other spending	18·3	15·9	22·8
Total	100·0	100·0	100·0

* i.e. two adults plus three or more children.
† i.e. the household taken as standard in constructing the Retail Price Index.

Using the above spending patterns, the Cost of Living Advisory Committee, which reported in 1968, then went on to establish a special cost-of-living index for pensioners, and the large-family/ low-income group. The Committee found that between 1962 and 1968 the general price index had risen by 20·8 per cent, but the pensioner index by 24·5 per cent. As a result of this finding the Government decided that in the future a special pensioner index should be published every quarter. This is now done – but even the new pensioner index has to be taken with a pinch of salt. As Table 1 shows, nearly one fifth of pensioners' income went on housing, compared with a bit over one tenth in the case of the average household. It should be noted that housing is excluded from the calculation of the pensioner price index. Yet from 1962 to 1974 the cost of housing to the consumer rose by 145 per cent compared with a 124 per cent rise in the general price index. Presumably housing is not taken into account because supple-mentary benefit pays the rent for about two million retired people. It is scarcely a good reason, since another three million old people pay their own housing costs.

At the same time the Government decided that there was no need for a special cost-of-living index for large families on low incomes. The basis for this decision was that between 1962 and 1968 the cost of living of this group had risen only fractionally faster than for the average household. It should be noted, however, that the large family estimate was based on the income group £10 to £20 a week. It is likely that a pattern rather closer to that of pensioners would have been found if large families on, say, less than £16 a week had been studied.

There are a number of other weaknesses which make the Retail Price Index a misleading guide to the cost of living of low-income groups. Certain items of expenditure are omitted in calculating the index–income taxes for example, contributions to pension funds, and trade-union subscriptions. A particularly important omission is the employee's share of the national-insurance stamp, a large and unavoidable item in the budget of any household with one or more of its members in employment. In the period since 1948, whereas the Retail Price Index has doubled, the cost of the national-insurance stamp has risen by three and a half times.

The Index reflects only the national average of price changes and thus may conceal considerable local variation. So far the Government has resisted pressure to publish separate retail-price indices for the various regions.* Yet the average national price for a particular item may vary widely from the actual prices charged in different areas in Britain. For example in March 1970 the Department of Employment collected 856 quotations for the price of tomatoes being sold in shops all over the country. The average price being charged was 15p a pound; but only 80 per cent of the quotations fell within a range as broad as from 13p to 20p per pound and the remaining quotations were either above or below these limits. For Cheddar cheese, 20 per cent of the quotations fell outside the range 15p to 20p per pound. The prices of most items show a comparable range of variation.

No account is taken of the fact that prices per item tend to be higher for people on a low budget buying small quantities or that

---

* The main opposition to regional price indices comes from the Confederation of British Industries. Yet the Retail Price Advisory Committee, reporting in August 1971, found, for example, that food prices tend to be 4–8 per cent higher in Scotland; and that the average amount spent in travel to and from work varied from 95p in the North of England to £1·75 in the South East of England. And the regional variations in rents and house prices are well known.

many people on low incomes are not able to get about so freely because of age or disability or family responsibilities and therefore do more of their shopping at the high-price corner shops, rather than at cut-price supermarkets.[3]

Rents are counted as if everyone were getting the full means-tested rebates to which they are in theory entitled. Yet survey evidence suggests that only 70 per cent of council tenants get their full rebate entitlement, and only one quarter of people renting unfurnished property from a private landlord.[4]

The use of conventional cost-of-living indices to assess the adequacy of social security provision is, at best, a recipe for arriving at wildly over-optimistic conclusions. But the technical deficiencies of this type of approach are closely linked to much broader questions about the nature of poverty. In a period when a degree of economic growth is taking place and in which living standards are rising, any social group whose purchasing power rises less than the average will experience a fall in its living standards relative to other groups. The first question to ask about those sections of society which depend on social security is not whether their incomes rose faster than the cost of living, but whether benefits have risen as fast as average earnings. It is not a very impressive national achievement that the living standards of pensioners have somewhat improved since 1948, given that the benefit levels were established initially at a very low level.

Often in academic discussion about welfare a distinction is made between the absolute and relative concepts of poverty. On an absolute criterion the poor are those who have insufficient resources to achieve some fixed standard of living. In the 1930s in Britain there was a good deal of research undertaken to establish basic minima of diet, clothing etc. below which physiological efficiency could not be sustained. It is now generally accepted that absolute definitions of poverty, however 'scientific' the appearance they present, are simply irrelevant to social realities. People's lives revolve round the social relationships in which they are involved. The complex deprivations summarized in the term *poverty* cannot begin to be measured in terms of the calories in a daily diet. Only some kind of relative conception of poverty is in any way illuminating. Poverty is an inability to achieve a standard of living allowing for self-respect, the respect of others, and for full participation in society.

In the last analysis to be poor is not just to be located at the tail end of some distribution of income, but to be placed in a particular relationship of inferiority to the wider society. Poverty involves a particular sort of powerlessness, an inability to control the circumstances of one's life in the face of more powerful groups in society. All this, however, should not be taken as an argument that money is irrelevant, either to the social problem of poverty, or to the problems of the poor. One of the most prevalent and comforting of middle-class doctrines about the nature of poverty is that it is not lack of money, but inability to manage what resources one has, which is the root cause of poverty. On this view the solution to the problem of poverty lies not so much in an improvement in income, but in the moral retraining of the poor. It is true that in this century as compared with the nineteenth, the supposed necessity of re-educating the poor tends to be discussed less in the religious-authoritarian language of moral improvement and more in the blander idiom of lay psychoanalysis. The poor may appear to suffer from lack of money, but nevertheless the underlying cause of their predicament is attributed to a defective personality structure, inability to relate to others, and impaired capacity to make realistic judgements of self and others. Such views still have a certain prevalence among social workers, especially of the more traditional sort, and in a more diluted and moralistic form are still widely entertained in middle-class social milieux. Yet it is the existence of such attitudes, allied to the social power to translate them into organizations for 'dealing' with the problem of poverty, which gives an essential clue to the meaning of the experience of being poor. It is to be dependent for needed assistance on social agencies which have the power to investigate your personal life, can involve you in bureaucratic complications, and can stigmatize you as immoral or inadequate according to *their* standards. Sometimes you may be helpfully and courteously treated by the officer from the Ministry or the social worker or the hospital receptionist. But in any case, how you are treated is very largely out of your control. The arbitrariness of circumstance is a dominant theme in the experience of poverty.

The British system of social security is only partly concerned with the prevention and relief of poverty. Lack of money is only one element in a complex of deprivations which make up the experience of poverty. But money is a crucial element.

> Money is a generalized source of power over people through a right to control over goods and services, As such, money is one of many kinds of power. Poverty, therefore, is one of many kinds of powerlessness, of being subject to one's social situation instead of being able to affect it through action.[5]

At the very least, an adequate income may enable a person more easily to evade social situations in which he is placed in a position of enforced dependency on the decisions of other more powerful persons.

It should now be clear why an absolute definition of poverty is meaningless. A social group whose command of economic goods and services remains fixed over time in a society in which average living standards are rising will experience a relative decrease in social power. Such a group will be increasingly open to invasions of privacy and self-respect from more powerful groups. Obviously even those at the very foot of society in contemporary Britain enjoy a standard of living that is somewhat higher than that of the poorest in Victorian society a hundred years ago and much higher than the norm in many underdeveloped societies today. But to recognize this is no justification for adopting a less urgent view of poverty in contemporary Britain.

Another, and more sophisticated, misconception is that once a relative view of poverty is adopted it follows that poverty cannot be abolished, since in any society where complete social equality does not prevail the label of poor can always be given to the 10 per cent or 20 per cent of the population who come lowest in the hierarchy of income. If the absolutely poor need not always be with us, surely the relatively poor, by definition, cannot vanish. A refinement in formulation is needed. A relative notion of poverty implies that the extent of poverty in a society can only be estimated in terms of the degree of *general* social equality that exists. The more inequality there is between standards of living and of privilege at the top and the bottom of a society, the larger is the number of people which it is reasonable to define as poor. For this, as well as other reasons, it is impossible to discuss the adequacy of a social security system, without taking account of the overall social distribution of income and capital, and without asking whether Britain, in economic terms at least, is becoming a more or less equal society.

In Chapter 1 I gave some figures showing that basic social security benefits are still the same proportion of average manual wages as was the case in 1948. Can it be assumed from this that pensioners and other non-working groups have fully shared in the general rise in working-class standards of living over this twenty-seven-year period? Such a conclusion rests on the assumption that, since 1948, the cost of living has risen no faster for low-income groups than for groups with average incomes. The facts are otherwise. The single-person pension may still be 20 per cent of the average working-class wage just as it was in 1948. But the cost of the basic essentials which figure more heavily in the pensioners' budget has risen a great deal faster than the average run of prices. Thus, in terms of relative standard of living, the pensioner has lost out and continues to do so. It is highly probable that the same holds for other low-income groups, including low-wage earners, as well as those on social security benefits.

When politicians compare benefits with price trends, or with the movement of wages, they can manage to evade the simple issue of whether or not social security benefits are sufficient to meet the needs of those who depend on them. A similar kind of evasiveness underlies discussions about the numbers of people in poverty. But lack of basic research is only one reason for the arbitrariness of such poverty estimates as are possible. Exactly what level of weekly income is to be selected as marking off the poor from the not poor? The question is unavoidable in any account of the adequacy of a social security system – and yet no tidy answer can be given. To speak of 'poverty' is not just to apply an objective and purely descriptive label. Unless it is argued that poverty is an inevitable feature of any society, or that the poor must be held solely responsible for their own deprivations, then to define poverty is to take a political stand. Embedded in the concept is an implicit demand for social action to eliminate injustice and human waste. And from any judgement about whether poverty is on a limited scale – or whether it is widespread – flow very different political conclusions. Limited poverty can be abolished by marginal social reforms. If the volume of poverty is very considerable, then it cannot be abolished without a radical restructuring of society. In the latter case the elimination of poverty is inseparable from a comprehensive attack on the broader pattern of social inequality.

The Official Poverty Line

In recent years the usual practice among research workers and politicians has been to rely on the Supplementary Benefits Commission for a definition of poverty. The SBC has a set of minimum rates of weekly income, which it uses in deciding whether or not to give money to an individual or family. Poverty, on this definition, is a weekly income below the SBC minimum. This looks like an unambiguous criterion, and yet in fact it is anything but. The SBC has a great many poverty lines, and which one will apply in a given case depends on the particular circumstances of the family being considered for supplementary income. On the whole the better off a person is the larger is the weekly sum which the SBC considers the minimum necessary for his needs.

Firstly the rules of the SBC allow people to have small amounts of income from certain sources, without the supplementary allowance being reduced. For example, a person is able to earn up to £4 a week from a job or to get up to £4 a week in war pension or industrial disablement pension, without affecting the supplementary allowance. These are meagre sums, but for anyone with income from any of these sources, the effect is that in their case the poverty line is £4 higher than the basic minimum. Out of the total of people on supplementary benefit, the number who have extra cash which the Board would disregard is quite minute. Of the 2·6 million supplementary allowances being paid at the end of 1968, only half a million went to people who had any income whatsoever apart from national-insurance benefits. Out of this half million more than half were retired people with an occupational pension, generally very small.

Characteristically the treatment of people with capital is rather more generous. If a person owns a house, its capital value is disregarded. If claimants have some savings, it is by no means expected that these should be completely eaten away before the owner becomes entitled to supplementary benefit. A person can have up to £1,200 of capital without reduction in SBC benefit. Thereafter 25p will be docked off the supplementary allowance for each £50 of capital. Out of 2·6 million SBC claimants at the end of 1968, 1·5 million had no capital assets and another 425,000 had less than £100 of savings. About 360,000 had capital to the value of more than £325 but the average income produced by these assets was only 57p for a household per week. One final disregard is worth mentioning; the annuity paid to a holder of the Victoria Cross or George Medal is not deducted from the supplementary entitlement.

All told about one in three of SBC claimants has income from savings, earnings or pension, which is disregarded in the calculation of supplementary allowances. Of those who have some disregarded income the effect of the disregard is to leave them with an average of 90p each above the minimum basic scale of the SBC.*

In disregarding certain types of income, the Government is not so much motivated by generosity, but rather by a concern for incentives. The argument is that without disregards people would have less incentive to contribute to superannuation schemes, or to take poorly paid part-time jobs, or (presumably) to risk their neck for a Victoria Cross. However, irrespective of motives, the consequence is that for some people, the effective minimum poverty line is higher than the basic-scale rates, without the

* In November 1968, 870,000 claimants had a total disregarded income of £753,000.

163

claimant having to prove that he has extra needs above the average. The fact that one in three of supplementary claimants has some other income which is disregarded cannot justify any complacency about the effectiveness of the present supplementary system. Two out of three claimants have no income beyond what is provided in social security. For many of the remainder the extra income that is disregarded is no more than a few shillings a week. There are, however, a lucky few who have the full entitlement to supplementary benefit, although their final weekly income is several pounds above the SBC minimum scale. Thus in practice the SBC operates a whole range of poverty lines, and more favourable treatment is given to certain groups, not because they need more money, but because they already have extra bits of income.

There is also another reason why, for some, the effective poverty line is higher than the basic scale of allowances. The SBC have a system of extra payments, referred to officially as 'discretionary allowances'. These are awarded when the Commission accepts that there is need for a special diet, or for extra fuel where someone is unable to get out of the house because of infirmity, or if the house is particularly damp. The Commission has discretionary power to provide fares to visit a relative in hospital, to pay hire-purchase instalments for household equipment and furniture (provided the Commission considers it absolutely essential) or the cost of renting a safety gas cooker (but only if the claimant is old, disabled or infirm). They can make single payments to replace worn-out bedding or footwear (though not normally if the cost is less than one pound). Under extreme pressure they can even pay electricity and gas bills and rent arrears. They have also the power to help pay funeral expenses of a relative or friend of the claimant, though only if the claimant has first tried and been refused help from the local authority, the hospital, and local charities.

Lest all this sounds like a cornucopia of generosity, it should be noted that the discretionary system is one of the most arbitrary and meanly operated parts of the entire Welfare State. The SBC are most concerned that people should not consider these possible extra payments as in any way a right. Only the most fleeting and non-committal references to discretionary payments are made in the leaflets handed out by the Ministry to claimants. When dealing with people who are not infirm or crippled, the Ministry tries to reserve these additional payments for people it considers particularly 'deserving'. For example, at November 1973, 28 per cent of all claimants got an 'exceptional circumstances addition' – though if the Board's powers were seriously used in practice as they exist in theory, a great many more SBC claimants would qualify under one heading or another. The moralistic way in which these powers are used is suggested by the statistics of those who get the exceptional-circumstance addition. Twenty per cent of old people get such an addition and 34 per cent of the sick and disabled, but only 10 per cent of the unemployed group and 10 per cent of the group of women with dependent children, i.e. the divorced, separated, deserted, and unmarried mothers.

The discretionary powers of the SBC do, however, affect the way the poverty line is defined. As in the case of disregarded income, the effect is that once again for a minority the effective poverty line is rather more money than is allowed in the basic scale. This, in turn, raises questions about the criterion used by politicians and social scientists in arriving at estimates of the numbers of people in Britain below the poverty line. Why should this be calculated in terms of the lowest possible income thought necessary by the Supplementary Benefits Commission? Why not set the poverty line to take account of the £1 or £2 a week of extra income which is allowed to a minority?

But if the poverty line is drawn a pound or two above the basic SBC-scale rate, then the effect on estimates of the *number* in poverty is dramatic. There are very large numbers of people who have incomes that are only just above the minimum scale rates of the SBC.

In a much discussed estimate of the incidence of poverty in 1960, Townsend and Abel-Smith found numbers of households on national assistance whose effective income was 40 per cent above the basic scale (i.e. for a single person £1·60 a week above the minimum scale in 1960). Reasonably, therefore, the authors set their poverty line at this higher income level. Their conclusion was that:

In 1960, approximately 18 per cent of the households, and 14·2 per cent of the persons in the United Kingdom, representing nearly 7·5 million persons were living below a defined 'national assistance' level of living. About 35 per cent were living in households primarily dependent on pensions, 23 per cent in households primarily dependent on other state benefits and 41 per cent in households primarily dependent on earnings.[6]

This estimate of 7·5 million in poverty could, however, be reduced to 3·6 million by drawing the poverty line at a level only 10 per cent above the basic national assistance role. Using the same criterion – supplementary benefit basic scale plus 10 per cent – the Department of Health and Social Security reported a total of 7 million persons in poverty in 1972.[7] Thus, during the period 1960–72 it would appear that there has been almost a doubling of the numbers below, at, or only just above the basic supplementary benefit scale.

It is easy to see why in so much political discussion the SBC *minimum* scale has become sacrosanct as the accepted criterion for dividing the poor from the non-poor. Only if the lowest possible poverty line is taken as valid, does it become possible to suggest political solutions which do not in any serious way threaten the overall distribution of income and privilege throughout society.

The use of the SBC scale to define poverty is in fact an amazingly metaphysical criterion, which has, for example, one very odd consequence. If the Government should let their SBC scales lag behind increases in prices and wages, then there will be a decrease in the percentage of people defined as poor by that scale. The figures would show less poverty; the reality would be an increase in poverty. Equally, if the Government in a burst of generosity should improve their basic scale relative to average wages, then the numbers in poverty would show an increase.

In any case there is no good reason why official definitions of financial poverty should be accepted as having any special validity. Government policy is based on what it thinks can be afforded at any particular time rather than on judgements about the income people need to maintain any kind of decent existence.

From time to time Governments carry out surveys to find out the numbers of people below the official poverty line. But, since the Second World War, no British Government has ever carried out an inquiry to establish the minimum amount of income which people *need* or what sorts of sacrifices are imposed by inadequate income. There has not even been any official research into what special expenditures may be made necessary by disablement or handicap of various sorts, or by extreme old age, or by a long period on the poverty line.

Any suggestion that the existing poverty line is too low is very threatening to the selectivist proposals for minimum reform, because there are such large concentrations of people just on or just above the basic level of SBC scale rates. As soon as it is accepted that the poverty line should be drawn at the level which the SBC allows for people with investments or occupational pensions or Victoria Crosses, then the problem of poverty turns out to be a massive and structural characteristic of British society. And on this latter view, it becomes impossible to explain poverty or to propose strategies for its elimination without calling in question the entire existing pattern of inequality and privilege in Britain. In effect, an end to poverty becomes simply a way of speaking of an end to social inequality.

It is, of course, reasonable to say that among the many poor there are the smaller number of poorest, and that these should be the most immediate concern of politicians. But in most recent discussion the poorest have somehow ended up being presented as the only poor. Nothing but this concern to narrow down the political implications of poverty could explain why people have been content to define poverty in terms of the SBC basic scale.

CHAPTER 10

The Problem of Low Wages

Apart from the inadequacies of the social security system, the other main source of poverty lies in the low wages paid for a broad range of jobs in the British economy. In 1974, even including overtime payments, 10 per cent of men in full-time employment were earning less than the supplementary benefit poverty line for a family with two children. A further $1\frac{3}{4}$ million men got over this poverty line only because of overtime earnings. Despite all the campaigning and legislation about equal pay it is still the case that women on average earn half as much as men.

These are figures for wages, and do not include the family allowances which are supposed to protect the families of low-wage earners from living at poverty levels. However, the latest, and very out of date, information provided by the Government in 1973 suggested that 50,000 families had a bread-winner in full-time employment and yet ended up with a total income below the poverty line.[1]

This total would be enormously larger but for the fact that a great many men with low basic wages work a great deal of overtime or are on shift work. Also, millions of families achieve a living income only because the wife goes out to work.

The average number of hours actually worked in British industry is still over 44 per week – i.e. not much less than the 47–8 hour week which was general throughout the inter-war period. Moreover, despite the impression conveyed by press attacks on British workers, the working week in this country is longer than in a number of comparable economies, with the exception of France.

Approximately one quarter of manual workers in Britain work more than 50 hours a week.

168

Table 1: Hours of Work in Manufacturing, 1972[2]

United Kingdom	44·2
West Germany	42·9
Japan	43·9
U.S.A.	40·9
France	44·4

In recent years there has been a substantial increase in shift work, and by 1968, 25 per cent of all workers in manufacturing were on shift work – as compared with only 12 per cent in 1954. There is much evidence suggesting that shift work imposes considerable extra strain on workers, both physical and psychological; basic rhythms of sleep and of eating are broken, family and other relationships are disrupted. In this respect large numbers of workers have experienced a deterioration in working conditions, and currently each year an extra 1½ per cent of the manual labour force is being switched over to the shift system. Yet it is remarkable how little extra money workers get to compensate for the extra demands of shift work – in many cases only about £4 a week. It would seem on the whole that trade unions have tended to concede shift work at bargain prices. However, basic wage rates for many jobs are so low that even limited payments for shift work help bring many families over the poverty line.

It is important to stress that quite large numbers of workers earn low wages, because in much public discussion it has been assumed that the real explanation for poverty among wage-earning families lies not in the lowness of wages, but in the largeness of families. The official poverty line varies according to the numbers and ages of children in a family. A very large number of children – say six or seven – would mean a poverty line for that family which might be roughly equivalent to the average industrial wage. If it is assumed that poverty in wage-earning families is heavily concentrated on those with exceptionally large families, the implication would then be that the fault lies not in the wage system, but in the unwillingness of certain sections of the population to limit their family size to reasonable proportions. On this argument a substantial part of the problem of poverty could be

P.E.B.–9

eliminated not by changes in the structure of society but rather oy educating the poor to take the strait and narrow path of birth control.

Historically this kind of argument has been one of the major recurrent themes in middle-class theorizing about the nature and causes of poverty. A direct line of descent can be traced from Thomas Malthus in the early nineteenth century to the contemporary Eugenic Society. Their case can be answered in two ways. First the association between poverty and large families is much more limited than they suggest. The 1966 official survey found an average family size of 3·3 children in the families identified as in poverty and yet with a bread-winner in full-time employment. This is only marginally above the national average family size. Two thirds of the group of families in poverty had three or fewer children.[3] Overwhelmingly therefore sub-poverty-line incomes were due to inadequate earnings and not to exceptional fertility.

However, it was also the case that 20 per cent of the wage-earning poor had five or more children. For a minority it would seem that many children cause poverty. But in fact it is much more likely that, insofar as there are causal mechanisms at work, they run in precisely the opposite direction: namely that poverty can lead to large families. The whole complex of deprivations which affect the poor – the struggle for housing, being forced to accept a pattern of low and unstable earnings, exclusion from educational opportunity – these and the like add up to exceptional social insecurity. It is a rational and sensible response to such insecurity to build up a large family which will provide resources of social and psychological support to its members. The conferences of the Eugenic Society resound with complacent discussion about the need to instil in the poor a disciplined attitude to birth control and to develop habits of rational prevision and planning of personal resources. It is certainly desirable that birth control should be freely and easily available. But, as a total programme for the abolition of poverty, birth control is strictly a non-starter. For the poor to convert themselves to middle-class values and strategies would be disastrous, given the insecurities they face. They are thoroughly sensible in relying on their own kin rather than on the uncertain benevolence of bureaucratic agencies of support and control. Besides, the enthusiasts for eugenic or Malthusian solutions to poverty take too little account of the possibility that the very poor *like* to have a lot of children, given that to be poor is to be excluded from many other kinds of social opportunities.

Why Low Wages?

Many people who are not directly familiar with the industrial scene find it difficult to accept that there are so many jobs in Britain which scarcely pay a living wage. The newspapers are continually deploring the strength and militancy of the trade-union movement and blaming the economic difficulties of the country on the ability of workers to make off with inflationary wage settlements. Clearly when unemployment is high there are various pressures operating to depress wages; when jobs are hard to come by workers are forced to accept jobs at unreasonably low wages. However, it is also the case that during the 1940s and 1950s, despite exceptionally low levels of unemployment, a large low-wage sector continued to persist in the economy. A crucial factor determining wage levels is the bargaining power of workers, and although this is stronger when there is no mass unemployment, it is far from equal as between different groups of workers.

A very wide range of factors affects the bargaining strength of workers, and only a few of the more important can be mentioned here. For a start it is often forgotten how limited and unevenly spread the membership of trade unions in Britain is. It is not perhaps unexpected that only one quarter of women employees belong to unions, but for men the tally is only a little over one half.

Secondly, although the absence of a union, or a low rate of union membership in a particular job, is usually a sign of weak bargaining strength, the existence of a numerically strong union is no guarantee that wage claims will be advanced in a determined way. Indeed it can be argued that one of the major social functions of union officials in capitalist society is to limit wage claims

171

to what is 'realistic', i.e. less than the maximum that could be obtained by militant bargaining. In a great many wage disputes in recent years workers have obtained for themselves a much better deal by rejecting the official advice of their unions and by holding out until the employers improved their offer.

Wage levels in Britain are determined by a combination of two sorts of processes. First there are wage bargains negotiated nationally between union officials and employers, or often combinations of employers controlling whole industries. These central negotiations tend to be concerned with minimum pay and conditions. But secondly, where particular groups of workers are well-organized in individual factories and other places of work, they are able in local shop-floor negotiation to obtain better-than-national levels of pay and conditions.

It frequently happens in local disputes involving strike action that a direct conflict arises between the full-time officials of the union and the shop stewards. Nineteen out of every twenty strikes in Britain are unofficial, i.e. carried out without the sanction of the trade-union head office. No strike pay is paid out unless a strike is official. Although exceptions can be found, shop stewards are on the whole responsive to the views of the workers they represent. Especially where mass meetings are held regularly during a strike, unofficial disputes offer examples of direct democracy in action which have no parallel elsewhere in British society. The effects of such localized bargaining show up in a phenomenon which the economists call 'wage drift', that is the difference between hourly wage *rates* and actual earnings per hour, leaving aside the extra income which comes from overtime. Wage drift is a measure of the extent to which local shop-floor pressure can build up earnings over the national minima achieved by official union negotiators. In recent years wage drift has accounted for about one third of the amount by which wages have been increasing year by year.

The large part played by local negotiations in determining the trend of wages results inevitably in a great unevenness in the pattern of wage increases. The effect is that earnings for the same type of job vary widely in different parts of the country, in work establishments of different sizes and degrees of efficiency, and even within comparable factories in the same locality. One piece of research carried out in 1967 showed that the difference in pay between workers doing comparable work in neighbouring factories was sometimes as much as 100 per cent.[4] In determining differences between total earnings, variations in basic hourly rates are also compounded by differences in availability of overtime.

The two types of wage bargaining – local and central – do not of course operate in isolation from one another. On the whole, in unions where workers tend to be well organized at the point of production, the national leadership of the union is correspondingly more militant in wage negotiations. The group of engineering unions is a notable example. On the other hand in unions where workers find it difficult to develop effective organization in the work place the national union leaderships tend to ask for less in the way of better pay and conditions and to press their demands less forcefully. The National Union of Public Employees or the General and Municipal Workers Union would be cases in point. But the net effect of such differences in the militancy and effectiveness of organization in the various unions is to maintain wide differentials between high- and low-paid workers.

Thus low wages persist in situations where workers are unable to exercise effective bargaining pressures; where there is no union organization or where union membership is limited in numbers; where the union leaders are unable or unwilling to take a militant line in central wage negotiations with employers; where local conditions are such that workers are unable to organize in a united way to bring pressure to bear on the management or on their full-time union officials.

There is a wide range of factors which can weaken the bargaining power of workers in particular industrial situations. The trend in all industrial societies towards large scale production and administration has been much discussed. What receives less notice is the fact that a great many people still work in very small enterprises. More than half of the industrial units in Britain have fewer than twenty-five employees. Out of a total labour force of just over eight million in manufacturing industry, more than one quarter are employed in establishments with less than a hundred workers. On the whole it is in the smaller working units that union organization is relatively weak, and pay and conditions relatively inferior.

A little unexpectedly perhaps, low-wage industries do not appear to have a particularly high percentage of unskilled workers. Probably this is partly because over the past two decades there has been a considerable decrease in the traditional earnings differential between skilled and unskilled jobs. Possibly also during the fifties and early sixties when unemployment rates were low, wages for unskilled work were pushed up by a shortage of labour, men preferring where possible to take factory jobs which, if they involve running machines, are usually classified as semi-skilled. (Between 1931 and 1961 the proportion of men in the population classified as unskilled labourers fell from 18 per cent to only 9 per cent.) More probably the whole concept of unskilled work is increasingly irrelevant given the realities of industry. By tradition unskilled work is thought of as the kind of job 'anyone' could do, yet the physical demands of such jobs are often severe and appear as relatively more so in a machine society.

Government Intervention

British Governments have always rejected proposals to introduce minimum wage legislation, such as operates with varying degrees of effectiveness in many other industrial societies.[5] Instead, in Britain, Government attempts to limit exploitation of low-paid workers have taken two forms: the long established Wage Council system and, more recently, a variety of experiments in incomes policy.

In 1909, after a public campaign against sweated labour in a number of industries, the Trade Boards Act was passed, by which the Government appointed autonomous committees to set minimum wages in industries where exploitation of workers seemed exceptionally gross. These bodies – called Wage Councils since 1945 – contain representatives of the employers, of the trade-union movement, and so-called independent members, usually academics or lawyers. At present there are Wage Councils for fifty-three industries, covering in all about three and a half million workers. Large numbers of workers in agriculture, catering, food production, hairdressing and retail distribution have their pay and conditions settled by Wage Councils. But the archaic character of the whole system is aptly suggested by the continued existence of, for example, the Ostrich and Fancy Feather and Artificial Flower Wage Council, and the Pin, Hook and Eye and Snap Fastener Wage Council. What the Councils do is find a compromise between the claims put forward by the union representatives and the counter proposals made from the employers' side. The independent members are there to ease along the process of conciliation. The legislation behind this system provides no clear guidance about what sort of criteria should be used in establishing pay levels and conditions, except that these should be 'reasonable' – whatever that means. The Government retains the power to refuse to accept recommendations made by a Wage Council. But generally in the recent past the agreed decisions of Wage Councils about minimum pay and conditions have been so eminently modest that Governments, however enthusiastic for wage restraint, have found no difficulty in accepting what Wage Councils have recommended. Such recommendations are embodied in an Order issued by the Minister for Employment which is legally binding on employers. Or at least in theory. The fact is that Wage Council minima are often ignored by the smaller employers, and among workers covered by the Councils, the average number of employees per firm is seven. The Department of Employment has a Wages Inspectorate whose job it is to check up on whether Wage Council awards are being observed by employers. In 1974 there was a grand total of 140 inspectors employed to supervise the wages paid in nearly half a million places of work. In 1972 this staff managed to inspect only 10 per cent of all establishments. As in other recent years they found roughly one in ten of all employers inspected to be paying less than the legal minimum laid down by the Wage Council. The powers of enforcement given by Parliament to the Wages Inspectorate are something less than terrifying. They can compel defaulting employers to pay arrears to their workers. But the maximum legal penalty for an employer caught in default remained in 1974 at the same level set by the original 1909 legislation – £20.

The Wage Council mechanism for pay negotiations is hideously cumbersome. The employers are able to stretch out negotiations over a much longer period of time than is the case in other forms of wage bargaining. Thus workers covered by Wage Councils receive pay increases at much less frequent intervals than most other groups of workers. Furthermore, when Wage Councils do eventually make pay awards, the percentage increase is almost always lower than the going rate for workers able to use normal methods of wage bargaining. The combination of lower increases less frequently awarded tends to leave Wage Council workers further and further behind in a period of rapid inflation.

Whatever may be the intentions behind the Wage Council system, in practice it is a mechanism for creating increasing poverty among the millions of workers it is supposed to help. It is a bleak commentary on the lack of commitment of the trade-union movement to the interests of lower-paid workers that the TUC is prepared to use its authority to help keep the Wage Council system in existence. If the trade unions were serious they would devote their energies and resources to spreading trade-union membership among workers at present covered by Wage Councils and would back these workers by all the necessary means in a struggle to improve wages and conditions. At another level it is depressing to find that, although millions of pounds a year are now spent on social research in Britain, there is a virtual total absence of academic inquiry into the composition and working of the Wage Council system. However in 1975 an independent Low Pay Unit was created and its Bulletins contain a devastating portrayal of the role of the Wage Councils.[6]

Incomes Policy

During the late 1960s the Labour Government undertook to use a different form of State intervention on behalf of low-paid workers. During the successive phases of the incomes policy from its inception in May 1965 until it petered out in 1969, the Government promised that exceptionally favourable consideration would be given to wage claims on behalf of low-paid workers. Indeed the low-pay exception was of great significance in Labour's attempts to justify and defend the incomes policy. When it was suggested that by trying to prevent wage increases Labour were doing no more than making the working class pick up the bill for the difficulties of British capitalism, the Government were able to point to the low-pay exception as proof that despite appearances the incomes policy was in reality an instrument of socialist planning. Ministers stated that a general restriction on wage increases, combined with special pay awards for the exceptionally low paid, would help reduce poverty.

The Government transferred the power to make decisions on specific wage claims to the Prices and Incomes Board. The PIB, while recognizing that its terms of reference included the requirement that it should operate a low-pay exception, proved fertile in producing reasons for not invoking this exception in numerous pay claims on which it was asked by the Government to adjudicate. At no point did either the Government or the PIB define exactly how much money per week was to count as low pay, nor what was the minimum wage to be aimed at, nor how much of an increase above the going average of wage increases would count as giving the promised 'special consideration' to claims from poorly paid workers. No attempt was made to seek out cases in which wages were intolerably low. Only at the point when claims for wage rises had gone through procedure and an increase was about to be conceded did the Government step in and refer the claim to the PIB for evaluation.

However, the PIB disliked the low-wage exception. From its inception it took the line that pay increases should be resisted unless justified by increases in productivity. In one of the last reports issued by the Board its position is plainly stated.

Insofar as improving the position of the low paid is one of the purposes of a productivity prices and incomes policy – which in our view it should be – the main remedy is to be found in the improvement of efficiency. Except in a minority of instances, therefore, we consider that the improvement in the position of the low paid can be subsumed in the general problem of improving efficiency.[7]

To insist on higher productivity as the universal criterion for pay increases means in practice to discriminate severely against lower-paid workers. Many are in service jobs in which output cannot readily be increased by the introduction of more efficient machinery. In any case it is the employers, not the workers, who decide on what technology is made available. Groups of workers who are weakly organized will very often be already worked so hard that no further intensification of effort can be exacted. There will be little in the way of what employers call 'restrictive practices' which can be bargained away in return for a pay increase. Not surprisingly then the PIB rarely found itself able to do much for the lower paid.

The Labour Government made no objection to the PIB's approach. Increasingly, as the incomes policy evolved, the Government began to say that the real answer to the low-wage problem lay in such measures as increased family allowances. The implication could be fairly drawn that the earlier justification of incomes policy as a device for ensuring greater equality was no more than propaganda to increase its political acceptability to the trade unions. In the end the gaff was blown by Harold Walker, an Under-Secretary at the Department of Employment, who informed the Commons on 26 March 1969 that: 'It is not a primary function of the Government Prices and Incomes Policy to redistribute income.'

During the first period of Conservative rule which followed, no incomes policy was attempted, but late in 1972, a complete freeze on pay, prices and dividends was introduced, and then, from April 1973, an approach to wage control apparently tailored to improve the relative position of the lower paid. This was the Stage II pay code which laid down a maximum limit on settlements of £1 per week per person, plus 4 per cent of the previous year's basic wage.

For the lower paid this was obviously more advantageous than the flat-rate percentage formulae of the Wilson Government. A

Stage II wage award would give an increase of 8·5 per cent to someone with £22 a week, but only 7 per cent on a wage of £33.

Subsequent evaluation has shown that Stage II improved the position of the lower paid by very little. For example, the settlement for male laundry workers was for an extra 9 per cent, whereas Ford workers got only 6 per cent. But in cash terms the laundry workers got only £1·21 of an increase; the car-workers at Ford got £2·20. Thus, in terms of straight cash, the gap between these two groups of workers actually widened. The reason was simply that the percentage advantage given to the lower paid was not nearly large enough to compensate for the wide differences in the basic earnings to which these percentages were applied. Before Stage II laundry workers were on a basic of £13 a week, almost a third of the basic for Ford workers.[8]

Stage III of the Conservative Government's pay policy was initiated in November 1973, and was continued till the following June by the Labour Government which won the Election of February 1974. This offered the trade unions a choice of accepting either 7 per cent or a flat-rate increase of £2·25 a week. The Government argued that by choosing the flat-rate option, any group earning less than £32 a week could improve its position by more than the standard 7 per cent.

What turned out to be of more significance for at least some groups of lower-paid workers was the threshold agreement which was a permissible feature of Stage III settlements. The arrangement was that if prices rose above 7 per cent, then for every extra 1 per cent on prices a flat-rate 40p a week would be paid. At the time when this provision was written into the Stage III legislation, the Heath Government was confident that price rises could be kept within the 7 per cent limit, and the threshold agreement was seen in Whitehall largely as a piece of window dressing. The Government was gambling and the operation came unstuck rather badly. Stage III coincided with a massive rise of prices on international markets, and especially of food prices. In Britain, the Retail Price Index rose by 18 per cent, and thus the threshold was triggered eleven times. Some eleven million workers, one third of the adult labour force, had negotiated threshold agreements, and by November 1974 were collecting an extra £4·40 a week. Since threshold agreements were particularly prevalent in the public sector of the economy where many groups of lower-paid workers are concentrated, the threshold arrangement resulted in a major, if temporary, improvement in the position of a large section of the low paid. However the impact of threshold deals was very patchy – e.g. by August 1974, 41 of the 50 Wage Councils had still not got threshold agreements in operation.

The general conclusion of expert studies is that throughout the various phases of incomes policy, the lower paid as a body have held their relative position, or at best improved it only marginally. The exception was in 1974 when there was a marked advance for some groups of lower paid. It is a sad comment on recent incomes policies that the improvement made in 1974 took place because of a miscalculation by Government. It is a mistake they will try not to repeat. Since the Stage III threshold arrangement lapsed in November 1974, the Government and employers have fiercely resisted the incorporation of threshold arrangements into subsequent settlements.

One weakness of these various incomes policies was that the percentage advantage offered to the lower paid was never large enough to improve their position in a radical way. The other was that the percentages and other criteria laid down by the Government were no more than permissible maximum settlements. The lower paid, along with other workers, were then left to fight for what the Government would allow. The employers were under no compulsion to make any improvements in wages. Thus incomes policies have left workers as dependent as ever on their own organized trade-union strength and militancy. If the lower paid have more or less maintained their relative position economically over the past decade, then the explanation lies not in any active assistance they have received from Government, but in improvements in the level and effectiveness of trade-union organization among such groups. Trade-union membership has been rising. The quiescent leaderships of many unions covering large numbers of badly-paid workers have been severely rattled by a spirit of impatience and willingness to fight among their previously demoralized rank and file. The process began in the 1969–70 period in a series of bitterly contested strikes involving local authority dustmen, clothing workers (mainly women) in Leeds, and glass-workers. The Post Office workers' strike of 1971 was the biggest strike that had occurred in Britain since 1926, in terms of its length and the numbers of workers involved. Since then millions of workers in other low-pay unions have shown their ability to take militant action – hospital workers, clerical workers in the public sector, building workers etc. It would be too much to say that the revolt of the lower paid has enabled them to do any more than maintain their living standards in the face of rapidly rising prices. But there is no other 'solution' to the problem of low pay except in more effective organization and more militant tactics on the part of workers concerned. If they wait for decisive intervention on their behalf by the Government, then they will wait for ever.

There are three reasons why an incomes policy has not been used by successive Governments to improve the position of lower-paid workers. Firstly, any serious attempt to do so would require a Government to define what counts as a low wage – a matter left entirely vague in all stages of the incomes policies. A Government posing as the champion of low income groups could not pick too small a weekly sum to define the low wage without running the risk of having its pretensions exposed. And to pick a more realistic wage level to represent the minimum would involve so many millions of workers in line for such substantial increases as to defeat the anti-inflationary objectives of incomes policies.

Secondly, the Government had to recognize that groups of workers who were strategically placed in the economy could break the wage freeze by the exercise of militant bargaining power. To counterbalance this possibility, the Government was inclined to take a tough line with the sections of workers who could not muster as much in the way of bargaining strength. Thirdly, there is the fact that to some extent the whole wage structure in Britain depends on what the lower paid get at the bottom of the pyramid. To raise the floor is to narrow the differentials claimed for extra skill or extra effort etc. In a capitalist society workers are obliged to mobilize around and fight on all sorts of issues whose significance would be much less in a socialist society run under workers' control. The issue of pay differentials within the working class is just such an issue. For recent Governments it was essential to limit special improvements to low-wage earners, for fear of intensifying militancy among higher-paid workers.

In the event, recent Governments have been able to convince comparatively few workers that their incomes policies have been either fair or equitable. The associated restrictions on higher salaries, rents, dividends, taxation and prices, are widely, and correctly, believed to have been largely ineffective. For example, most workers readily appreciate that restrictions on the distribution of dividends mean only that more profits are retained by companies and this in turn is reflected in the increased capital value of shares. Thus owners of capital lose nothing by an incomes policy. But if workers forgo a wage increase this represents a clear loss.

Given all these factors it has been extremely difficult to sell the incomes policy politically, and the task would have proved quite impossible if Governments had not been able to enlist the collaboration of the top leadership in the unions. This meant in turn that Governments had to run the incomes policy in ways which would help the union leaders to resist criticism and pressure from their rank-and-file membership. In the trade-union movement generally, and for the unions representing more skilled groups of workers in particular, the threat of a decrease in wage differentials is by tradition seen as providing an irresistible case for a wage increase. Had the Government appeared to be encouraging any substantial narrowing of wage differentials, the collaborative role of the union leaders would have proved even more difficult to carry out than it was. Workers show a healthy and justified resistance to policies designed to redistribute income *within* the working class only and which at the same time aim to reduce the share of national income going to wage earners. Equality is one of the values embedded in working-class culture, but the terms of the ongoing battle on issues of pay and conditions dictate that workers should fight first to increase wages at the expense of other components of national income such as profits, rather than becoming involved in projects for the redistribution of wages alone.

It is not to be expected that any Government whose main concern is with the efficiency of a capitalist economy is going to take effective steps to abolish the low-wage sector. The viability of the whole of our present economic system rests to an extent on the maintenance of a sector of the economy where exceptionally low wages and harsh working conditions are prevalent. Partly, as I have argued, this is because standards of pay and conditions of work at the bottom of the heap influence the pattern of wages farther up the scale, partly because the overall level of profit rests partially on low pay levels operating in the service sector of the economy and in jobs where the capital employed per worker is limited.

CHAPTER 11

The Contribution Myth

Unless you are directly affected there are few more tedious subjects to inquire into than the conditions which determine entitlement to particular national-insurance benefits. The Ministry of Social Security puts out dozens of different leaflets explaining the rights and obligations of various special social categories. There is a leaflet addressed to Share Fishermen and another for Company Directors, one for those employed in or about Places of Public Entertainment; there is even leaflet NI 146 which lists all the leaflets published by the Ministry. These details need not concern us here. But there are certain general questions to ask about the principles which underlie the relationship between contributions and benefits in the social security system as a whole.

I have already referred several times to the deep administrative gulf which is maintained between supplementary benefits, awarded only after a test of need, and national-insurance benefits, to which a person becomes entitled after paying a minimum number of weekly contributions into one of the schemes. The retirement pension, sickness and unemployment benefit, provision for widows and for maternity benefits, all of these fall within the contributory sector. The fact that such benefits have been in some sense paid for by a series of contributions is used to justify a very different administrative approach than is adopted in the supplementary benefits sector. A person's rights to national-insurance benefits are stated in detail in the leaflets and reports published by the Ministry: these rights are guaranteed by the legal system; there is a public tribunal, the National Insurance Commissioner, to which appeals can be made, and the published record of decisions made by this tribunal can be consulted by anyone who believes he has been unfairly treated. None of this applies in the supplementary sector, where the criteria on which benefit is awarded or withheld are largely kept secret, so that the claimant is in no position to know whether or not his treatment has been fair.

One of the main arguments of this book is that any serious programme for the elimination of poverty in this country must include the abolition of the Supplementary Benefits Commission. Wherever it exists in the social services, the means-test principle should be banished. As soon as people fall into some category in which inability to work is socially recognized, then they should have a right to an income. Such a right must be based on citizenship, not paternalism. Which means among other things that the right to an income has to be as clearly specified in law as the right to vote. The individual, or any organization on his behalf, must be able to challenge and test any administrative decision. At present the Supplementary Benefits Commission acts as its own judge and jury in any dispute – and as Lord High Executioner into the bargain. At the very minimum there must be a clear administrative separation between the system that pays out the money and the system whereby conflicts between the claimant and the Government are settled. The effect of the present arrangement is that, despite many attempts at reform, the supplementary system is still deeply tainted by the apparently charitable, but effectively deterrent, perspectives of the Victorian Poor Law.

By comparison national-insurance benefits are much more recognizable as providing social *rights*. Many objections can be raised about the particular rules which govern entitlement to national insurance, but at least the rules are publicly specified in the Ministry leaflets and in the published decisions of the National Insurance Commissioner.

When challenged to justify the quite different approach adopted in national insurance, as compared with supplementary benefits, officials and politicians always invoke the contributory principle. National-insurance benefits are a special case, because they have been bought and paid for by a record of contributions. The right to benefit is secured by an implied contract, arising out of a cash transaction.

I shall try to show that this argument is spurious, that the contribution principle is mythical, and furthermore that many of the anomalies and injustices that arise in the national-insurance system can be traced back to attempts to give some appearance of substance to what is really a fiction – that a person's pension or unemployment benefit is in some sense directly paid for by the national-insurance stamp which he and his employer have purchased week by week.

Virtually the whole cost of national insurance is directly financed by current contributions and virtually all contribution income is immediately paid out in the form of benefits. The system works on a pay-as-you-go basis.

It is misleading to think of the State scheme as analogous with private insurance. In both there is a collective pooling of risks, but there the similarity ends. A commercial scheme is actuarially sound if the accumulated fund is large enough to meet all claims outstanding at any given time. The soundness of a State scheme rests on the ability of a Government to compel the working population to support those who cannot work.

Still less does the contribution principle mean that the average contributor, plus his employer, has paid the full value of the benefits he is likely to receive in periods of incapacity for work. This is particularly true of anyone who lives long enough to draw an old-age pension for a few years. For example at the beginning of 1968 a man plus his employer contributing since 1948 would between them have accumulated £867 – a sum which includes allowance for interest at $3\frac{1}{2}$ per cent. This would be sufficient to finance a pension of only £1·80 a week in the case of a man aged sixty-five, and of less than £1·40 for a married couple at retirement age.[1] Thus, at the very most, only 40 per cent of the pension being paid in 1968 could be regarded as paid for by contribution.

It follows that the range and levels of social security benefit available at any time are determined not by the record of past contributions of an individual or even of a whole generation, but rather by the month by month decisions of the Government in power. Given the very large sums of money involved, especially in the provision of retirement pensions, it follows too that the main factors affecting the adequacy of benefits are what the Government thinks the economy can afford and certain more narrowly political considerations. It has often been noted that there is a correlation between the timing of general elections and the timing of increases in pensions and other benefits. There were seven General Elections between 1948 and 1970. In each of these elections, except in 1950, there was a pension increase during the election year or in the year immediately before. Between 1948 and 1950 there were nine increases in the basic old-age pension and on six of these occasions there was an election expected within the following twelve months. (One might almost conclude that old people would be better off if general elections were more frequent, irrespective of the political outcome of elections.)

Despite its unreality the contribution principle has become one of the sacrosanct elements in British social security. An example will illustrate the lengths to which officials will go in sustaining the myth. Towards the end of 1962 Mr Reginald Maudling, who was then Chancellor of the Exchequer, decided that the economy needed a quick and substantial injection of extra consumer purchasing power. The situation was unusual for, in general, post-war governments had been preoccupied rather with cutting back than increasing consumer demand and the Chancellor found some difficulty in thinking of an appropriate technique.

Mr Maudling did, however, have at least one very good idea just before Christmas 1962. This was to pay out the higher pensions and national insurance benefits which the government had promised for 1963 several months before the increase in contributions. If Maudling's idea had been accepted a large temporary stimulus worth several hundred million would have been applied when it was most needed. Later when contributions were raised, the stimulus would have been cancelled out in a way that everyone would have regarded as fair, and could not possibly be denounced as stop-go. The Chancellor asked the Ministry of Pensions officials to his room, but he was defeated by administrative difficulties of unbelievable obscurity. Somewhere in the background, one feels sure, was the moralistic belief that if the link between contributions and benefits were to be broken, even if only for a few months, the whole myth of an insurance scheme would be shattered beyond repair.[2]

The various national-insurance benefits differ a good deal in the minimum contribution qualification. For example a man qualifies for a retirement pension if he has insurance stamps for three full years, plus an average of fifty weekly contributions for every year that he has been in the scheme. (Contributions are credited for weeks of sickness or unemployment.) What is important to realize is what happens if contributions are deficient. Benefit will be cut accordingly; but unless the claimant has other resources, any cut in benefit will create a correspondingly greater entitlement to supplementary benefit. In such cases the State merely pays in a different way. Public money is only saved to the extent that the applicant has private resources, occupational pension etc., which lift his income above the poverty line. Given the large number of retirement pensioners and other groups dependent on social security, who have no other substantial resources beyond what the State provides, it becomes very arguable whether the contribution qualification is worth preserving. So far as employed persons are concerned, qualification for benefit is not an indispensable incentive to keep people paying national-insurance contributions, since not to do so is an offence against the law. These doubts grow sharper when consideration is given to the vast and expensive task that is involved in administering a contribution system.

The contribution principle requires that a separate and detailed record has to be kept of the contribution history of the entire working population. The effort involved is breathtaking. Even by 1958 the Ministry of Pensions record office in Newcastle had become the largest purely clerical establishment in Europe. Today it covers 64 acres and employs 10,000 staff. Here is an example of the sort of work they do. Every time someone makes a claim for a national-insurance benefit,

A card called a 'shuttle card' is punched in the local office and sent to Newcastle. There it has to be channelled to one of a hundred sections each of which holds ledgers containing a quarter of a million individual records. (Each section is run by a team of 20 clerks.) The sections correspond with the last two digits of a national insurance number, so that the records of all insured persons whose number ends with the figures 69 are held by the same team. A clerk takes the shuttle card, looks up the ledger, records on the card whether the contribution conditions are satisfied (after consulting a thick manual of instructions in case of doubt) and sends it back through a pneumatic tube to be dispatched to the local office.[3]

Each year this operation is carried out for nine million claims for sickness benefit, and four million more for unemployment and maternity allowances. A quarter of a million cards reach Newcastle in a normal week, rising to two or three times as many during epidemics. Regular information from employers is used to keep up to date the 25 million individual contribution records. Every time anyone cashes a national-insurance order, the cancelled slip is returned to Newcastle for checking – a million slips a week, and double that number at peak periods.

All this is very impressive and apt to leave the outside observer in a state of paralysed amazement. Nevertheless it is mostly a huge waste of effort. When someone's contributions are deficient, national-insurance benefit is reduced accordingly – and this reduction will in a great many cases create a corresponding entitlement to supplementary benefit. The 22,000 officers of the SBC take over the operation of income support from the 30,000 officers of the national-insurance sector. Another and more personal investigation of the circumstances of the claimant then begins. The savings made by the operation of the contribution principle in national insurance are more than counterbalanced by the heavy administrative expenses involved in means-testing.

A contribution principle cuts in two ways, including some people and leaving out others. For certain social groups the operation of the contribution principle means complete exclusion from any form of national-insurance benefit. One of the largest of such groups is the chronic sick – those who, because of physical or mental handicap, extending usually from childhood, have not been able to work, or at least not for long enough to qualify for national-insurance benefits. Some 135,000 disabled and handicapped people, of working age but incapable of work, are wholly dependent on supplementary benefit and get nothing from national insurance. Their incomes are of course limited by the poverty-line standard used by the SBC. It is clear that permanent disablement or handicap must involve many exceptional expenses for those afflicted and for those who look after them. (More than half of this disabled group live with relatives or friends.) Some of these are eligible for an Attendance Allowance, but this is paid only when the level of disability is so great as to require constant assistance and nursing. There is in fact no up-to-date and comprehensive information available about the living standards of major categories among the disabled. A recent report by the Government on social security provision for chronically sick and disabled people manages to avoid any reference to current income levels among this population.[4]

Women who work full-time in the home are excluded from some of the key forms of coverage provided by national insurance. One of the worst disasters that can befall a family in Britain is long-term sickness or disability affecting a non-employed wife or mother. In extreme cases a constant attendance allowance may be payable. But no coverage of any sort is provided by the husband's insurance. As a consequence the family may be involved in all kinds of extra expenditure, without any sort of assistance from national insurance. And so long as the husband remains in full-time employment, the Supplementary Benefits Commission is forbidden by statute to offer any help. Yet, despite the fact that this is one of the most glaring gaps in British social security, there has been so little official concern or investigation that no accurate estimate has ever been made of the numbers of families in this plight. The Disablement Income Group have suggested tentatively that probably about 200,000 housewives are disabled enough to be incapable of employment. The sick or disabled housewife with a working husband still remains outside the framework of the whole social security system, a double victim, both of the contribution principle and of the rule withholding supplementary benefit from families with a bread-winner at work.

What causes particular bitterness in the case of seriously handicapped or disabled people is that, if they enter hospital, all expenses of treatment and care are met by the health service. Yet, if the family make an effort to keep a disabled wife at home, the social security system offers no serious help.

Women

I have just referred to the particular vulnerability of families in which a full-time housewife becomes handicapped or is afflicted with some kind of long-term sickness. But this is only one of the more glaring disadvantages suffered by women under present social security provision. So long as entitlement to social security is based primarily on contributions made during paid employment, whole categories of women are left without adequate provision. The ability of women to accumulate adequate contribution records is severely limited by two factors. The average wage paid to women for full-time work is less than half of the average wage paid to men and the working life of women is much shorter than that of men, because of the need to care for children and to run a house. The Government has organized social security on the principle that what counts is financial contributions made during employment. And a housewife is officially defined as non-employed.

The operation of the contribution principle hits hard at a number of large categories of women. Widows with children form only one part, and not the largest, of a wider group of fatherless families. The DHSS reckons that of all dependent children in the country, about 8 per cent belong to fatherless families, the main groups being as follows:

Table 1: Fatherless Families[5]

	Number of families	Number of children
Single mothers	90,000	120,000
Separated	190,000	360,000
Widows	120,000	200,000
Divorced	120,000	240,000
	520,000	920,000

There is evidence that one-parent families are the fastest growing group in long-term poverty. Excluding widows, who get a national-insurance benefit, one half of the rest are on supplementary benefit and are mostly dependent on this benefit as their major source of support. Of those not on supplementary benefit, around 15 per cent live below the official poverty line, scraping along on maintenance payments and part-time earnings. Single women, widows excepted, have no rights under national-insurance schemes, and unless employed and paying the full contribution are thrown back on the mercy of supplementary benefit.

For once it is not Beveridge who is to be blamed for the lack of provision for the children of divorced or separated women. Beveridge in his report took a clearcut line:

> Divorce, legal separation, desertion and voluntary separation may cause needs similar to those caused by widowhood . . . From the point of view of the woman loss of her maintenance as housewife without her consent and not through her fault is one of the risks of marriage against which she should be insured; she should not depend on National Assistance. Recognition of housewives as a distinct insurance class, performing necessary services not for pay, implies that if the marriage ends otherwise than by widowhood she is entitled to the same provision as for widowhood, unless the marriage maintenance has ended through her fault or voluntary action.[6]

Beveridge therefore incorporated certain provisions for separated and deserted wives into what he called the 'Housewives Policy' part of his scheme. Characteristically, however, it was in imperialistic rather than welfare terms that he justified the special status given to housewives in his Plan: 'In the next thirty years housewives as mothers have vital work to do in ensuring the adequate continuance of the British race and of British ideas in the world.'[7] Naturally not every mother could be held fit for such a High Mission, hence Beveridge excluded from benefit rights under the Housewives Policy any woman held guilty of causing a marriage breakdown. Thus he adopted good behaviour rather than need as the criterion for entitlement. Beveridge supports the position by invoking the principle of commercial insurance that a person cannot insure himself against a contingency which he deliberately causes to happen.

By introducing the moralistic irrelevance of who might be innocent and who guilty in desertion and separation, Beveridge effectively destroyed any chance of getting provision for separated wives into the eventual legislation. The post-war Labour Government, naturally enough, refused to land the national-insurance authority with the task of allocating responsibility for marriage breakdown in cases where the divorce courts had not already done the job – and promptly dropped the whole thing as unworkable. In any case the country's moralists would have protested bitterly against any scheme which involved giving benefit as of right to people guilty of marriage breakdown. The Government played safe therefore and decided that, if need was urgent, such cases would be dealt with by the National Assistance Board, which would provide cash and stigmatization in appropriate quantities.

In the absence of assured national-insurance rights women and children affected by marital separation are one of the most exposed and insecure groups in our society. The wife may apply to a Court for a Maintenance Order for herself and the children. The Courts generally make a rather low award because they know a high award will make it more likely that the husband will vanish. The Court cannot order a man's wages to be deducted until the wife reapplies and can prove maintenance is at least four weeks in arrears. Maintenance is then reassessed by the Court, which sets a (usually high) protected-earnings rate.

The maintenance can only be paid out of the margin of income received by the man in any week above the 'protected earnings'. The wife loses her entitlement to maintenance if the husband does not earn more than the protected earnings rate in any week. Furthermore, the husband is entitled to have his earnings made up to the protected earnings rate for any week in which his earnings are below this rate from the margin of his income above this rate in subsequent weeks, before he is liable to pay maintenance to his wife.[8]

Employers find the requirement to deduct earnings expensive and troublesome and it appears that frequently the husband is sacked. Or the husband may change his employer. The lengthy process must then begin again.

The Court must restart the proceedings after the woman, or the police, have found the husband, a task which may be extremely difficult. By this time, three or four months later, arrears have accumulated and the difficulty or recovering them may be insuperable.[9]

In all this process it is often the wife whose Court award is at a level above the official poverty line who is in the greatest difficulty. If her award is below the supplementary benefit scale the Commission can give her a regular allowance and take over the task of pursuing the husband. But if her order is above supplementary benefit level she must go to the Court to collect money, then to the Commission, if the money is not waiting for her at the Court, and so on, week after week.

Much the same applies to women with illegitimate children who have an Affiliation Order from the Court, making the father liable to pay for the support of the child – he is under no obligation to support the mother.

The numbers of husbands and fathers who have vanished or who default repeatedly on payments are very large. The latest available figures appeared in the Finer Report on One Parent Families.[10] In 1970 there were 59,500 cases in which supplementary benefit was being paid but the father or ex-husband was paying nothing. In a further 15,000 cases the man involved had disappeared. Thus despite the obsession of the SBC with defaulting relatives and the pressure they put on claimants to pursue and take legal action against defaulters, these efforts produce only a limited amount of cash. In such cases in 1970 the SBC paid out £93 million, the women were able to get £8 million from the men, and the SBC a similar sum. No estimate is available of the cost to the State of tracking down defaulters. In 1972 the SBC had 116 men sent to prison and 292 fined for maintenance default.

This area of social security – insecurity would be a more accurate term – is particularly dominated by a narrow and vindictive moralism. It is perfectly obvious what is required as minimum provision, namely that an adequate allowance should be paid for all fatherless children, irrespective of the cause of fatherlessness, and also an allowance to maintain the mother who looks after the children. These payments should be the direct responsibility of the Government and should not in any way depend on what the father can pay and when he can pay and whether he will pay. If it is thought necessary to levy a contribution on the father, then that should be a separate operation negotiated by the State directly with him. The responsibility for collection should be transferred to the Inland Revenue, who have in any case to keep track of people for income-tax purposes and who can exact payment without troubling the employer, simply by varying the income-tax coding.

But it can also be argued quite cogently that the father in many cases might as well be left out of the whole matter. After all, it can be assumed that a large part of the massive non-payment indicated in the table above can be attributed not to the selfishness and greed of fathers, but to their attempts to meet obligations – to other families. Everybody knows that society would operate more smoothly if marriage breakdown were confined to the upper income groups, who have the resources to manage these things with due consideration for the needs of everyone involved. The numerous moralists who wish to persuade the lower income groups of the advantages, material and spiritual, of a 'respectable' way of life are perfectly entitled to express their views. What is unacceptable is that these views should dictate a legal structure of social security provision which causes endless misery to those at the receiving end.

As a single example from a mass of evidence, here is part of a report by a child-care officer.

I recently accompanied a 17-year-old unmarried mother to her local supplementary benefits office. She had not received her supplementary allowance that week, and so had no money whatsoever and could not afford the bus fares to visit her baby which had been admitted to hospital.

The officer who interviewed us immediately asked about the putative father whom the girl had not seen for many weeks. She asked how long the girl had known this man, and the date when they had first had sexual intercourse. She went on to ask how many times they had had intercourse, where, and the date of the last occasion. She made a note of what the young girl said each time she replied.

The cubicle in which we were interviewed was thinly partitioned from two other cubicles, one of which was occupied. But this did not seem to deter the officer from her questioning. Neither did my presence. She questioned this young mother about the most intimate aspects of her private life, as if it was something she did every day.

The young girl was naturally very upset. Throughout the interview she was close to tears and totally unable to answer the more personal of these questions. Yet her distress seemed to go unnoticed by the interviewing officer who after all was only doing her duty as laid down by that part of the 'Liable Relative Code' which the Supplementary Benefits Commission keeps secret and which no MP or the public may see.

The total time spent at this office was two and a half hours: time which this young mother could have been spending with her sick child. At the end of this interrogation she received a total of £1 9s. – £1 for pocket money for herself, and 9s. to visit her sick child in hospital three times that week.[11]

The present treatment of separated wives and women with illegitimate children is hypocritical to the core. Ostensibly its purpose is to make sure that the man pays the price for his moral delinquency. But in fact all along the line, it is the mother and the children who suffer, and their predicament is directly due to clumsy efforts to use the social security system as a weapon of retribution, not of welfare.

Defenders of the present system argue that the Government must take every precaution against encouraging an increase in the rate of breakdown in marriage and in the evasion of paternal responsibilities. But as we have seen, the penalties are ineffective on those they are supposed to fall on, and in any case it is unlikely that future financial penalties have much effect on motivation in the complex of tensions that lead to the breakdown of marriage.

The Supplementary Benefits Commission, like its predecessor the NAB, has become notorious for the humiliations it inflicts on separated or unmarried women with children. The SBC has a rule that if a woman is cohabiting with a man he is supposed to support her. Thus the cohabiting woman loses any entitlement to supplementary benefit. The normal method used to establish cohabitation is that the SBC officer comes early in the morning, insists on entry and searches the premises for clothes and similar evidence of male visitation. The woman and the neighbours are questioned. The officer can, if he wishes, cancel the supplementary allowance, leaving the woman destitute. Her only recourse is an appeal which may take weeks to be heard.

The SBC officer is in a very strong position. The social relationships which any girl looking for a husband gets involved in can be used on the basis of hearsay gossip as damning evidence of prostitution. Neither when withholding benefit nor at an appeal does the officer have to offer real proof of his suspicion. An Appeal Tribunal is not a court of law, merely three local dignitaries who decide which side they think is lying. After the money is cut off a girl may well be forced into financial dependence on a man, in which case the decision of the SBC officer can, of itself, produce confirmation of his original allegations.

These are the sordid outcomes of a rigorous application of the contribution principle, and the refusal to acknowledge that looking after a child is a job of work, whether the mother is married or not married.

The Finer Committee reporting in 1974 recommended the creation of a new social security benefit for one-parent families, a guaranteed maintenance allowance (GMA). This would be means-tested, but administered by a specially created agency and not by the SBC. For mothers without other resources the GMA would provide a standard of living slightly above the present supplementary benefit poverty line. Where the single parent went out to work, the first £4 a week of earnings would not affect the GMA. Thereafter for each extra £1 earned, the GMA would be cut by 50p. However, the allowance for each child included in the GMA (and equivalent to 33 per cent more than the normal family allowance paid to two-parent families) would not be affected by the earnings of the single parent. Single parents getting a GMA would not be entitled to get maintenance payments from ex-husbands etc. These would be collected instead by the agency administering the GMA.

Clearly these proposals represent an advance on current

provision. Their total cost was estimated by the DHSS to be around £200 million, that is a 4 per cent increase in the present expenditure on social security. So far (1975) the Labour Government has implemented none of the recommendations of the Finer Report with the minor exception of the extension of the family allowance to the first child in one-parent families.

However, there are important questions to be raised about the Finer proposals. It is extraordinary in view of the accumulated mass of evidence about the ineffectiveness and injustices of means-tested welfare that the Committee appears to have given no serious attention to any other technique for allocating benefit. Yet there is a strong case for paying the new allowance to all one-parent families, and taxing it back from the few with high incomes. The Report of Finer Committee is a very long and detailed document. Yet this crucial question is dismissed in one brief paragraph (5.103). Peter Townsend has commented as follows:

Benefits awarded only after a test of means are notoriously inefficient. Many people who are eligible in principle for them do not in practice apply. And the more the rules of eligibility are relaxed or simplified to encourage application the more arbitrary and unfair are the different amounts paid. Again it seems administratively more wasteful to apply a test of means to, say, 80 per cent of adults who are eligible for benefit than to recapture the benefit back from the other 20 per cent paying more than trifling amounts of tax.[12]

A further serious criticism arises from the proposal to cut benefit by 50p for every £1 of earnings. The Finer Committee noted that a single parent going out to work would also have to pay income tax and national insurance, and concluded that the net value of earnings to such a person would be 41p. The Committee entirely ignored the effect of losing the right to other means-tested benefits if a single parent started earning. Yet, through the whole band of income from £21 a week, right up to £50 a week, a single parent with a Finer GMA would pay tax or lose benefit at a minimum rate of 86p per £1. In the band between £25 and £28, the loss would be 94p in the pound.[13] Given the extra expenses of going out to work, it would be effectively impossible for a single perent to improve her standard of living by taking a job. In the end the Finer proposals further underline the deep gulf which separates provision in the contributory sector from the greatly inferior provision in the means-tested schemes.

The Contribution Principle Ignored

Having illustrated some of the ways in which the contribution principle has been obsessively defended at the expense of various groups whose needs for social security are urgent and blindingly obvious, it remains to add that on occasion the contribution principle has been casually ignored. A notable example involved the treatment of the so-called late entrants into social insurance.

As pointed out above, many millions of people were already contributing to the various schemes of social insurance which operated before the Beveridge system was set up in 1948. A decision had to be made about the terms on which those not contributing to the earlier schemes would be admitted to the Beveridge scheme. Partly it was a social class question, since the earlier schemes had not required people earning above a certain income and in middle-class occupations to be contributors. The mass of mainly working-class contributors (together with their employers) had accumulated reserve funds in the various schemes, which by 1948 totalled nearly £200 million. On a strict contribution principle only the very youngest of the middle-class groups beginning to contribute for the first time in 1948 should have been entitled to full old-age pension rights when they eventually retired. But, instead, it was decided to allow full pension rights to the middle classes after only ten years of contributions. Between 1948 and 1958 the maximum total contribution which anyone could have made to the scheme was £160. For the new 1948 intake, who retired in 1958, a married couple could buy with this sum pension rights worth £200 a year which, only eleven years later in 1969, were worth double that amount. For someone aged fifty-four in 1948, who lived to the age of seventy-three, an investment of £160 brought a return of £1,857 in pension rights. It was also the case that someone paying contributions for the first time in 1948 immediately became entitled to the whole range of national-insurance benefits other than the old-age pension. The middle-class recruits thus inherited a full share in the £200-million fund accumulated by working-class contributions and, especially in the case of old-age pensions, received a substantial subsidy from the whole body of people contributing to the scheme after 1958. The rights and wrongs of this arrangement are not an issue here. The point being made is that a massive encroachment of the contribution principle was accepted in the interests of a social group which contained most of the best-paid and wealthy individuals in the age groups affected.

Historical Development of the Contribution Principle

In general the conception of a contribution principle is derived from the model of commercial insurance. Historically the idea of running a State social security scheme on the model of commercial insurance derives from Germany. In that country in the 1880s the introduction of social-insurance schemes, in particular in 1889 for old-age pensions, had formed part of Bismarck's strategy to combat the rise of the socialist movement. But the particular pattern of national insurance which emerged in Britain was greatly influenced by the quite exceptional extent to which other, non-State, forms of insurance had developed in nineteenth-century Britain.

First there were the friendly societies, to which working men contributed in pennies every week and which mainly provided sickness benefit. By the turn of the century nearly 24,000 separate societies or branches were officially registered with a total of more than four and a half million members.[14] Allowing for some duplication of membership, nearly half the adult males in Britain belonged to a friendly society. Leading societies such as the Manchester Unity of Odd Fellows and the Ancient Order of Foresters each had well over 700,000 members, while the Hearts of Oak had 400,000. The friendly societies were institutions of mutual insurance, not run for commercial purposes.

The commercial form of mass insurance was centred round the

provision of death benefit. It is well known that a horror of a pauper's funeral was widespread in Victorian society. Capitalizing on this dread were the industrial insurance companies which employed a vast network of agents to collect weekly contributions on the doorstep. The largest and wealthiest company in this class of business was the Prudential which owes its origins to the cholera epidemic of 1848 to 1849 and which by 1911 had accumulated £77 million of working-class savings.[15] The high-pressure sales tactics of the industrial-assurance companies were phenomenally effective and by 1911 there were forty-two million policies for funeral benefit in existence.

In the early years of the century politicians trembled before the political influence of the friendly societies and the insurance companies. Their tens of thousands of agents knocked on millions of doors every week and were thus regarded as able to influence electoral opinion in a very direct way. Neither of these two types of saving institution was sympathetic to the advent of State social security as a competitor for working-class savings. Their influence was sufficient to delay the introduction of State-run social security in Britain for nearly a generation later than in Germany. Indeed the advent of the first old-age pensions in 1908 was only possible because of the increasing financial difficulties in which the friendly societies were becoming involved around the turn of the century. The decrease in working-class death rates which occurred in that period had thrown into disorder the actuarial calculations on which the societies had based their contribution charges. The friendly societies did not offer old-age pensions, but the provision for sickness benefit operated as an equivalent for working-class groups, for whom in fact the concept of retirement had yet to be invented. Around the turn of the century more friendly societies' members were living on to claim sickness benefit at older ages. Even so, though the societies were unable to resist the introduction of social insurance against unemployment and sickness (National Insurance Act of 1911) they still had enough political steam to compel Lloyd George to pay for their support by making the societies the official collecting and payment agencies under the new scheme.

To this day commercial insurance draws heavily on working-class savings via the industrial sector of the business, and private insurance is still one of the most powerful of the business lobbies in British politics. The friendly societies, though in 1965 they still had as many as five and a half million members, are now politically negligible. Their heyday was in the late nineteenth century. But their existence as autonomously created institutions for working-class thrift impressed many later reformers such as Beveridge as a justification for creating a State social security system, providing only minimum subsistence benefits obtainable on the basis of a contribution. In arguing the case for pensions to be provided out of contributions, rather than out of general taxation, the 1969 White Paper repeated in essentials the same arguments as were used by Beveridge in his 1942 Plan which laid the basis of the present national-insurance system. In 1969 the Government explained that: 'People do not want to be *given* rights to pensions and benefits; they want to *earn* them by their contributions.'[16]

In 1942 Beveridge had argued that:

benefit in return for contributions, rather than free allowances from the State, is what the people of Britain desire. This desire is shown by the established popularity of compulsory insurance, and by the phenomenal growth of voluntary insurance against sickness, against death and for endowment, and most recently for hospital treatment. It is shown in another way by the strength of popular objection to any kind of means test. This objection springs not so much from a desire to get everything for nothing, as from a resentment at a provision which appears to penalise what people regard as the duty and pleasure of thrift, of putting pennies away for a rainy day. Management of one's income is an essential element of a citizen's freedom. Payment of a substantial part of the cost of benefit as a contribution irrespective of the means of the contributor is the firm basis of a claim to benefit irrespective of means.[17]

It is an interesting argument. Unless 'earned' by a payment labelled 'national insurance contribution', a benefit is to be regarded as a free handout. This applies even if the benefit is mainly paid not out of the contribution but out of general taxation which everyone pays. Citizenship creates no rights, nor does payment of taxes, nor the unpaid work of the housewife, nor the helplessness of the permanently handicapped. Beveridge was a lifelong Liberal and his arguments are a classic example of the degrading reduction of liberal values to those of the capitalist market system. In the end rights are seen as created only by the ability to buy them, cash down.

Next it is argued that the growth of mutual benefit societies, friendly societies, and industrial insurance – to an extent which certainly made Britain unique – proves that the British people want their State insurance system to be as similar as possible to a commercial pattern. Yet it is clear from contemporary witnesses, including Beveridge himself, that the funeral insurance was run mainly by profit-making companies which operated by badgering housewives to take on more expensive policies than they could keep up. As for the friendly societies, their success probably rested on reasons quite different from those which Beveridge imputes. Brian Abel-Smith has commented as follows on the friendly societies:

The major motive force was the desire for mutual aid among the working classes – to help other working people in their current troubles in the same way as you would expect them to help you. But middle-class observers interpreted those developments as forms of 'thrift', by which was often meant the personal accumulation of wealth.[18]

Hence of course the phoney equality of the flat-rate benefit and flat-rate contribution principle recommended by Beveridge, adopted by the Attlee Government and still largely in force to this day. The poor man pays in a large proportion of his income, the rich man a trivial proportion of his, and everyone gets the same uniform benefit, which is not enough for a man to live on when he has no other resources, but is useful pin money for the rich.

Finally there is Beveridge's argument that the contribution principle allows the system to dispense with the hated means test and gives 'a firmer basis to benefit'. As we have seen, the contribution principle is used to justify a more secure claim to national-insurance benefit – but only to a level of benefit which is determined by arbitrary political decisions. In the event reliance on means-tested supplementary benefits has grown steadily over the twenty years since the Beveridge system was instituted. Indeed, with the exception of the unemployed, supplementation of national-insurance benefits has now a much larger role in social security than was the case in the inter-war period. In the twenties only 9 per cent of old-age pensioners got additional outdoor* relief and never more than 10 per cent of those on sickness benefit. At the end of 1968 29 per cent of retirement pensions and 15 per cent of the recipients of sickness benefit received income support from the Supplementary Benefits Commission.

What I am arguing for is the abolition of the distinction between the contributory and non-contributory sectors in social security and the operation of the whole system on a unified basis. Contributory national insurance carries with it two sorts of privileges: (a) the right to benefit irrespective of the amount of other financial resources at the disposal of the recipient, and (b) that the individual's rights are publicly specified in detail and guaranteed by a system of administrative law. I have argued that the preservation of the contributory distinction is expensive because of the need to maintain and refer frequently to the contribution records of millions of people, and furthermore that the contribution qualification excludes from national-insurance benefit large categories of people in need, who should have firm right to benefit and who in most cases need more financial support than is allowed by the poverty line for supplementary benefit. In addition we have seen that the relationship between contributions and benefit for the whole mass of people insured under the State scheme is a very arbitrary one, since the level of benefits at any time is dependent on decisions made by the Government in power and not by the volume of contributions built up in the past.

On the other hand the non-contributory supplementary scheme is both inefficient and expensive. A great many people who are in need do not get it, either because they are excluded from consideration by the rules of the SBC, or because they are unaware of their entitlement, or because they are unwilling to apply to the

* Money given without the necessity to enter the workhouse.

SBC for help. There is no valid reason why applicants for supplementary benefit should not have their rights to benefit guaranteed at least as firmly as claimants for national-insurance benefit, given that the latter have not 'paid for' their benefits in any real way.

As was illustrated at length in Chapter 6, lower income groups pay a much higher proportion of general taxation than is often supposed. Why is this kind of contribution less privileged than the sort made via the national-insurance stamp?

What I am criticizing is not the notion of some special tax which is earmarked for social security, but rather the attempt to maintain an artificial and spurious connection between a person's individual contribution record and his entitlement to benefit. The distinction may seem obvious, but it has been consistently ignored by those who set out to defend the present system. They explain that, if the national-insurance contribution were to be abolished, the consequent increase in general taxation would be greater than the electorate would tolerate. The present system cannot be changed in principle: 'because people are prepared to subscribe more in a contribution for their own personal or family security than they would ever be willing to pay in taxation devoted to a wide variety of different purposes'.[19] The assumption is that people are fooled by the jargon of national insurance into thinking of the contribution as fundamentally different from a tax. There is no empirical evidence to support this view, which is only credible if one is prepared to assume an astonishing stupidity in the electorate. Most people are perfectly familiar with the main argument developed earlier in this chapter – namely that a contribution buys a right to social security benefits, but at levels and on conditions determined by the Government of the day. Notice how, in the Government statement quoted just above, only two alternatives are stated; either a personal contribution or a tax which may be used for many other purposes than social security. The third possibility is simply excluded, namely a tax specially earmarked for social security purposes. What is left out is the notion that people might find it 'a duty and a pleasure' to pay out money to support the old, the widowed and the sick, if they could be sure their money would be used for that purpose and no other.

Official thinking on this question also makes the convenient assumption that, if the contribution system were scrapped, taxation rates would rise for the mass of people. It is not so frequently pointed out that the scrapping of the contribution principle would make it easier to finance social security to a much greater extent by extra taxation of the richer sections of society. Earlier, in Chapter 6, considerable evidence was quoted to suggest that there is now ample scope for massive redistributive taxation at the expense of the rich. They of course are enthusiastic supporters of the contribution principle, which minimizes redistribution from higher to lower income groups, and it is their interests which are primarily reflected in official support for the contribution myth.

CHAPTER 12

Social Security and Labour Discipline

At any one time only about half of those who are unemployed are entitled to receive unemployment benefit; the rest are forced to rely on supplementary benefit. By far the most important reason is that unemployment benefit is not paid for periods of unemployment lasting more than twelve months and thus the long-term unemployed are excluded. However, a variety of other circumstances can lead to disqualification from unemployment benefit for a period, if the authorities decide that the individual worker is to be held responsible for his own unemployment. Benefit is withheld for a period of up to six weeks in cases where the worker is regarded as having left his job voluntarily or has been sacked because of an offence known as 'industrial misconduct'. It is not generally appreciated just how broadly these rules are defined by the national-insurance authorities.

This part of social security is governed by a system of administrative law centred on the National Insurance Commissioner. He is a lawyer, employed by the Government, who adjudicates in disputes between the individual and the national-insurance authorities. Cases come to the Commissioner for settlement when one of the parties involved appeals against the decision made by a local national-insurance appeals tribunal. The decisions made by the Commissioner are final, and are published by the Government, together with a brief indication of the circumstances of each case and of the grounds on which the Commissioner arrived at his judgement. The day-to-day decisions made by all national-insurance officials are to a great extent based on the rules laid down by the Commissioner.

'Industrial misconduct' is a very strange sort of crime. It is only a worker who can be accused of it, never an employer. Furthermore a worker accused of industrial misconduct is placed in a difficult position, for the National Insurance Commissioner has ruled that, 'proof is not restricted to such evidence as would be admissible in a court of law . . . hearsay evidence which would not be admissible in a court of law may be accepted in proceedings before the Commissioner.'[1]

In general a worker is held to be guilty of industrial misconduct if he is dismissed by an employer for dishonesty or negligence in his work. The basic precedent was laid down by the Commissioner in 1950. 'A labourer employed by British Railways was dismissed after being fined £5 for stealing a piece of sacking from them of the value of 1s. 4d.'[2] The national-insurance authorities then enforced a further penalty of two weeks loss of unemployment benefit. Normally the disqualification from unemployment benefit is for six weeks: in this case the penalty was less since the sacking was worth only 1s. 4d. and the man involved had believed that the sacking was worthless and that no one would object to his taking it.

On the face of it, in such cases disqualification from benefit seems like triple jeopardy, since the offender has already been fined, and dismissed – three punishments for one crime. The National Insurance Commissioner gets round this point as follows:

The object of the provision for disqualification is not to punish the insured person but to protect the insurance fund from claims in respect of unemployment which the insured person has brought upon himself by such misconduct as might have been expected to lead to dismissal. It follows that the fact that the insured person has been fined or dismissed for his offence is not in itself a reason for reducing the period of disqualification.[3]

Other examples of industrial misconduct are a breach of the rules at work and negligence in the performance of work. If a person is sacked for absenteeism or lateness for work, this also counts as industrial misconduct. It is also misconduct if a man employed as a driver loses his licence, because of some offence against the Road Traffic Act, and loses his job as a driver. And a judgement made in 1957 extends the concept of industrial misconduct as follows:

A lorry driver was dismissed because he ceased to hold a driving licence following conviction for being under the influence of drink while in charge of a motor-car. The car was his own and the offence committed after working hours. It was held that he had lost his employment as a result of his misconduct although the offence was not in the course of his employer's business and did not arise out of it.[4]

Another precedent was created in 1953 and concerned a crane driver who was also a shop steward. This man was dismissed because he refused to operate his crane on a jetty which had been blacked by his trade union. The National Insurance Commissioner decided that this refusal was a case of industrial misconduct and unemployment benefit was withheld for six weeks.[5]

The concept of 'industrial misconduct' has been more recently extended in a judgement issued in 1971. The case concerned a single man in his thirties who was employed as a gardener by the Parks Department of a Corporation. He appeared in Court on a charge of what the law calls 'gross indecency' with another man, pleaded guilty, and was fined £10. The offence was not committed during his employment or on his employer's premises. However, the Corporation sacked him. Whereupon the local national-insurance officer disqualified him from unemployment benefit for six weeks, and the local appeals tribunal concurred when the matter was referred to it.

On appeal the National Insurance Commissioner pointed out that the relevant section of the National Insurance Act refers only to 'misconduct' as a grounds for loss of benefit rights:

the word 'industrial' does not appear and has never appeared in the statute. The commonest cases of misconduct are in the employment, but it has long been accepted that this is not essential. If a person loses his employment by reason of misconduct which has a sufficient connection with the employment, it may not matter that it was committed outside the employment . . . there are some employments where the employer has a legitimate interest in the conduct of employees even outside the employment. One example may be that of a person who holds a special position, e.g. a school teacher. Another may be that of an employee of a government department or local authority who rightly feel that their employees should maintain a high standard of conduct at all times.[6]

That the National Insurance Commissioner reduced the period of disqualification from benefit to one week is less important than his further extension of the doctrine of misconduct.

It is important to emphasize that the judgements in all these cases are used as precedents and are treated as binding by all national-insurance officers in routine decision-making. In effect what is happening is that the national-insurance system is used to back up the disciplines exercised by employers, by imposing further sanctions against disobedience or negligence.

Unemployment benefit can also be withheld for up to six weeks in cases where it is held that a worker left his job 'voluntarily without just cause'. A key example concerns a woman employed as a canteen assistant, subject to a satisfactory medical examination. She refused to undergo an X-ray test, on the grounds that other employees were exempt, and was dismissed. It was held that she left her employment voluntarily without just cause and unemployment benefit was withheld for two weeks.[7] As this case makes clear, a person can be sacked and yet still be held by the insurance authorities to have left voluntarily. The Commissioner explains that: 'There are various ways in which an employee may invite dismissal; and if it appears that he has in accordance with his own desires brought about the termination of his employment he may properly be held to have left voluntarily.'[8] One precedent of great importance was set by the Commissioner in a case involving some actors.

An actor and his colleagues in a repertory company presented the directors with an ultimatum that if certain conditions were not met, they would leave their employment. The directors treated the actors as having given notice to terminate their employment. It was held that the claimant voluntarily left his employment without just cause. Although he may have had cause for complaint about his conditions he and the other actors belonged to an Association, and he ought first to have tried to have his grievance remedied through the proper channels. Six weeks disqualification.[9]

However, although the Commissioner expects an employee to use union negotiating machinery, he is less enthusiastic about other aspects of union activities. In 1951 a trade-union member gave up a job with a non-union firm because his union objected to a particular demarcation of duties. It was held in this case that the worker had left his employment without just cause and he lost his unemployment benefit for six weeks. According to the Commissioner, 'there was no justification for leaving when he did, simply because the firm with which he was employed did not follow the practice laid down by the rules of the union'.[10] On the other hand, when dealing with non trade-unionists, the National Insurance Commissioner shows rather more benevolence.

An electrician, not a union member, left his employment voluntarily rather than yield to pressure to join a trade union. In this case it was held that the electrician's action was reasonable and that he had just cause for leaving his job.[11]

In should be added that to deprive someone of unemployment benefit has been a more serious penalty since 1966 when the earnings-related unemployment benefit scheme was introduced.

Of course a person who loses the right to unemployment benefit is still able to apply for a supplementary allowance. However, here also there is a penalty. If unemployment is due to industrial misconduct or leaving a job without just cause, then it used to be the case that the unemployed worker would have his benefit cut by a fixed sum of 75p a week. For many years the employers' associations argued that this penalty was insufficiently severe, in particular because the amount by which it kept the family below the official poverty line had been reduced, relatively, by inflation. The first Wilson Government accepted this view that supplementary benefit should be cut still further in cases of industrial misconduct. At the point when they lost the General Election of 1970 Labour had legislation going through Parliament which would have increased the industrial misconduct penalty to £1·65 a week. Following this precedent the Heath Government raised the penalty still further. The situation in 1975 is that the unemployed worker found guilty of industrial misconduct or leaving a job without just cause will have his benefit cut by 40 per cent of the rate for a single person. At the benefit rates prevailing in 1975 this would mean a loss of £4·80 a week in supplementary benefit.

The contribution principle is also set aside in cases where workers are laid off and thus unemployed because of a strike. Here too the unemployment insurance system is clearly biased in favour of the employing classes. Unemployment benefit is in no circumstances paid to workers on strike. In addition, a worker who is laid off because of a strike can only get unemployment benefit, if he can prove that he is not 'participating in or financing or directly interested in the trade dispute'. This was the wording in Labour's 1946 National Insurance Act and it is a very broad and inclusive definition. Until 1935, legislation provided that the merits of the dispute might be taken into consideration in determining right to benefit, but by the Unemployment Insurance Act of 1935 the disqualification was laid down for *any* dispute and this has not been changed by subsequent laws. If a trade dispute causes a man to be unemployed because there is no work for him, he will receive unemployment benefit only if he can show that his earnings and conditions of work will not be affected by the result of the strike. No matter what a person's job is, if he belongs to the same union as any group of workers on strike at his place of work, he is held to be financing the strike. If a person is sacked from a job and within the next twelve days his former workmates go on strike, then he loses his right to unemployment benefit. In some quite metaphysical way, the dismissed worker in such a case is held to be 'directly interested' in the dispute. The term 'trade dispute' is also extended to disputes between workers. The precedent lays down that, if a man does not go into work because he has been turned back by pickets, he cannot be given unemployment benefit – on the grounds that he is 'involved in a trade dispute' with the pickets.[12]

The whole legal basis of these regulations has been questioned by at least one distinguished specialist in Labour Law.

The interest of the worker need not even be substantial or of great magnitude so long as it is direct. Where in a demarcation dispute between platers and shipwrights, platers' helpers were thrown out of work by a stoppage, the National Insurance Commissioner decided that the latter had not proved that they were not 'directly interested' in the dispute since each worked as a team with his plater and was therefore interested in the work available. The Court of Appeal, to which this case was taken twice, refused in 1964 to disturb this decision, saying that in any case the final arbitrator of such matters under the Act was the Commissioner and the Court could not interfere; but one judge commented that he did not disagree with the decision. It may be wondered whether the social security statutes have not gone too far in this matter, and whether the same definition of 'trade disputes' really is appropriate here as for other legal problems. For example, it is hard to see why a man on strike in pursuit of a 'grudge' or of a political dispute should suffer less (a possible maximum disqualification of six weeks for 'misconduct') than the striker pursuing an industrial dispute. And, even more, why the striker's helper, unemployed by a stoppage in which he cannot avoid having a 'direct interest', and which he cannot help 'financing' if he pays union dues in that union, should lose his benefit.[13]

As in the case of industrial misconduct, there are also limitations on the supplementary-benefit rights of workers on strike or laid off because of a strike. The worker is entitled to nothing in respect of his own needs and can only claim on behalf of his wife and children. Thus a single person on strike or laid off because of a strike in which he has an interest is liable to be completely disqualified from supplementary benefit. However, since 1900 it has been a rule that means-tested assistance can be paid for the wife and children of a man on strike. In effect the striking or laid-off worker is made dependent on his wife and children and the effect is simply that family income is reduced well below the poverty line. The purpose of these rules is to allow the State to appear as neutral in industrial disputes, although it is a heavily qualified neutrality, given that exactly the same rules hold in cases where workers are locked out.

The Heath Government decided to step up the social security penalties imposed on workers on strike or who are laid off because of a strike. Until 1971 it was the case that a worker on strike was allowed £4·35 a week from strike pay, tax refunds etc., without deduction from the supplementary benefit he could claim in respect of his wife and children. Only above £4·35 was there a 100 per cent deduction, so that if a worker on strike had, say, £5·35 a week, then £1 would be deducted from the supplementary benefit. The Social Security Act of 1971 reduced this £4·35 disregard to only £1 a week. Thus any income which a striker has above £1 a week now means a corresponding reduction of supplementary benefit. For a great many workers on strike, the effect was to cut family income by £3·35 a week.*

It has not, however, been the case that the social security has been offering massive financial support to workers on strike. In 90 per cent of strikes no supplementary benefit is paid. This is because nine out of ten strikes last less than two weeks, and in most cases the wages held in hand by employers for the last two weeks at work will keep families above the official poverty line and so disqualify them from means-tested assistance. In strikes lasting more than two weeks, only 20 per cent of the workers involved have been getting supplementary benefit for their families in recent years. This is a very low figure and suggests either substantial non-application by strikers, or that the SBC are successfully resisting such claims. In 1970 the total supplementary benefit paid to strikers was £2·5 million, roughly £1 per week per striker. However the immediate background to the passage of the Social Security Act of 1971 was the Post Office strike. In this – admittedly the biggest strike since 1926 – £3·5 million was paid out in supplementary benefit, mainly because there was no strike pay and no tax refunds, since the Post Office tax clerks were themselves on strike.

The fact that tax refunds can mean a corresponding cut in supplementary benefit entitlement is a further piece of discrimination against strikers. A person gets a tax refund when he stops work, because under the PAYE system he is immediately in the position of having overpaid tax in his previous period at work. Normally an overpayment of tax is regarded by the authorities

* Incidentally, if the wife is working, only the first £2 a week of her income is disregarded. Anything she earns above that is taken off the supplementary benefit at a 100 per cent rate.

as a form of savings. Thus a person who becomes unemployed can get a tax refund of up to £1,200 without any loss of supplementary benefit entitlement. In this case the tax refund is treated as savings. But, when a man is on strike, any tax refund is treated as income and, as a result of the 1971 Social Security Act, will lead to a loss of supplementary benefit if the refund is anything over £1 a week. The only way of avoiding this rule is to strike in April at the start of the tax year before enough tax has been paid to qualify for a refund.

There is one further way in which the 1971 Social Security Act limits the social security rights of workers on strike. Normally, after a long strike, workers will have to wait for one week, or more usually two, before the first pay packet comes along. Generally workers obtain a sub (i.e. wages paid in advance) to tide them over. However, in 1969 after a strike on Liverpool Docks the workers involved realized the advantages of claiming supplementary benefit rather than a sub. Unlike the sub, supplementary benefit is not subject to tax and does not come out of the wage packet. News of this discovery spread fast. In 1968 the amount paid out in social security *after* strikes ended was £80,000, in 1970 £900,000. The Conservative Government chose to regard this as an abuse of the system and, in line with their general policy of weakening the ability of workers to sustain strikes, they closed the loophole. The 1971 Social Security Act provides that any supplementary benefit paid to families of strikers in the week or two following the conclusion of a strike will be reclaimed from the employer. And the employer in turn has been given the power to dock the money out of the wage packet.

In all of the above cases social security rights are limited by the introduction of disqualifications which reflect the interests of employers. Both supplementary benefit and the national-insurance system have been adjusted to back up the disciplines exercised by the employers and by the labour market. Given that the economic system which we live under offers to a great many people no more than monotonous and poorly paid jobs, it is surely wrong to use social security rights as part of the armoury of sanctions and penalties which keeps people at work, or prevents them from improving their position by walking out of a job or by going on strike. The right to benefit should depend on need, and not be greater or less depending on the cause of unemployment. Particularly as regards the restrictions on unemployment benefit described above, the contribution principle is being consistently contravened. The various legal precedents which I have quoted may seem clearcut enough. But in the nature of things these rules have to be applied in all sorts of cases involving special circumstances. Thus even if the claimant knew of the existence of and were able to interpret the Index and Digest of Decisions of the National Insurance Commissioner, he would still be in the dark about how these regulations might be applied in his particular case. The effect is therefore to allow officials the same kind of power of arbitrary decision as operates universally in the supplementary benefit part of the system.

CHAPTER 13

Conclusions

Over recent years there has been a wide-ranging debate between the advocates of universalism and selectivity as alternative principles around which the present Welfare State might be reorganized. The selectivist case rests on two observations about the way the Welfare State in Britain actually works. (1) That the level of benefits and services provided as of right to everyone is pitifully low and, in the case of social security, leaves millions in poverty among those who have no other income except what is provided by State social security. To the extent that national-insurance benefits are provided on a universal basis to everyone who is old or unemployed etc. then benefits cannot be made substantial enough to bring all of them above the poverty line except by a large increase in the proportion of national resources devoted to social security. This would mean moving in the direction of a socialist society, and selectivists oppose socialism on political grounds. (2) Selectivists point out that a good deal of the money spent within the present Welfare State goes to people whose income is already substantial. The universal principle of equal rights for all, irrespective of need, tends to have the effect in practice that social inequality is sustained or even increased. Equality of social security entitlement means that the rich become richer by receiving the same benefits which leave the poor in poverty. In a recent statement of selectivist theory it is pointed out that 'two thirds of the total value of State social benefits goes to households where the amount of taxes paid is equal to or more than equal to the benefits paid'.[1] The conclusion is drawn that 'most social expenditure goes to people for whom the two way traffic of levying money in taxation then paying out benefits is abortive because they receive no net transfer from higher income groups'. Thus these writers confirm what has been one of the main arguments of this book, namely that the social security system is based only to a very limited extent on the vertical redistribution of income – from richer to poorer. At present social security is a system whereby the State redistributes income from certain parts of the individual's life cycle to other parts.

The exponents of selectivity have encouraged a much overdue recognition that there are only two clear alternatives to the present untenable structure of social security. Either there has to be a much wider extension of the selectivist principle or a radical reorganization of social security in terms of a thorough-going universalism. The present compromise structure combines only the worst of both approaches – poverty at one end of the scale, and a generous array of additional rights for the already well-off.

By contrast with selectivity, the defence of the universal principle has suffered from a lack of clear definition of what precisely is involved. Ostensibly universalism implies that whenever a person falls into a category in which need is officially recognized – unemployment, old age, sickness, etc. – then an adequate income is paid as of right, and without taking into consideration any other financial resources which a person may have. In this sense there are virtually no universal elements in the British system of social security. National-insurance benefits are paid only to people who achieve the minimum contribution qualifications and therefore non-employed groups are excluded, as would be recent immigrants. The family allowance more nearly approaches the status of a universal benefit, although even here this benefit is subject to taxation, and therefore its net value to the individual family varies according to the level of its other income. Thus neither the Beveridge scheme, nor the earnings-related schemes of recent Labour Governments, were fully universal. They offered benefits as of right only to contributors. I have argued earlier that a social security system which sets out in a serious way to eliminate poverty must be based not on a contribution principle, but simply on citizenship. Or more precisely, since it is now the case that citizenship is not extended to everyone living in the country whose skin is not of a certain colour, that full social

218

security rights should be extended to all members of the human race who happen to be living in Britain. Administrative decisions can then, with enormous saving of money, be confined to the simple question of whether or not a person falls within the appropriate categories of old, sick, unemployed, or with full-time domestic responsibilities looking after children, sick people, old people, etc. In no other way is it possible to guarantee the fundamental equality of status which is essential in a democratic society.

Because of the way in which the universal principle was implemented by Beveridge and by the post-war Labour Government, universalism is often taken to imply a flat-rate level of contribution and a flat-rate level of benefit. The issue here rests squarely on the degree of equality which holds in the distribution of income and wealth in the society as a whole. In a highly unequal society the flat-rate principle is plainly a recipe for sustaining or even amplifying inequality. Social security looms so large in the economy as a whole that a contribution system which is graduated or steepened as income rises can be a powerful instrument for increasing equality. As we have seen in earlier chapters, it was only by quite extraordinary ingenuity that first Beveridge, and then successive post-war Governments, have prevented social security from exercising a considerable influence in levelling post-tax incomes. As to benefits, a flat-rate principle operates perfectly fairly, provided it is not superimposed on top of substantial inequalities in other sources of income which people may possess in periods when they are non-employed. No doubt, even in the sort of socialist system I am describing, there will be some people who would wish to have relatively more income when non-employed than when at work and will want to make the necessary savings. There is nothing in socialist theory which opposes such arrangements for personal savings, since they need in no way depend on the existence of capitalism. What is unacceptable to socialists is the present system, in which accretion of personal wealth can grow to enormous dimensions and in which the possession of wealth confers extraordinary power to control and dispose of social resources.

My argument is thus that the opposition between universalism and selectivism resolves itself into an argument about whether to create a more or less equal society. The universal principle cannot be combined with the elimination of poverty, except by massive redistribution of resources away from the wealthier classes. We are currently living with the ugly consequences of a sustained historical attempt to achieve what is not possible. It is not simply that there are rich and poor. It is rather the case that some are rich *because* some are poor. I do not believe that selective social services which work by using means tests to identify the poor can be combined with the basic equality of status which is one of the determining characteristics of a democratic society.

As I have shown earlier, occupational pension schemes have provided a source of investment capital of growing importance. In both the public and the private sector the extraordinary tax privileges accorded to pension funds have made pension rights a substantial element in the remuneration of top managerial and professional personnel. The interests of employers, and of the social groups who benefit from top-hat pension rights, have combined with those of the commercial insurance companies to create a political lobby of exceptional strength, committed to the defence of the private sector in insurance. As a consequence it remains a virtually unchallenged position in official circles that the private insurance sector is sacrosanct and that extensions and reforms in the State scheme can only be carried out within limits set by the private sector. Thus the State scheme tends to become residual, attempting to make effective provision for social groups and categories of need which employers have no direct interest in providing for. It is likewise accepted, also without question, that massive subsidies from the tax-payer should be placed at the disposal of the individuals and institutions for whose benefit private and occupational pension schemes are run. The same is true of the generous sick-pay schemes which are becoming an increasingly significant feature of managerial privilege.

As I have argued earlier, what is required is that the private pension schemes should be incorporated into a reconstituted State scheme. At a stroke this would make available to the whole of the population dependent on State social security the annual subsidy of about £2,000 million which at present is used to enhance the pension rights of beneficiaries of occupational pension schemes – and which is distributed amongst those groups in such a way that the larger the individual's prospective pension, the more generous the tax subsidies he receives. It is true of course that a large number of people are now contributing to occupational pension schemes and, as happened when Labour's National Superannuation scheme came before Parliament in 1969, an impressive propaganda campaign can be whipped up by the suggestion that the State is going to rob people of their hard-earned occupational pension rights, without compensation. But the plain truth is that for the mass of manual and lower-paid white-collar workers, the pension rights offered by the occupational schemes are very limited indeed, and can only appear as a privilege to be cherished, when compared with the inadequate provision offered under present schemes of State social security. The majority of workers stand only to gain from the nationalization of the occupational sector, provided that the consequent reorganization of State social security is carried out with the object of providing adequate benefits paid as of right, and financed on the basis of a redistributive taxation and contribution system.

The nationalization of the private-pension sector is not presented here as an alternative to an overall redistribution of income and wealth, but rather as one of the techniques whereby redistribution could be managed. The greater the degree of social-class inequality in a society, the more complex, anomalous and inequitable must be its social security provision. So long as incomes during periods of non-employment are a great deal lower than for individuals in employment, then the reproduction in the non-employed population of the same degree of inequality as exists in the working population has the effect of leaving a great many people exposed to poverty whenever incapacity for work arises. The average income for men in employment is now around £60 a week, but retired couples have an average income of less than £20 a week. If the distribution of income for the old is the same as for men in employment, then a large proportion of the retired population is pushed down below any tolerable subsistence level. In other words a social security system, even one providing only a minimum subsistence income, is inconceivable without at least some redistribution of income from higher to lower income groups. In previous chapters I have traced the efforts of successive Governments to minimize the degree of income redistribution involved in social security. The consequences are evident: an official poverty line which is set at an intolerably low level; a wage system and a series of social security schemes which leave millions of people below the poverty line; a system of welfare administration which relies increasingly on means-tested, selective welfare provision such as that offered by the Supplementary Benefits Commission; and, as one result of the spread of the selective principle, a welfare system of growing complexity, which is for that very reason increasingly ineffective, since many potential beneficiaries are unable to achieve the knowledge, skill and persistence necessary to obtain what they are theoretically entitled to. It is clear also that increasing reliance on selective social services means a growing difference in status between the majority in society who can fend for themselves and a large minority who are forced into daily dependence on the goodwill of welfare officials. Selectivity is a recipe for the creation of second-class citizens.

It remains to discuss whether it is politically practicable that the sort of redistributive programme which I have outlined might be implemented. Given the record and proclaimed attitudes of the major political parties in Britain the policies advocated in this book must appear fairly utopian. Certainly this is the case if it is assumed that all political possibilities are exhausted by what the established parties are prepared to promise or to carry out. Irrespective of the cogency of the arguments in favour of universalism or selectivity – or which of the two alternatives the electorate might prefer if offered a clear choice – it is clear that in hard political terms the selectivists have been winning hands down over the past decade.

The Conservative Government of 1970–74 was deeply committed to a selective approach. During this period the Tories made two major additions to the long list of means-tested schemes already in operation: the Family Income Supplement, discussed earlier, and the rent rebate scheme introduced in 1972 for all council tenants and for those renting unfurnished from private landlords. Legislation by the Labour Government which took office in 1974 perpetuated the Tory rent rebate scheme (which Labour had vilified in opposition) and extended it to the furnished sector of housing.

The Labour Party position in the selective–universal debate is profoundly ambiguous. Officially the Party is committed to the defence of the universal principle as embedded in Beveridge-type welfare. In practice, however, recent Labour Governments have oscillated unsteadily between the two alternative principles. A means test was introduced in the rates rebate scheme started in 1966, and when family planning provision was extended in the same year, it too was made subject to a test of means. Labour Governments have been indifferent to the steady growth in the numbers of people compelled to apply to the Supplementary Benefit Commission. And Labour have not attempted to replace the massive array of local authority means-tested schemes, for education maintenance grants, school uniform grants, day nurseries, children in care, residential accommodation for the elderly, food and clothing for people with tuberculosis, chiropody services, etc.

At the same time, Labour have experimented with earnings-related social security. As applied in the 1966 legislation for extra sickness or unemployment benefit and in the 1975 pensions scheme, this is certainly universalism of a sort. Benefits are calculated on the basis of contribution levels and not reserved for those defined as having exceptional needs for extra income. As a solution to the deficiencies of present social security provision, the fatal flaw in these schemes lies in the fact that redistribution of income is non-existent in the sickness and unemployment schemes and limited in the new pensions scheme. As implemented by recent Labour administrations, the earnings-related principle is simply a device for projecting into the non-working section of the population some of the equalities which exist in the employed population. The pension scheme enacted by the 1975 legislation will result in no reduction during the 1970s in the numbers of pensioners below the official poverty line, and will produce only a limited improvement in the living standards of the elderly, this improvement taking several decades to come fully into effect.

What are the prospects that Labour Governments in the future will take a more socialist direction in welfare and taxation policy? I believe that the social-democratic programme of accepting capitalist society in all essentials, while attempting to modify it by moderate and gradual reforms, is becoming increasingly unrealistic as a practical political strategy. Competition for world markets is growing fiercer. The lowering of international tariff barriers, and the increasing tendency to over-production in important sectors of the world economy, create mounting difficulties for British capitalism, which is lagging badly in terms of growth and investment. The reformist approach of the Labour Party means in practice that they must give first priority to assuring the viability of the capitalist system. Short of some British economic miracle, it would seem that a future Labour Government, even less than in the 1964 to 1975 period, would not be able to divert extra resources into the social service sector. All the signs are that the demands of the balance of payments and the profit and investment requirements of big business would be more pressing than during the late 1960s. Reformism is no longer practical politics.

Nor is it on the cards that the Labour Party will abandon its traditional allegiance to social-democratic doctrines of moderate, marginal and gradual reform. The left wing of the Parliamentary Labour Party is now a great deal weaker in numbers, ability, socialist convictions and in terms of active constituency support than was the case when the Bevanite left was operating in the 1950s. Labour Members of Parliament and constituency activists are a great deal more middle class in social composition than at any previous point in the Party's history.

Thus there is no reason to expect that a Labour Government will introduce egalitarian legislation. If politics began and ended with the major parties, the outlook would be bleak. However, the whole history of the development of the Welfare State in this country is a standing illustration of the fundamental importance of extra-Parliamentary forces. The major welfare advance of the nineteenth century, the public-health movement, was carried through, because the upper classes began to appreciate that epidemics and diseases could not be confined to the slum areas of the big cities. As scientific research began to expose the mechanics of transmission by which diseases spread, so the upper classes realized that their own skins were at risk unless efforts were made to provide a healthier environment for the working class. Hence the public health policies of the Victorian era with their close attention to problems of sewage, water supply, drainage, cemeteries and slum housing.

The foundations of modern social security were laid in the period 1906 to 1911. Two factors in particular provided the stimulus behind Liberal legislation to provide school meals, medical inspection of school children, old-age pensions and, in 1911, social insurance against unemployment and sickness. One was fear of the rise of the Labour movement and of socialist doctrines of social transformation. The British ruling class sought to imitate the tactics of Bismarck who in the 1880s had introduced schemes of social insurance in an attempt to buy off popular support for the rising movement of German social democracy. As A. J. Balfour, later to become leader of the Unionist Party, explained memorably in 1895, 'Social legislation is not only different from socialist legislation; it is its most direct opposite and effective antidote.'

Secondly, during the early years of the twentieth century, the upper classes in Britain became deeply concerned about the question of what was then called 'national efficiency'.[2] Only with the greatest difficulty had the Boers been defeated in the war of 1899 to 1901, and doubts about British military effectiveness were increased when it was discovered that only two out of five of the young men whom the army wished to recruit for service during the Boer War were physically capable of being turned into soldiers.

In this period competition with Germany in trade and imperialism was intensifying and the prospect of a land war against

225

Germany seemed to be approaching. This threat added impetus to fears that physical standards in the British working class were deteriorating. There were in addition more general uncertainties about whether, without social reforms, the ruling classes in Britain would be able to drum up sufficient popular enthusiasm to support a conflict with Germany. It was also about this time that the more forward looking industrialists began to realize that a modern economy could not be run unless the health of workers was improved. Here again the rapid development of a powerful and efficient economy in Germany seemed to offer an example to be followed.

It was at the insistence of the military that the Liberal Government in 1906 and 1907 initiated legislation for the feeding and medical inspection of schoolchildren. Big business was not on the whole unsympathetic to the introduction of old-age pensions in 1908, or to the advent of unemployment and sickness insurance in 1911.

But probably it is the inter-war period which carries the greatest significance for those concerned about defending, in the 1970s, the limited advances which have been achieved in the field of welfare. In the period from 1918 to 1926, one can point to a whole series of modest but useful developments in the social services: the start of programmes of council housing, from 1920 payments of extra unemployment benefit when a man on the dole had a wife and children, and the introduction in 1925 of social-insurance benefits for widows and orphans. After 1926 and right up to the outbreak of the Second World War, there were no significant advances of any sort in the pattern of social security provision. On the contrary for most of this period the main concern of the Government was to attack and limit the financial provision made for the unemployed. The same lack of progress is apparent in all the main sectors of the Welfare State, with the sole exception of housing, where there was a fairly extensive programme of council-house building in the late thirties.

It was 1926 which marked the decisive break in inter-war welfare development. The reason is not hard to seek. Until the General Strike the upper classes, with the example of Russia fresh in everyone's memory, feared the possibility of mass unrest and working-class revolution in Britain. The outcome of the General Strike largely set those fears to rest. The working class was heavily defeated and defeat provoked profound divisions within the Labour movement. The leadership of the trade-union movement had proved themselves ready to fight in the last ditch in defence of capitalism, and in the few years after the General Strike trade-union membership dropped enormously. For the next decade and a half the ruling classes were firmly in command of the economy and the social order. They had no need to generate popular support for their rule by making any serious concessions in the way of social services.

The implications for the 1970s are plain enough. It remains the case that two factors above all determine the possibility of radical advances in welfare provision in periods when national economic growth is lagging: either a concern for what used to be called 'national efficiency', which today would be most effectively expressed by the political agencies of big business, or a mounting tide of industrial unrest, especially if this were tending to take on more coordinated political forms such as growing support for revolutionary socialist organizations.

There are no signs that big business believes that the efficiency of its labour force would be improved, or its problems of industrial relations made easier to manage, by the sorts of redistributive welfare policies argued for in this book. On the contrary, commercial and business interests would resist radical redistribution to the death. The reason is simply that any serious attempt to lessen poverty makes it more difficult to sustain in existence the large sector of employment in which exceptionally low wages and poor working conditions are prevalent.

Yet from the point of view of capitalism the low-wage sector helps to underpin and stabilize the whole structure of wages and the conditions of employment of the working class. The employers can tolerate no serious threat to the disciplines of the labour market and the competitive values which support the very existence of capitalism.

These considerations must deepen one's pessimism about

whether the Labour Party can initiate any thorough-going reforms in the welfare field. At no point in its history has the Labour Party shown any disposition to enter into sustained conflict with big business and its international allies. The limitations of the Labour Party extend equally to those forces in the welfare arena who look to the Labour Party to carry forward their cause. The Child Poverty Action Group has established itself as one of the more efficient pressure groups in the margins of British politics. The research it carries out is invaluable and it provides a continual and useful service of documentation of some of the grosser defects of social security provision. But its political horizons are limited to the traditional Fabian tactic of polite persuasion of leading politicians. The CPAG has not sought to forge the sort of campaigning links with the trade-union movement, and especially with rank-and-file workers, which would give it serious political clout.

The rapidly expanding ranks of social workers offer an even weaker source of political pressure. During the first thirty years of this century most organizations of social workers fought every advance in the State provision of welfare services with the greatest bitterness.[3] Even now there appear to be few social workers who believe that the interests of their actual or future clients might be advanced by a revolutionary change in the class structure of society. Even at a more mundane level the majority of social workers do not seem to accept it as part of their duty towards the people they are ostensibly trying to help, to make sure that their clients are obtaining their full entitlement to all available social security benefits. In recent years there has been an enormous development of training courses for prospective social workers. Few of these courses inculcate a critical and militant attitude towards the administrative structures of the State, nor the detailed practical knowledge of the maze of schemes, regulations, qualifying conditions etc., required to fight effectively for social security entitlement. The vast mass of social workers remain indifferent to the broader possibilities of radical reconstruction of the Welfare State and appear content with the limited role they are offered in the present social order – i.e. the impossible task of trying to limit some of the damage to individual lives, which is a necessary feature of class society. It may be that in a socialist society there would be personal problems which social workers could help solve. What one can say is that most of the individual problems which social workers currently set out to solve are essentially of the sort generated by a society which is not organized on the basis of people's needs.

It is immensely difficult for groups dependent on the welfare services to organize themselves in defence of their own interests or to agitate politically on welfare questions. There is no kind of equivalent to the work place in which organization becomes easier to the extent that workers are concentrated together and subordinated to a single and visible authority. Furthermore the very inadequacy of social security benefits tends to involve those dependent on them in a miserable day-to-day struggle just to keep going. The system encourages an individualistic struggle to manage and a short-range time perspective, rather than purposeful collective organization. Old-age pensioners illustrate the point vividly. Of the total of seven and a half million only about three quarters of a million belong to old-age pensioners' associations. Those associations tend to be small and very numerous, confined to limited residential areas because pensioners are limited in mobility – not least by lack of money for bus fares. The individual associations tend to be primarily social in their focus, rather than political. The National Federation of Old Age Pensioners' Associations is thus a very loose organization and is largely controlled by people of middle-class background. Given the numerical strength of the pensioner population, its political weight is pathetically limited. There is terrible bitterness among the old at the treatment they are accorded. But this bitterness has as yet no adequate political expression. There is no question that pensioners could be organized very much more effectively than at present, and that effective political campaigns carried out by the old could have enormous effect in encouraging popular hostility towards an economic and political system which imposes a position of poverty-stricken inferiority on the old. I believe that we may hope for a much greater degree of political mobilization on the part of the old during the 1970s, but it must be said that there is little sign of it at present.

This is less the case among other groups dependent on social security. Recent years have seen the growth of a claimants' and unemployed workers' movement which by mid 1971 had branches in many towns and cities. Local branches vary a good deal in character. Some consist mainly of unemployed workers, while others include also unmarried mothers, people who are sick or disabled and other groups who over long periods are forced into depending on social security for an income. (So far comparatively few old-age pensioners have become active in claimants' unions.) The objectives of this type of union movement are twofold. First, to assist individual members to secure their full social-security entitlement by pooling the collective strength and knowledge of the system of the membership. Second, to develop and press for a programme of radical reform of existing provision. Abolition of means tests; work or full maintenance for the unemployed; an adequate income for all those who cannot work: those are the main slogans of the claimants' and unemployed workers' movement. Most branches in the movement are anxious to form links with established trade unions and trades councils, but in many cases full recognition has been withheld by these bodies. However, in a few localities the claimants' movement has certainly won the respect of some unofficial sections of the Labour movement because they have been able to assist groups of workers on strike to obtain the limited social security benefit which is allowed to workers participating in a strike. The claimants' unions have had to fight a major battle with the Supplementary Benefits Commission to win the right to negotiate on behalf of their members. The Commission prefers to take the line that its relationship with the individual claimant is a private and confidential one. It has usually tried to ignore the expressed wishes of members of claimants' unions that the union should represent them. However, most claimants' unions have developed sufficient solidarity to force the social security authorities to negotiate on individual cases.

The claimants' and unemployed workers' movement is a most

hopeful development, and one which deserves the full support of all who oppose the present system of welfare provision. The great weakness of groups dependent on the Welfare State is their isolation from and lack of links with the organized Labour movement, which alone could have the strength to effect real changes in the structure of society. It will be very much easier to create such links if unemployed workers and other categories of claimant can develop militant organizations of their own, even if only, as at present, on a small scale. The Unemployed Workers' Movement of the inter-war period, which for example organized the celebrated Hunger Marches, illustrates the point. The militant activities of the inter-war movement, plus its close connections with the Communist Party, provoked the hostility of the Labour Party and of many trade-union leaders. But the Unemployed Workers' Movement was able to win recognition from broad sections of the working class, and helped to make the plight of the unemployed and of the depressed areas a political issue of overwhelming importance. It is unlikely that the inter-war movement of the unemployed could have attained the necessary degree of cohesion and national impact without the support and sponsorship of a national organization of revolutionary socialists such as the Communist Party was in the early 1920s.

I believe this is also a necessary condition for the effective development of the contemporary movement. That the activities of the inter-war unemployed movement did not have a more profound effect on the welfare system and did not force greater concessions from the ruling class must be ascribed to two factors: first the defeat of the working class in 1926 which removed the central threat to the ruling order of capitalism, and second, that after about 1925, the revolutionary impetus of the British Communist Party was increasingly held back by the anxiety of Stalin to seek an accommodation with the capitalist classes in the West. Thus began a process which has gone on ever since and which has in effect turned the British Communist Party into a reformist party following, like the Labour Party, the path of Parliamentary gradualism.

Prospects in the Welfare State are likely to be profoundly

affected by current developments in working-class politics. There has been an enormous rise in militancy among workers. One result has been the appearance, largely under pressure from rank-and-file trade unionists, of a distinct left-wing current within the official trade-union bureaucracies. This current is particularly exemplified by the leaders of the two largest unions, Hugh Scanlon of the Engineers and Jack Jones of the Transport Workers. These men do not act as militant socialists, but they are willing to talk about the need for radical reorganization of society in stronger terms than is normally heard from trade-union leaders. Jack Jones in particular, during the winter of 1970 to 1971, made many speeches about the desperate plight of the old, and some of the financial resources of his union were used to support a propaganda campaign for higher pensions. But neither Jack Jones nor any others among the left-wing trade-union leaders seemed prepared to lead a campaign on welfare issues which would involve any form of militant *action*. And yet to anyone familiar with the current mood of rank-and-file workers it is clear that a properly prepared fighting campaign – especially on the issue of old-age pensions – would evoke enthusiastic support from workers, extending possibly even to a willingness to take some form of strike action on a national scale. However, any massive trade-union campaign on welfare issues involves necessarily a direct challenge to the prerogatives of the State. The traditions which predominate in official trade-union circles stand flatly against any such challenge.

It is not out of the question that trade-union leaders might be pressured into a willingness to use industrial action to back demands for better social services. In Italy in the past two years there have been major strikes over housing and pensions. But British trade-union leaders would move in this direction only under the strongest pressure from the mass of their union membership. Trade unions are very far from democratic in structure. The necessary pressure within the unions can only be generated if shop floor militants can become a good deal more strongly organized than at present. The growth of bitterness and fighting spirit among workers is being fuelled by Tory policies in welfare, as well as by unemployment, rising prices and by Government attempts to attack and weaken trade-union bargaining power. But at the same time the capacity of workers to fight back is weakened by fragmentation and lack of organization – by lack of contact between militants in different work-places, unions, industries and regions. Working-class militancy at present lacks political expression. There is an urgent need for the creation of a political party of revolutionary socialists which can link together all those forces which in industry and elsewhere are opposed to the capitalist system.

There can be no question that the tempo of class conflict is rising sharply in Britain. The signs are clear: a strike rate which is without parallel since the 1920s; the fact that strikes are becoming more massive in terms of the numbers of workers involved, and in their duration; a high and rising rate of unemployment accompanied by rapid inflation; and an increasing receptivity on the part of workers to socialist ideas. There is now above all the prospect that a new left-wing party can be created over the next few years, which will be socialist and therefore revolutionary in its objectives, and which, even initially, will have a large enough working-class membership and sufficient popular support to establish itself credibly on the national political scene. Short of such a development, little in the way of radical advance in welfare is to be expected.

Thus it is not my conclusion that old-age pensioners and other welfare groups can look for no appreciable improvement in social security provision this side of a socialist revolution. In the past the ruling class have showed themselves willing to make concessions in social services and in redistribution of income – but only when they feared increasing popular opposition to their rule. Such a threat is offered as industrial militancy begins to find direct political expression in a revolutionary party which can then pose the alternative of a transformation of existing society. Faced with opposition on this level, neither a Labour nor a Conservative Government would dare treat the old, the sick and the unemployed as they do at present.

But even then it would be a question only of reforms and of

patching up improvements in existing provision. Poverty cannot be abolished within capitalist society, but only in a socialist society under workers' control, in which human needs, and not profits, determine the allocation of resources.

For the immediate present, the urgently needed reform of the Welfare State remains contingent on the mobilization of the working class as an independent force in British politics.

References

Chapter 1

1. R. H. S. Crossman, *Paying for the Social Services*, Fabian Society, 1969, p. 1.
2. Department of Health and Social Security, *Annual Report for 1973*, HMSO, 1974.
3. Ministry of Pensions, *Financial and Other Circumstances of Retirement Pensioners*, HMSO, 1966.
4. In a letter from DHSS to Brian Sedgemore M.P., 13 May 1974. Reported in a useful survey by Ruth Lister, *Take Up of Means Tested Benefits*, Child Poverty Action Group, 1974.
5. Ministry of Social Security, *Circumstances of Families*, 1967.
6. Ruth Lister, op. cit.
7. *Low Pay Bulletin*, No. 1, January 1975.
8. A. B. Atkinson, *Poverty in Britain and the Reform of Social Security*. Cambridge University Press, 1969, p. 38.
9. *National Income and Expenditure 1963–73*, HMSO, 1974, Tables 1, 44, 45.
10. *Social Trends*, No. 5, 1974, p. 91.
11. Office of Health Economics, *Old Age*, HMSO, 1968.
12. *Hours of Work, Overtime and Shiftworking*, National Board for Prices and Incomes, 1970.
13. *Social Trends*, No. 5, 1974, p. 102.

Chapter 2

1. Beveridge Report, HMSO, Cmnd 6404, 1942, Appendix F, para. 16.
2. Fisher Committee, *Report of the Committee on Abuse of Social Security Benefits*, Cmnd 5228, 1973, p. 175.
3. Ministry of Social Security, *Annual Report for 1966*, HMSO, p. 53.
4. A. B. Atkinson, *Poverty in Britain and the Reform of Social Security*, Cambridge University Press, 1969, p. 38.

References

5. R. H. S. Crossman, *Report of Labour Party Annual Conference of 1962*, p. 104.
6. Fisher Committee, op. cit., p. 191.
7. ibid., p. 180.

Chapter 3

1. Janet Beveridge, *Beveridge and his Plan*, Hodder & Stoughton, 1954, p. 161.
2. B. B. Gilbert, *The Evolution of National Insurance in Great Britain*, Michael Joseph, 1966, p. 43.
3. W. Robson, *Social Security*, Allen & Unwin, 1943, p. 361.
4. ibid., p. 355.
5. Beveridge Report, Appendix A, para. 83.
6. ibid., p. 170.
7. ibid., Appendix F, para. 16.
8. ibid., p. 170.
9. Quoted by N. Harris, 'The Decline of Welfare', *International Socialism*, No. 7, 1961.
10. A. Briggs, *Seebohm Rowntree*, Longmans, 1961, p. 106.
11. S. Rowntree, *The Human Needs of Labour*, second ed., Longmans, 1937, p. 61.
12. ibid., p. 78.
13. The complete dietary is reproduced in K. Coates and R. Silburn, *Poverty: The Forgotten Englishmen*, Penguin Books, 1970, p. 23.
14. This £2·65 would include the family allowances which Beveridge proposed should be introduced as an adjunct to his scheme.
15. Beveridge Report, p. 87.
16. ibid., p. 87.
17. ibid., p. 88.
18. *The Times*, 9 November 1953.
19. *Hansard*, House of Lords, Vol. 182, 1953, col. 677.

Chapter 4

1. *Let's Go With Labour for the New Britain*, Labour Party, 1964.
2. *The National Plan*, H M S O, Cmnd 2764, 1965.
3. R. H. S. Crossman, *Paying for the Social Services*, Fabian Society, 1969, p. 16.
4. *Hansard*, 24 May 1966, col. 341.

5. *Hansard*, 17 June 1966, col. 1907.
6. *Observer*, 16 August 1970.
7. V. George, *Social Security*, Routledge & Kegan Paul, 1968, p. 190.
8. *Economist*, 18 April 1970, p. 66.
9. In a Commons speech by Sir Keith Joseph on 10 November 1970.
10. *Hansard*, 5 March 1971.
11. *Poverty and the Labour Government*, Child Poverty Action Group, 1970.

Chapter 5

1. N. Kaldor, *Economic Journal*, No. 53, 1943.
2. 'The Incidence of Taxes and Social Service Benefits in 1968', *Economic Trends*, February 1969, p. xviii.
3. T. Lynes, *Pensions Rights and Wrongs*, Fabian Society, 1963, p. 11.
4. ibid., p. 12.
5. For a fuller explanation for the refusal to inflation-proof graduated pensions, see Sir John Walley, *Social Security*, 1972, Ch. 11.

Chapter 6

1. 'Incidence of Taxes and Social Security Benefits', *Economic Trends*, December 1974, p. LXVII.
2. *Inland Revenue Report*, Cmnd 4262, January 1970, Table 40.
3. *Economic Trends*, February 1965 and February 1970.
4. *National Income and Expenditure*, 1974, Tables 39 and 52. About half of the total given for rates is paid by households.
5. *Economic Trends*, February 1971.
6. 'Incidence of Taxes and Social Service Benefits', *Economic Trends*, December 1974, Table 2.
7. On the regressiveness of rates, see D. Nevitt and P. Roberti, 'In Search of the Determinants of Rates and Gross Values', *Policy and Politics*, Vol. 2, March 1974.
8. A. B. Atkinson, *The Economics of Inequality*, 1975, Ch. 4.
9. M. Meacher, *New Statesman*, March 1971.
10. J. R. S. Revell, *The Wealth of the Nation*, 1967.
11. In P. Townsend and N. Bosanquet, *Labour and Inequality*, 1972.
12. Reported in the *Guardian*, 17 December 1973.
13. *Economic Trends*, February 1971, Table 2.
14. *Social Trends*, No. 4, 1973, Table 174.

References

15. *Proposals for a Tax Credit System*, Cmnd 5116, October 1972.
16. *Select Committee on Tax Credits*, Vol. 1, House of Commons 341, June 1973, p. 12.

Chapter 7

1. *Britain Belongs to You*, 1959.
2. D. E. Butler and R. Rose, *The British General Election of 1959*, Macmillan, 1959.
3. For a sparkling account of Wilson's electioneering, see Paul Foot, *The Politics of Harold Wilson*, Penguin Books, 1968.
4. B. Abel-Smith, *Labour's Social Plans*, Fabian Society, 1966, p. 9.
5. *National Superannuation and National Insurance*, HMSO, Cmnd 3883, 1969, para. 175.

Chapter 8

1. Government Actuary, *Occupational Pension Schemes*, Fourth Survey, HMSO, 1972.
2. *National Superannuation and Social Insurance*, HMSO, Cmnd 3883, 1969, p. 35.
3. Government Actuary, op. cit., p. 4.
4. T. Lynes, *French Pensions*, Bell, 1967, p. 108.
5. *Journal of the Institute of Actuaries*, 1959.
6. T. Lynes, 'Labour's Pension Plans', *Fabian Tract No. 369*, 1969, p. 27.
7. *Annual Abstract of Statistics*, HMSO, 1969, p. 345.
8. *Committee on the Economic and Financial Problems of Provision for Old Age*, HMSO, Cmnd 9333, 1954, p. 62.
9. *Inland Revenue Statistics*, HMSO, 1970, p. 137.
10. National Prices and Incomes Board, *Report No. 107*, HMSO, Cmnd 3970, 1969, p. 8.
11. *Strategy for Pensions*, Cmnd 4755, September 1971, p. 5.
12. ibid., p. 23.
13. ibid., p. 22.
14. *Better Pensions*, Cmnd 5713, September 1974, p. 27.
15. ibid., p. 12.
16. ibid., pp. 3, 6.
17. *Sunday Times Business News*, 23 March 1975.
18. The Conservative Party did not vote against the Social Security Pensions Bill after the Second Reading debate in the House of Commons.

Chapter 9

1. T. Lynes, *National Assistance and National Prosperity*, Bell, 1962.
2. *Cost of Living Advisory Committee*, HMSO, Cmnd 3677, 1968.
3. For further details about the Retail Price Index see Ministry of Labour, *Method of Construction and Calculation of the Index of Retail Prices*, HMSO, 1967 and *Report of the Cost of Living Advisory Committee*, HMSO, Cmnd 3677, 1968.
4. Ruth Lister, *Take Up of Means Tested Benefits*, Child Poverty Action Group, 1974.
5. W. C. Haggstrom, 'The Power of the Poor', in F. Riessman *et al.*, *Mental Health of the Poor*, The Free Press, New York, 1964, p. 217.
6. B. Abel-Smith and P. Townsend, *The Poor and the Poorest*, 1965.
7. Reported in F. Field and P. Townsend, *A Social Contract for Families*, Child Poverty Action Group, 1975, p. 15.

Chapter 10

1. House of Commons, 5 February 1973.
2. *DEP Gazette* and *Social Trends*, 1973, p. 197.
3. Ministry of Social Security, *Circumstances of Families*, 1967, Ch. 3.
4. D. Robinson, *British Journal of Industrial Relations*, 1967.
5. Summarized in NPIB, *General Problems of Low Pay*, Cmnd 4648, April 1971, p. 8.
6. The address is Low Pay Unit, 9 Poland Street, London, W.1.
7. NPIB, *Fourth General Report*, Cmnd 4130, 1969.
8. M. Young (ed.), *Poverty Report, 1974*, Ch. 2.

Chapter 11

1. G. D. Gilling-Smith, *The Complete Guide to Pensions and Superannuation*, Penguin Books, 1967, pp. 40–41.
2. S. Brittan, *The Treasury Under the Tories*, Penguin Books, 1964, p. 256.
3. R. G. S. Brown, *The Management of Welfare*, 1975, Ch. 4.
4. *House of Commons Papers No. 276*, 1974.
5. Child Poverty Action Group, *Poverty*, No. 31, Winter/Spring 1975.
6. Beveridge Report, p. 134.
7. ibid., p. 53.
8. M. Wynn, *Fatherless Families*, Michael Joseph, 1969, p. 59.

References

9. ibid., p. 60.
10. The financial and legal insecurities of one parent families have been thoroughly documented in the *Finer Report of the Committee on One Parent Families*, Cmnd 5629, July 1974.
11. Letter in the *Guardian*, 17 November 1970.
12. Child Poverty Action Group, *Poverty*, No. 31, 1975, p. 31.
13. ibid., p. 28, for the details.
14. B. Gilbert, *The Evolution of National Insurance in Great Britain*, Michael Joseph, 1966, p. 167.
15. M. Bruce, *The Coming of the Welfare State*, Batsford, 1968, p. 112.
16. *National Superannuation and Social Insurance*, HMSO, Cmnd 3883, 1969, p. 12.
17. Beveridge Report, p. 11.
18. M. Ginsberg (ed.), *Law and Opinion in England in the 20th Century*, Stephens, 1959, p. 350.
19. *National Superannuation and Social Insurance*, HMSO, Cmnd 3883, 1969, p. 18.

Chapter 12

1. *Index and Digest of Decisions of the National Insurance Commissioner*, R(U) 2/60 HMSO.
2. ibid., C.U. 190/50.
3. ibid., C.U. 190/50.
4. ibid., R(U) 7/57.
5. ibid., R(U) 41/53.
6. ibid., R(U) 1/71.
7. ibid., R(U) 16/52.
8. ibid., R(U) 16/52.
9. ibid., R(U) 33/51.
10. ibid., R(U) 18/52.
11. ibid., R(U) 38/53.
12. ibid., R(U) 2/53.
13. K. W. Wedderburn, *The Worker and the Law*, Penguin Books, 1965, p. 283.

Chapter 13

1. A. Christopher and others, *Policy for Poverty*, Institute of Economic Affairs, 1969.

2. The matter is excellently discussed in one of the best books ever written about the British Welfare State: Bentley Gilbert, *The Evolution of National Insurance in Great Britain*: Michael Joseph, 1966.
3. See for example C. L. Mowat, *The Charity Organisation Society 1868–1913*, Methuen, 1961, or K. Woodroofe, *From Charity to Social Work*, Routledge & Kegan Paul, 1962.

Index

Index

More about Penguins and Pelicans